A DIVIDED PARADISE

An Irishman in the Holy Land

DAVID
LYNCH

A DIVIDED PARADISE
First published 2009
by New Island
2 Brookside
Dundrum Road
Dublin 14
www.newisland.ie

ISBN 978-1-84840-013-9

British Library Cataloguing Data. A CIP catalogue record for this book is available from the British Library.

©Map of Lebanon and map of Israel/Palestine on page viii appears by kind permission of Julie Lynch.

Book design by Inka Hagen
Printed in the UK by CPI Mackays, Chatham ME5 8TD

New Island recei̶v̶e̶
The Arts Counci̶l̶

10 9 8 7 6 5 4 3 2

'No race possesses the monopoly of beauty, of intelligence, of force, and there is a place for all that at the rendezvous of victory'

Aime Cesaire, (1913–2008)
French West Indian poet and political leader.

'No other conflict carries such a powerful, symbolic and emotional charge, even for people far away. Yet, while the quest for peace has registered some important achievements over the years, a final settlement has defied the best efforts of several generations of world leaders. I too will leave office without an end to the prolonged agony.'

Kofi Annan, in his December 2006 exit address as Secretary General of the United Nations.

'Fanatics have their dreams, wherewith they weave
A paradise for a sect'

John Keats, 'The Fall of Hyperion - A Dream'

To my parents, David and Marie

Contents

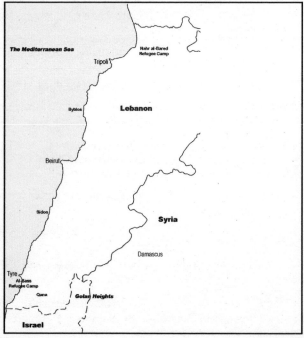

Timeline

Some Key Events in the Modern History of Palestine and Israel

1897 – First Zionist Congress held in Switzerland.

1909 – Tel Aviv established north of Jaffa.

1917 – Balfour Declaration issued, announcing British support for a 'Jewish homeland' in Palestine.

1918 – British seize Palestine following the defeat of Ottoman Empire in First World War.

1920 – British Mandate over Palestine established by League of Nations.

1929 – Significant riots between Arabs and Jews as Jewish immigration to the Holy Land grows.

1931 – Jewish paramilitary force, the Irgun, is established.

1936-39 – Arab Revolt against growing Zionist power in the region is eventually defeated by British and Zionist forces.

1939-45 – Second World War. Six million Jews die in the Holocaust.

1947 – Britain hands over responsibility for Palestine to the United Nations (UN).

November 1947 – UN proposes the partition of Palestine into separate Jewish and Arab states.

1947-48 – The Nakba (Catastrophe), and the exodus of over 750,000 Palestinians from their homes. Refugee camps in Lebanon, Syria, Jordan, the West Bank and the Gaza Strip take them in.

14 May 1948 – Israel's establishment proclaimed by their first Prime Minister David Ben-Gurion.

1948-49 – First Arab-Israeli War.

1954 – Palestinian resistance group Fatah founded and quickly becomes the largest faction within the Palestine Liberation Organization (PLO).

1956 – Israel, along with France and Britain, attacks Egypt following the nationalisation of the Suez Canal.

1967 – Israel spectacularly defeats Egypt, Jordan and Syria in 1967 War. Israel conquers the West Bank, Gaza Strip, Sinai Desert and the Golan Heights. Following the victory, Jewish settlements are constructed in the West Bank and later in the Gaza Strip.

September 1970 – Jordanian forces attack PLO strongholds in Palestinian refugee camps in Jordan and thousands die. The period is later called Black September. PLO leadership is forced out of Jordan and eventually relocates to southern Lebanon.

1973 – Israel defeats Egypt and Syria in Yom Kippur War. Israeli victory is less conclusive than in 1967.

1977 – The right-wing Likud party wins Israeli general election ending decades of Labour Zionist control. The building of settlements in the West Bank and Gaza intensifies.

1978 – Egypt and Israel sign Camp David Peace Accords. The Sinai Desert is returned to Egypt, and Egypt fully recognises the Israeli State.

1982 – Israel invades Lebanon. The PLO and its leader, Yasser Arafat, are forced out of Beirut.

1987 – The first Palestinian uprising, the 'intifada', explodes in the occupied territories.

1990-91 – First Gulf War. Iraq launches SCUD missiles at Israel.

1993 – The Oslo Accord is signed between the Israeli government and the PLO. The first peace agreement between Israel and Palestine.

1994 – Yasser Arafat triumphantly returns to Palestinian territory in Gaza, and the Palestinian Authority (PA) is established.

1995 – Israeli Prime Minister Yitzhak Rabin is assassinated by extremist Jewish rightwinger.

2000 – The Camp David peace negotiations between Israeli Prime Minister Ehud Barak and Yasser Arafat collapse. In September the second intifada begins on the streets of the occupied territories.

February 2001 – Likud Leader Ariel Sharon wins Israeli general election.

September 2001 – Suicide attacks by AI-Qaeda on United States kill almost 3,000 people.

2002 – Operation Defensive Shield takes place, with Israel attacking the Palestinian cities on the West Bank.

2003 – United States military lead an invasion of Iraq.

November 2004 – Arafat dies in Paris. Mahmoud Abbas becomes leader of PA and PLO.

January 2005 – Mahmoud Abbas wins Palestinian presidential election.

August 2005 – Gaza Disengagement. Jewish settlers are removed from the Gaza Strip.

January 2006 – Hamas wins Palestinian Legislative Council (PLC) elections.

January 2006 – Israeli Prime Minister Ariel Sharon suffers a major stroke, ending his political career.

March 2006 – Kadima wins Israeli elections and Ehud Olmet becomes prime minister.

July – September 2006 – Border skirmishes lead to Second Lebanon War. Israel invades southern Lebanon and attacks cities including Beirut. Hezbollah fires rockets at northern Israeli towns and cities.

May – August 2007 – Lebanese forces attack Nahr al-Bared Palestinian refugee camp to destroy a small terrorist cell. Political instability continues across Lebanon with a series of car-bombings and assassinations in the capital and elsewhere.

June 2007 – Vicious street battles between Hamas and Fatah gunmen in Gaza spiral towards a civil war. Hamas takes full control of Gaza and Fatah takes the West Bank.

May 2008 – Israel celebrates 60th anniversary of its establishment with major celebrations and visits by international leaders, including US President George W. Bush. Palestinians mourn 60 years since the Nakba.

Preface

Israelis are enjoying their state's 60th birthday. There are barbeques on the beach, spectacular aerial displays over the Mediterranean coastline and military parades through public parks. The May weather is predictably beautiful for the Holy Land, and there is an atmosphere of excitement that belies the usual tensions in the major cities.

The local Hebrew media has produced bumper commemorative supplements to mark 60 years since the May 1948 foundation of the state. But it is the final of the Israeli 'Survivor' reality TV show, the upcoming Eurovision Song Contest and the gripping end to the Israeli soccer season that take up most tabloid print acreage and ordinary conversation.

Here in the secular parts of Jewish West Jerusalem morale is high. A technology-based boom continues, tourist figures have started to increase and violence within Israel has dropped dramatically. Maybe Israel at 60 is not a 'light unto the nations' as its most optimistic of supporters maintained it would be, but the surface of everyday life in Israel makes it feel like 'a normal country' as the first Prime Minister David Ben-Gurion had hoped for.

Twenty minutes' drive east from the packed cafes and restaurants of West Jerusalem's lively pedestrian streets and shopping malls is the occupied Palestinian West Bank. Stinging tear gas swirls in the air; deafening stun grenades, low-flying military helicopters, speeding Israeli army jeeps and the crackle of gunfire greet you.

Israeli soldiers clash with Palestinian protestors outside the Kalandia refugee camp.

The protestors carry the Palestinian national flag and large cardboard keys. The keys symbolise the refugees' homes, lost 60 years ago. For while Israeli Jewish society happily commemorates 60 years since the Israeli Declaration of Independence, the exact same historic moment marks the beginning of the Palestinians' national tragedy.

Their *Nakba* (Catastrophe) also occurred in 1948, and demonstrations, public meetings, literary readings and art exhibitions are held across Palestinian society to commemorate the event. The Nakba is mourned in the occupied territories of the West Bank and the Gaza Strip, within the Palestinian refugee camps in the neighbouring Arab states and among the Arabs who live in Israel, who make up one fifth of that country's population.

In the occupied West Bank, some of the protests descend into violence as Israeli troops blast tear gas and fire rubber bullets at demonstrators. Later that evening, off-duty Israeli soldiers will sip their coffee in the bars of West Jerusalem while watching the Israeli soccer State Cup Final on outdoor TV screens.

Two peoples, two narratives, two realities.

But behind the clear contrast in the everyday divided experience of Israelis and the occupied Palestinians, there is a more complex, interconnecting story. Israel is not a country just like any other.

This book weaves together personal experiences, anecdotal evidence, traditional reportage and historical and political analysis. It is based primarily on my stay during the summer of 2005 in the West Bank Palestinian town of Bir Zeit. During that period I studied Arabic at the local university and wrote a series of articles for *The Sunday Business Post* on life under occupation and the 'Gaza Disengagement', when the Israeli state pulled Jewish settlers out of the Gaza Strip.

I returned to the Holy Land in March 2006 in order to cover the Israeli general election and life in the occupied territories for *Daily Ireland*. There had been a shock result in the Palestinian election in January of that year when the Islamic party, Hamas, rose to power. In May 2007, I travelled to Lebanon to gain an understanding of what life was like for Palestinian refugees in that region. At the time, tensions between the various factions in that divided country were growing, with car bombs exploding regularly in the capital Beirut. The Lebanese Army was bombing a Palestinian refugee camp in the north of the country in what they claimed to be an operation to destroy a small terrorist cell.

My most recent trip to the Holy Land came a year later, to cover the 60th anniversary celebrations for Israeli Independence and the parallel Palestinian mourning of six decades since their Nakba.

The contemporary world contains a long roll call of oppressed peoples whose circumstances demand our interest, sympathy and support. From the Kurds, who remain stateless and the victims of repression by various nations, to the Tibetans whose occupied country is under increasing centralised military control from Beijing. There are many others whose stories hardly ever generate newsprint.

Over the past decade, still more occupied peoples have joined the list of those who wake in the morning, peer out from their windows and see foreign troops on their land. War is being unleashed in their midst, from the Iraqis, to the Chechens and the Afghans to mention but a few.

Such national bondage is not a new historical phenom-enon, but since the era of colonialism through today's imperialism, it has rapidly intensified. The indigenous populations of the American, Australian and African continents were early victims. In Europe, in the nine-teenth century, the high-profile struggles for independ-ence by the Irish and the Poles captured the imagination of progressive, left-wing individuals and political move-ments. The twentieth century witnessed a whole series of successful anti-colonial struggles sweep across Africa and South East Asia. Yet despite the end of the Cold War, justice and freedom does not reign freely within a 'new world order' dominated by the United States.

Africa, with its famines, wars and pandemic diseases, is the contemporary home to those who suffer most desperately under the iniquitous global system. But it is in the Middle East where the forceful and bloody military actions taken by western powers and their client states to shape the world in their selfish interest are most clearly at work to the objective observer. The conflict between the State of Israel and the Palestinians is the long-standing touchstone issue in this region.

The Palestinian struggle for freedom inspires millions of Arabs and others across the globe who also fight against occupation and tyranny. This struggle has become for some a singular example of all the injustice in the world. It is an explosive political situation that contains within it all of the basic elements of oppression, inequality, hegemonic power and resistance. A 'solution' to the conflict based on justice is therefore believed by millions to be a prerequisite to world peace and stability.

In this context, the primary role of journalists should be both to bear witness to the complexity of events and to attempt to write truth in the face of power. Those in the modern world who have access to almost unassailable economic control and military might have little need for ever more literary and media support. Therefore, the conflict on which this journalistic-historical account focuses is one of the complex lives on both Israeli and Palestinian streets.

It is difficult to conceive how anyone who is aware of the facts or who has experienced them at first hand could not be clear in their minds as to who the principal victims and oppressed are in this particular situation.

Yet some still support the occupier. These include the political leadership of the world's only superpower who has for many decades pursued a policy that lends unlimited support to those who occupy and take land, while also attacking, denigrating and deriding those who live under occupation or who are exiled in refugee camps.

This book, while honestly attempting to portray the often hurt, diverse and divided everyday existence in Israel, will unashamedly and sympathetically chronicle that which has lost the most over the past six decades of Middle Eastern history – the tragic Palestinian nation and its defiant, inspiring people.

David Lynch, Jerusalem, 2008.

1

Under Fire in Bil'in

The angry demonstrators stood within inches of the soldiers. They were chanting loudly, screaming straight into the faces of the young armed men who were partially hidden under their large, green helmets. The soldiers seemed unmoved, barely twitching despite the close-range sonic onslaught. Their eyes showed no signs of fear or anger; many covered them with dark sunglasses. The bright Middle Eastern sun glistened against the armoured jeeps.

I was standing on a rock a couple of metres behind the front line of protestors, trying to get a better view. A rotund, thirty-something stranger wearing a keffiyeh tight around his neck, was standing beside me. He turned to me, smiled and asked where I was from.

'Ireland.'

'Ireland, wow! Have you gone to any of the Irish bars

in Tel Aviv? Some of them are very cool,' he said.

'No. Are you from Tel Aviv?' I asked.

'Yes.'

I paused for a second.

'Are you Jewish?'

'Yes,' he laughed.

I had found myself in some odd situations during the first month of my stay in occupied Palestine, but this was already competing to be one of the most surreal.

I was positioned within the main body of a protest in the small West Bank village of Bil'in. A line of determined-looking Israeli soldiers had prevented our group, numbering approximately 200, from walking any further along the road north out of the village. It was Friday afternoon, following Muslim prayers, and the intense sun blazed above. The situation was peaceful, but there was an unmistakable tension along the narrow dusty road.

This was not where I had expected to spark up a conversation with a Jewish resident of Tel Aviv regarding the social highlights of his city, and certainly not an Israeli Jew wearing the black and white scarf that, more than any other item of clothing, symbolises the Palestinian struggle for independence.

'I only stayed a couple of nights in Old Jaffa south of Tel Aviv when I got here last month,' I said.

'Oh yeah, Jaffa can be very nice. But you should come to Tel Aviv as well – it is not too far away. There are many Irish bars – it would be like home for you, maybe,' and he laughed again before continuing. 'Molly Bloom's is a great Irish bar. You would love it, coming from Ireland. I was there on St. Patrick's Day this year. They had to close the street in front of the bar, there were so many people. You could go outside and drink plenty of Guinness,' he said while motioning his two hands up to his open mouth as if drinking deeply from a black and white creamy pint. He chuckled.

I was not really in the mood for laughing. I was at that moment questioning my sanity, wondering why I had decided to attend the protest.

The weekly demonstration held in the village situated approximately 16 kilometres west of Ramallah had begun five months previously, in February 2005.

What the Palestinians call the 'apartheid wall', the Israelis refer to as the 'security fence', and what the International Court of Justice had ruled to be simply illegal, was due to be constructed through large swathes of Bil'in's hinterland. The imposing structure, hundreds of kilometres long, had already begun to dominate the arid landscape in many parts of the West Bank.

Local residents claimed that the Wall would 'steal' much of the villagers' land, and cut Bil'in off from other Palestinian economic centres. In short, it would be a calamity, and weekly demonstrations had been organised to try to stop it.

'What are you doing over here?' the man from Tel Aviv enquired.
    'I am working and studying. I am learning Palestinian history and colloquial Arabic at Bir Zeit University, you know the place? It's just outside Ramallah. I am also a journalist and I am filing stories for a paper in Dublin from here.'

'What stories?'

'Well, this week I'm working on an article about these gatherings and protests in Bil'in. I think I might now focus on the Israelis who attend them. Israelis like you, I suppose.'

He smiled and nodded his head.

I peeked over the Israeli man's shoulder and focused on the increasing friction at the front of the protest. A line of some 20 fully-armed Israeli troops stood two deep, blocking our way across the narrow potholed road. The bulk of the demonstrators were local Palestinians, but there was also a minority of Israeli and international peace activists. Near the back of the march was a small group of young people who had travelled from the Basque country. They were in high spirits, chanting in broken English, Arabic and flowing Basque. I did, however, speak to one pretty Basque woman with long black hair who bemoaned the fact that most people, even at the Bil'in march, mistakenly believed herself and her comrades to be Spanish.

The protestors clapped and chanted anti-occupation slogans in Arabic, Hebrew and English. As we marched briskly forward, our intended destination was the disputed area on which the Wall was due to be constructed. However, the Israeli military had long since deemed this part of Bil'in to be militarily sensitive and out of bounds for the local residents. They did not intend to allow us through and had declared the protest illegal.

More soldiers had now spanned out to the right and left of us, taking up positions among the sparse olive tree grove. The protestors' chanting had ceased. Other Israel Defense Force [IDF] troops stood on mounds of dirt alongside the roadway, filming the demonstration with their hand held digital cameras. A number of protestors stood a short distance from the Israeli lines, filming the soldiers with their own video cameras. Whatever was going to happen would be extensively recorded, from all perspectives.

The weekly Bil'in protest almost always ended in Israeli army attacks, which were then subsequently given high profile coverage in the Arabic media. The previous Friday, a 24-year-old local Palestinian, Ramzi Yasin, was shot in the head causing him extensive injuries. It was later reported that he had serious brain injuries that had caused him lasting sight problems. A number of other protestors were also hurt during the Israeli action.

The marchers once again renewed their chanting and furious clapping. Some were shouting directly at the soldiers, or waving huge green, black, white and red Palestinian flags. Others carried the banner of the Israeli peace group, Gush-Shalom. A Palestinian man in a wheelchair was at the front of the protest, screaming at the Israeli soldiers in Arabic. He moved his wheelchair violently back and forth against the front line of troops, waving his arms angrily. The rocky, uneven road was anything but wheelchair-friendly and this man had to push determinedly down upon the wheels to make any progress.

Organisers addressing everyone in the village community centre prior to the march had told us that this protest was to be peaceful. No stones were to be thrown at the army lines by anyone involved in the demonstration. One speaker asked people not to run if the IDF began to fire on us.

'It is more dangerous when everyone runs together,' explained a member of the global Palestinian support organisation, the International Solidarity Movement (ISM), sporting dreadlocks and an American accent.

To my militarily untutored eye, it now looked like the soldiers were starting to move into some pre-planned formation. Troops marched out even further to the east and west of the road, worryingly outflanking the tight knot of protestors. It was difficult to get a sense of how many Israeli troops had been deployed or where exactly they were in relation to the demonstration. I was feeling more than a little trapped.

'You look nervous, my friend. You are not used to this sort of thing in Ireland? It's a dangerous place, no? You hear all the news reports of violence … I suppose not as much now.'

'Well, not at the moment and not in the part of the island I am from anyway,' I said.

'You have peace now, yes?'

'Well, yes,' I answered quickly.

'That is great. I am happy for you and your people, we can only pray that peace will eventually come here one day as well. But as we stand here, that day looks very far away,' he said nodding his head and pointing towards the IDF.

'You have been to Bil'in before?' I asked the friendly Tel Aviv resident. I was beginning to think I should be more professional, stop worrying and ask some questions.

'Oh yes, many times.'

'You do not worry? Not at all?' I asked.

'About what?'

'Getting shot,' I said directly.

'Well, it is not so dangerous for the Israeli protestors really. They will try not to hurt us. It would look very bad in the media back home. But for the Palestinians, the locals, yes, it is dangerous.'

'What about for foreigners?' I asked selfishly.

'Hmm. You are somewhere in between.'

'Journalists?' I asked, thinking that I might get my National Union of Journalists membership card out and hang it prominently around my neck.

'You are also somewhere in between,' he playfully giggled like the Bil'in veteran that he obviously was.

'Why? How so "in between"?' I enquired anxiously.

'Well, sometimes you do get hurt – it's hard to say. Don't worry too much about it, you are here now. There is nothing much you can do now, is there?'

He smiled again, this time sympathetically.

I wanted to ask him about his motivations for being in Bil'in. Why was he not using his final hours before the weekly Jewish holy day, Shabbat, to walk along the beautiful, idyllic Tel Aviv promenade on the Mediterranean, rather than spending it here in the occupied territories? Why was he trying to defy the law and his own military to take part in an illegal protest? It was also potentially dangerous for Israeli citizens to travel outside the Jewish settlements in the West Bank. What were his feelings about the current state of the Israeli 'peace movement'?

But more pressing concerns shaped my questions for now.

'Do they always fire on the crowd?' I asked.

'Yes, always,' he said honestly.

'But how does it start?'

'They say they are attacked. They lie.'

'Are you sure nobody throws stones?'

'Well, yes, eventually the local teenagers sometimes start throwing them after the soldiers attack us. I have no problem with that, some do. They feel like they are protecting their village from the army, even if it is only with stones. I understand that. Anyway – stones, can they do so much harm? Look how protected the soldiers are and look what they fire back at us.'

'Still, it would surely be better for the organisers if none were thrown at all,' I said.

'Well maybe, yes. But they are not thrown until the protestors and the villagers are attacked. Anyway, look what we are doing. We are building this Wall on their land. We are stealing their land. Why? Because we can. This is the real tragedy here. When I think of what our people have been through, and now what we are doing to another people, it makes me angry.'

He again pointed towards the mass ranks of Israeli armed forces. Jeeps had brought more troops to the scene from behind the Israeli lines. The crowd was again chanting loudly in Arabic, Hebrew and English: 'Free Free Palestine' … 'This Wall has got to fall' … 'Free Free Palestine.'

'You drink in Molly Bloom's, so?' I asked.

'What? Say that again,' the Tel Aviv man replied. He couldn't hear me above the growing communal chorus.

'You like Molly Bloom's?' I shouted louder.

'Ah yes, Bloom's. A great bar. I will give you my email address and number – if you ever come to Tel Aviv, maybe we can meet up?'

'That would be cool. It's interesting, you might not know, but Molly Bloom was Leopold Bloom's wife.'

'Ah yes, *Ulysses*, James Joyce,' he said quickly.

A rush of pathetic literary patriotism enveloped me as I heard the Irish literary classic mentioned in a West Bank village. It briefly took my thoughts away from the burgeoning tension around me.

'You know it?' I asked smiling.

'Of course,' he said nodding and grinning back.

'The main character in the book is Jewish. I studied it while in college back in Ireland, there is a lot in it about Irish and Jewish identity and stuff like that,' I said rapidly.

'Yes. I have seen a copy of it in Hebrew. I think I read that it was only translated in the 1980s.'

'Hebrew! How do you translate passages like "shite and onions" into Hebrew!' I said, laughing.

There was a female scream from the front of the march. I forgot about Joyce and focused on Bil'in. There was some slight pushing and shoving between a couple of protestors and troops. Suddenly there was a deafening explosion to my left. My left ear began ringing. Then there was a quick, razor-sharp piercing pain. I thought that maybe my ear drum had burst. I bent forward and rubbed the left-hand side of my face. It felt like I was bleeding from my ear, but it was only sweat that rolled down my left cheek. To my right I saw some of the protestors running. There was another shattering sonic bang ten metres or so down the dusty path towards the village. The loud explosions from stun grenades signalled the beginning of the Israeli push. I was dazed and substantially deafened. I stood up straight and looked back at what was left of the front line of the protest, the group rapidly dwindling in number.

Protestors were now running past me, back towards Bil'in as the Israeli attack developed. The Israeli soldiers began advancing methodically. They walked around the

Palestinian man still screaming from his wheelchair. A combination of fear and foggy confusion kept me stationary. As I stood rooted to the spot, there was another large explosion. A stun grenade erupted close by. Small brush fires had started on either side of the road in the tinder-dry grass. At that moment I heard a low, soft thud and I saw something sail over my head. A tear-gas canister landed a few feet away. It exploded. There quickly followed a series of further thuds as more tear gas was lobbed into the clear blue sky over the heads of the fleeing protestors. The majority of demonstrators had begun to retreat quickly towards the village. I was still unsure on my feet and highly disorientated. My hearing was muffled. Somebody pushed into my back. I moved forward unsteadily. Another protestor standing close to me roared in English to nobody in particular.

'They are starting to fire from the trees.'

Something in that roar shook me from my momentary paralysis and broke through my partial deafness. I started to run, fast, towards Bil'in. The thick smoke from the tear gas was swirling in my path. A cloud of heavy gas now hung over the village's northern periphery. I ran through it. Behind me I could hear the mumbled cries of people shouting and screaming. I looked quickly behind and saw a number of Israeli soldiers break free from their front lines and chase retreating protestors. Some carried long batons and heavy riot shields and swung out violently at fleeing protestors.

From the edge of my line of vision I spotted the Israeli soldiers who had taken up positions adjacent to the road. They were crouched down on their knees, taking up firing positions amongst the olive trees and behind the small broken walls surrounding tiny plots of farmland. Some were cocking their guns towards us.

Having read and studied so much about this conflict in the previous months and years only one salient fact crystallised clearly in my head: the IDF has a consistent killing rate in the West Bank. The vast majority of victims are of course Palestinian, but it also has a record of killing foreigners and journalists. Since October 2000, ten foreign citizens have been killed by the Israeli military, and there have been some high-profile cases, such as the fatal shooting of British filmmaker James Miller in 2003.

I stumbled along as fast as I could. I saw a young woman who had fallen to her knees on the dust road. She was starting to vomit. A fellow protestor had gripped her shoulder and was desperately trying to lift her and pull her towards the village. Another clearly distressed and not so young man was holding his face and moaning.

Then it hit me.

My face grew progressively numb. My eyes felt like they were contracting and excreting some sort of ooze with great difficulty. I had to stop. The tear gas had got me. The gas was rapidly paralysing part of my face. I took a bottle of water from the pocket of my combats and tried to walk forward. Then I stopped again, holding the bottle open ready to pour into my cupped hand to throw onto my face.

I could not remember whether you're supposed to throw water on your eyes or not after being hit by tear gas. Something had been said at the meeting before the protest march began. But I could not focus clearly enough to remember. The blasts from the stun grenades continued behind me. They were starting to get closer. My mind was swirling with undefined fright, noise and pain. My face felt like it had been invaded by some silent numbing conquering army, bringing nothing but stinging pain in its wake.

There were a series of further explosions, again some metres behind. People were still running past me. I dropped my water when I began to run. Clasping my hands over my face I tried to race forward in self-imposed darkness over the rocky road, peeking painfully through my burning eyes. I could hear people fleeing, chanting, shouting and screaming both past me towards the front line, and by me into the village. The tears streamed down my cheeks as I rubbed my face furiously. I continued running unsighted.

After maybe 80 or so metres it got quieter; I could still hear the sound grenades and the thuds from the tear gas canisters being fired, but now from a somewhat safer distance. I slowed down to a walk. My eyes felt like they had been dipped in vinegar. The pain was building again.

I then felt a light pull on my left arm. I did not remove my hands. Something pulled me again this time a little harder. I stopped. I removed my hands from my face and opened my eyes slowly.

In front of me stood a small smiling Palestinian boy in a ragged short sleeve t-shirt and shorts. He was holding a wide tray full of sliced onions. He pointed at the two pieces of onion shoved up his nose. I grabbed two slices of onion and with some force sent both of them north-wards up my nostrils.

'Suckran kitiir (thank you),' I mumbled in my rudi-mentary Arabic, thanking him as he ran off to help oth-ers, delivering sliced onion to pained protestors.

I rapidly looked around through my almost fully closed eyelids. I seemed to be well away from the main contingent of protestors and close to the houses on the northern edge of Bil'in. The man from Tel Aviv who I had been talking to earlier was nowhere to be seen.

I saw a large flat rock to my right and it was with some desperate relief that I went and sat down hard upon it.

*

Bil'in is a rural village of some 1,800 residents. It is much like any other West Bank village. Local life is sus-tained, as it has been for generations, by agricultural living, particularly olive harvesting. Its bumpy, cratered, dry streets are common across the Palestinian territories occupied by Israeli forces, a place where major infra-structural investment in modern road surfaces is almost wholly restricted to roads which only Israeli Jews may use. The rhythm of its everyday existence is equally average, with a life built around the cycle of Islamic and Christian worship, and seasonal agricultural labour. This peaceful timetable is randomly shattered by military incursions and the unpredictable vagaries of life spent living under an occupation. The town is located approx-imately five miles east of the 'Green Line', the invisible, globally recognised border between Israel and the lands that it has occupied, including the West Bank and the Gaza Strip, since the 1967 War.

The Israeli military occupation is an integral feature of everyday life in Bil'in, as it is in hundreds of similar Palestinian villages, towns and cities across the West Bank. The locals learn to live with frequent army raids, military checkpoints and night-time arrests. Adjacent to the village are a number of Jewish settlements. These settlements, which Palestinians cannot enter, have wide, modern, suburban-type roadways, housing estates, functioning sewerage and plumbing systems, and sometimes, in a region plagued by water shortages, swimming pools. Many have facilities that the people of Bil'in could only dream of.

Since the 1967 War, successive Israeli governments have continued to build settlements for Jewish residents in the occupied territories. Over the past two decades, settlement construction, deemed illegal under international law, has risen sharply. By 2004 there were in excess of 400,000 Jewish settlers living on the Palestinian side of the Green Line. Due to the construction of the settlements and the vast road and military networks they have spawned, the Israeli authorities now directly control 60% of West Bank land. The Israeli military has de facto control over the rest of the West Bank, despite the very limited power exercised by the Palestinian Authority (PA) in some urban areas. The Jewish settlements near Bil'in are built on part of that Israeli-controlled land.

A complex web of modern motorways and tunnels connect these settlements to the major Israeli cities, like Tel Aviv and Jerusalem. Though Jewish settlers are permitted to use these roadways, Palestinian motorists are banned. Large-scale Israeli military installations have been built on the Palestinian West Bank to provide security for the illegal settlements and to facilitate military operations throughout the territories.

Bil'in's colourful mosque on what passes for its main street is certainly more aesthetically pleasing than many of the mundane white mosques dotted along the undulating hills of Palestine. However, when you walk past the numerous half-built two-storey white buildings and look out from the edge of the town over the West Bank, there is nothing particular to distinguish this village from any other.

Despite appearances, Bil'in is in fact significant to the greater picture of the Middle East. The trials and tribulations of this tiny place have since February 2005 been regularly splashed on the front pages of Israeli, Arab and international papers, and the town has hosted international conferences focused on the Wall and the Israeli occupation. West Bank residents have been known to affectionately refer to Bil'in's inhabitants as 'Palestinian Gandhis', for the villagers welcome peace activists from across the globe with open arms. They have suffered sustained military attacks by the Israeli army, but in the face of this, Bil'in has become a byword for a potential paradigm shift in the politics of resistance within the occupied territories, a cause célèbre for Palestinian solidarity activists and supporters around the world. For some, the town is now a pivotal example of sustained peaceful protest, and a regular forum for new ideas and developments in the Palestinian resistance. This progression has taken root from the widespread dissatisfaction among Palestinians and their supporters with the Palestinian leadership during the second intifada.

In 1987, a major Palestinian uprising against the Israeli occupation began. What is referred to as the first intifada (literally 'shaking off' in Arabic) witnessed strikes, demonstrations and peaceful protests across the Palestinian territories against occupying forces. (Although rather simplistically, the lasting international image of that uprising tends to be of a lone Arab boy throwing a stone at an Israeli tank.) Israeli troops had permission to shoot at unarmed Palestinians who raised their national flag. The first intifada won the Palestinians much international support as the nature of the uprising starkly exposed the massive military gap between the occupier and the occupied. The intifada petered out in the early 1990s as the peace talks that eventually ended in the Oslo Accords were signed.

The second intifada began in late 2000, and was characterised more by militarised resistance by Palestinians. It was sparked by a visit of the then Israeli right-wing opposition leader, Ariel Sharon, to the mosque compound of the Temple Mount in Jerusalem, a place holy to Muslims. Sharon was conscious of the violent reaction that his heavy footsteps would ignite, as he crossed that sacred ground. That said, the roots of the uprising had been watered for many years prior to Sharon's intentionally provocative visit.

The roots of the second intifada took hold as a result of Palestinian disillusionment with the Oslo Accords signed in 1993, the collapse of the Camp David peace talks in 2000 and the continued Israeli occupation. This disillusionment and resulting violence was captured by the Western media in footage of Israeli civilians killed by Palestinian bombings. In thinking of violence in the Holy Land, most in the West can call to mind horrific images of human remains strewn across public streets, the bodies of innocent Israelis who moments before had been eating in restaurants and dancing at discos, killed by Palestinian suicide attacks.

Suicide bombings did indeed play a significant role in the second intifada, a role they had not during the first. However, the second uprising was also characterised by mass civil disobedience and widespread military resistance to the Israeli army, which was not always reflected in the international media coverage. The second intifada also saw a continuous stream of vicious Israeli military attacks on Palestinians on a scale much larger than that of the 1980s. The crude arithmetic of the second intifada's body count displays clearly that Palestinian civilians suffered the most.

A great deal of blood has been shed on both sides of the Green Line since the outbreak of the second intifada. Between October 2000 and May 2008, over 4,700 Palestinians have been killed by Israeli security forces within the occupied territories, with a further 65-plus killed within Israel itself. Of those killed in the territories, over 940 were minors. In Israel, more than 480 civilians have died at the hands of Palestinians, with a further 236 killed within the territories. Over 300 members of the Israeli security forces have also died during the second intifada.

Many Palestinians and solidarity activists rejected the so-called 'militarisation' of the most recent intifada as both ethically questionable and politically foolish. Others have invested little hope in 'peace talks' between the leaders of the PA and Israeli government officials. This despair followed a series of false negotiated dawns which had inspired much hope but ended with no justice and no peace. It was in this context of disappointment, discussion and debate about the future that in early 2005, Bil'in, an innocuous, historically unimportant Arab town, became the focus of peaceful mass action based on Israeli-Palestinian solidarity with international cooperation. The converts to the movement inspired by Bil'in pointed to its fresh thinking and activism within a resistance that seemed strategically directionless and badly led in the face of Israel's military might.

In the summer of 2002, then Israeli Prime Minister Ariel Sharon gave the go-ahead to what Israel calls a 'security fence'. The radical idea behind this massive project had swirled around Israeli military and political circles for some years. The Israeli government argued that its construction would prevent Palestinian suicide bombers from targeting civilians in Israel's urban centres. They said it was to be built close to and sometimes along the Green Line. The authorities also promised that it was a 'temporary' measure.

Among Palestinians living behind the monumental construction that now weaves its way across hundreds of kilometres of the Holy Land, the perception was of course very different. Political leaders called it simply a 'land-grab' by Israel, taking still more Palestinian territory. They argued that the Wall was not in fact destined to be built along the Green Line, but rather, deep inside the West Bank, thus stealing Palestinian land. It would also serve to cut off villages, choking the economic and social life of the many towns situated close to its route.

Almost six decades since the creation of the Jewish state, nothing quite summed up current Israeli-Palestinian relations like this 400-mile barrier.

Firstly, the Wall is a physical expression of the iniquitous relations between both sides. Israel can, without any practical opposition from the PA, and in the face of international pressure to desist, build its Wall inside the West Bank – essentially wherever it wants. The Wall encircles Palestinian towns, cuts off communities and families, and, the PA argues, it completes the strangulation of the already enfeebled Palestinian economy. It is a unilateral act carried out by the Israeli government without any consultation with the Palestinians, and despite an International Court of Justice 2004 ruling that its construction is, in fact, illegal. It is a physical manifestation of Israel's occupation and oppression of the Palestinians.

Secondly, it is a visible representation of the Israeli fear of Palestinian suicide bombings that partially fuelled the right-wing shift within internal Israeli politics and society since 2000. An opinion poll widely published and commented upon in Israel in March 2006 showed that a significant number of Israelis did not want to have any interaction with Arabs at all. The poll reflected an intensification of trends that had been outlined in previous data.

This survey conducted by the Israeli Geocartographia on behalf of the Centre for the Struggle Against Racism made some shocking findings: nearly half of Israeli Jews said they would not allow an Arab into their home. Forty-one per cent said that they would like segregation of social facilities, much like the 'petty apartheid' that had existed in the old South African state. Forty per cent said that they would like to see the government help to 'remove' the Arab population that lives within Israel's borders.

During the peace process in the early 1990s, much of the overtly optimistic rhetoric on both sides was about 'coexistence' and 'cooperation'. This sort of dovish jargon has since been binned. The failure of the process to provide peace and justice has led to intense disillusionment among both Israelis and Palestinians. The majority of those who describe themselves as part of the Israeli peace camp now speak in terms of 'separation' as the only viable path to peace, as do many Palestinians.

For example, Peace Now, the central non-party political group at the heart of the peace movement in Israel, does not oppose the Wall per se. Rather, it argues that it should not be built within the West Bank, but on the Green Line.

The Israeli security establishment highlights as a success the decrease in Palestinian suicide attacks since the construction of the Wall started. The Palestinian side maintains that it was the 2006 decision by Hamas to abandon suicide attacks that has lowered the number of bombings. But with the support of Israeli citizens in the face of international pressure, and with Palestinians relatively powerless to stop it, the foundations of the Wall were begun in 2002 and its construction continued into the summer of 2008.

The Palestinian body politic was paralysed. They could do nothing to prevent the continued building of this Wall on its territory. There were some localised, almost spontaneous sparks of resistance on a micro level among Palestinian villagers. One such village was Bil'in. Local activists claim that the Wall, if completed, would cut off 60% off the town's farmland. The land which the villagers describe as 'stolen' would then become the site for a new Jewish 'city', established following the planned extension of five existing Jewish settlements in the locality.

*

While sitting down on the rock just outside Bil'in, I watched young Palestinian teenagers gather in a huddle. I was trying to get my thoughts together and deal with the pain in my face. I saw the teenagers move apart. They then separated out among the olive trees on both sides of the road at the edge of the village.

I could see a number of them take slingshots from their jeans' pockets. As if one, they began to fire stones from the impressively large slingshots, swinging wildly and yet carefully controlled over their heads. The speed at which the slingshots were loaded and released was mesmerising. This was no scattergun approach. With a sharp flick of the wrist, at just the right time, the stone was released swiftly, hurtling towards the Israeli soldiers.

In what was essentially an attempted counter attack on the Israeli forces moving down the road towards the village, the local teens took to the fields. Each stood a few feet from the other, fanning out in a curved line away from the road. There was a constant level of whistling going on between them, pointing and shouting as tactics were brought to bear.

I tried to control my breathing somewhat by bending forward. The effect of the gas continued to linger. I pulled out my ventolin inhaler and took a quick blast. I looked around at the reaction among the protesters clustered in small groups of four and five, up and down the road. It was mixed. The young local Palestinians seemed unfazed. Some of the Israeli pacifists looked calm as well, but others were clearly distressed, particularly from the effects of the tear gas. Some internationals were getting sick. People were walking around with large clumps of tissue paper shoved into their ears to deal with the deafening sound grenades. I quickly did likewise.

I thought back to the famous pictures from the first intifada in which the young Palestinian boys bravely threw rocks at Israeli soldiers and tanks through a haze of tear gas. I could not recall any of them having onion stuffed up their nose and toilet paper crammed into their ears. I was sure I looked quite undignified sitting there, tears streaming from my painfully gassed eyes, my skin red raw from the sun, the onion and tissue topping it off.

After a few minutes I had gathered my head together. The onion, somehow, had eased the pain produced by the tear gas. The majority of the protestors, including the few international students from Bir Zeit University who also attended, had not run back as far as I had. I was starting to feel a little embarrassed at the swift and excessive nature of my retreat.

I stood up with a little difficulty and began to walk north again towards the chanting. The front of the march had retreated, but it was still 50 metres or so in front of me beyond a slight left-hand bend. Every so often I could hear the distinctive swoosh from the olive trees as the slingshots were spun and swung at tremendous speed.

Just as I made it to the soft turn on the road I heard more people roaring, followed by the powerful blasts of a number of grenade explosions in quick succession. I then heard the crackle of gunfire. Around the bend charged many marchers, kicking up the dried sand and choking dust from the road as they retreated. I turned around instantly and ran with them towards Bil'in.

As we fled, I could see two or three tear gas canisters sail high into the air above me to the right. Two exploded within the olive trees. And then one landed just in front of me. With a bang the gas emanated and I ran straight through the cloud. This time I had decided to run all the way to the village.

I started to sprint alongside a larger group of demonstrators fleeing the Israeli barrage. The shouting from the Palestinian stone throwers became more rapid from the trees. A series of tear gas canisters again twirled above our heads ready to drop down and land in front of us. They exploded as we reached the first houses on the north side of the village; a greyish cloud of gas was hanging around Bil'in's centre. As we went through it, I saw an elderly Palestinian woman covering her mouth with her headscarf, wailing to herself as she shuffled slowly up her front garden to her door.

For the first time since the start of the Israeli attack, burgeoning anger, rather than instinctive fear, became my most pervasive emotion.

'Slow down! Stop here!' one of the organisers motioned with his arms as we entered Bil'in running.

I walked up the gently sloping hill towards the middle of the village. Most of the protestors came up to the hilltop or stood along the edge of the road. The front line of Israeli army troops had reached the foot of the hill. The majority of the local villagers had gone into their homes, their doors and windows closed tight. A couple of Palestinian drivers, who had chosen a tremendously inappropriate time to negotiate the narrow roads of Bil'in, were parked at the top of the hill. A decrepit truck had also stopped, with its potentially combustible cargo of some 20 home gas canisters exposed in the back and clinking ominously together. I eyed the vehicle warily, attempting to restrain my imagination which had already sped wildly out of control, with visions of stray bullets and tear gas hitting the truck's load and causing a massive explosion.

'They are firing the rubber bullets,' someone shouted.

The 'rubber' part of the bullet is a very thin veneer over a deadly steel ball fired at high speed from a specially adapted machine gun.

I moved right to the top of a field on the slope of an olive grove. The Palestinian stone throwers had now retreated into this field surrounded by tiny white houses. I could hear the small but deadly rubber bullets breaking the branches of the trees as the army fired in at them. From the bottom of the slope the army unleashed a further wave of tear gas and stun grenades, penning us in. At the same time, the continual spray prevented the Palestinians from leaving the trees.

By now the marchers were clearly separated from the local teenagers.

'We need to go over and stand beside the soldiers who are firing. We should jump up and down behind them and try to put them off. Look over there, they are firing at the Palestinians in the olive trees,' said a young Israeli man to a few people who were standing around. He looked like an organiser and he spoke in English. I must have looked at him as if he had four heads, because after registering my open mouth and lack of reply he moved on to try and convince someone else of what sounded to me like a ludicrous, if brave, proposal.

Despite my growing rage at the vicious Israeli invasion of Bil'in, getting as far away as possible from the people firing at us struck me as the best option, and the one I was most likely to follow; prancing around the IDF as it moved into Bil'in firing on the demonstrators was far down, very far down, on my list.

A young female international was walking slowly up the hill. She fell to her knees some 30 metres away from us and started to vomit. She was coughing furiously and was having severe difficulties breathing. Two people went over to her and carried her carefully towards a local house. A Palestinian ambulance, with its sirens blaring and lights flashing, drove past us at the top of the hill. It then descended slowly towards the Israeli line to retrieve an injured protestor who was caught up in the Israeli firing line. The Israeli army front line started to push into the olive trees, closer to the Palestinian youths. More troops began to climb the hill towards us.

*

In February 2005 the local 'Bil'in Popular Committee Against the Wall' launched a campaign of non-violent protests against the Israeli Wall. The weekly Friday demonstrations soon gained support from international groups as well as Israeli peace organisations.

There is much to recommend Bil'in from the perspective of those who oppose the Wall and support peaceful Israeli and Palestinian cooperation. Firstly, the weekly protests do seem to genuinely bring activists from the fringes of what is left of the Israeli peace movement in to common action with local Palestinians. This helps to create a moment of true Israeli and Arab connection in a region marked by an increasing surge towards dangerously deep and lasting separation. I heard young Palestinians cheerfully greet Israeli activists on the narrow streets of Bil'in with a 'shalom'; Bil'in on a Friday afternoon is probably the only part of the West Bank, save the Jewish settlements, where that iconic Hebrew word for peace would be uttered. While the Israeli political mainstream is dominated by the language of ethnic and national physical separation between Israelis and Palestinians, Bil'in proves every week that cooperation through struggle can be achieved, however briefly.

While there have been large protests across the West Bank against the unending construction of the Wall, Bil'in remains the only regular site of high-profile action. The first protest I attended there was also covered by international journalists and photographers as well as reporters from the Israeli liberal daily newspaper *Haaretz*. Pictures of the tear-gassed protestors wearing cardboard masks of Ariel Sharon were gleefully splashed on the front pages of the local Arab papers the following day. For the Palestinian protestors, attendance by Jewish Israelis was also helpful on a very practical level, as Israeli armed forces are more likely to dilute their military response to the protests when Israelis are marching. That said, the presence of Israeli Jews at the marches has not prevented continued casualties among Palestinians, and increasingly among Israeli activists.

Bil'in would be welcomed by many as an important site of cross-community work, and an admirable example of steadfast local resistance to the Wall's construction. However, some protestors at Bil'in are less encouraged. For some, their initial idealism and hope has been tempered by anger diluted with a sharp shot of depression following the Israeli military attack.

The two protests I covered were small, a few hundred at the maximum. The members of the Israeli peace camp who attended were exceptional people for many reasons. They differed from their fellow countrymen and women because they were willing to take personal risks and to break the law by coming into the West Bank to participate in such an action. But their numbers were tiny.

The number of Palestinians involved was also quite low, a phenomenon that is more difficult to explain. While the protest obviously garnered much passive support from local townspeople, only a minority of worshippers leaving the local mosque at the conclusion of Friday's prayers came to the march. Maybe a general weariness and a sense of hopelessness, widespread feelings that I encountered across the West Bank, had taken hold of the local Palestinians. Either that, or an understandable fear of the sometimes ferocious response of the Israeli military may have kept some away.

But on a wider political level, the Palestinian leadership seemed to be disinterested in the defiance shown at Bil'in each week. This was strange. I wondered why the Palestinian political leadership was not providing buses for people across the West Bank to swell the numbers at Bil'in. The sight of thousands of Palestinians marching alongside some Israeli peace activists against a structure that has been declared illegal by the international community would surely carry much moral force and capture the fickle imagination of the world's media. But this was not to be.

A top aide to Palestinian President Mahmoud Abbas, whom I interviewed in the summer of 2005, essentially dismissed the protests as a waste of time. Not all the Palestinian factions were so dismissive; leading liberal Palestinian politician Mustafa Barghouti had attended some of the marches, while a high-ranking member of Hamas on the West Bank, Hakam Yousef, also took part in the protest in early July 2005. But these were isolated occasions, and none of the major Palestinian parties have become involved in a sustained fashion.

The protests have also taken on a rather ritualised feel. They lack the dynamism and immediacy of a spontaneous show of popular street resistance to the occupation that was such a mainstay of the first intifada. This could all be viewed as a positive reflection of the stoic resistance mounted by the people of Bil'in, who have continued their struggle against the Wall's construction. But the weekly nature of the demonstrations has also been subsumed by the Israeli security forces.

Bil'in has become an important training ground for IDF soldiers learning the 'tools' of crowd control and subduing riot situations. The IDF have a ready-made, regular, real-life situation where they can test the most cutting-edge policing and military technology. The Israeli military industry complex is understandably one of the most advanced in the world. Israeli technological know-how has led to the supply of equipment for armies and police forces across the globe. The protestors and residents of Bil'in have the dubious honour of being real-life guinea pigs every Friday afternoon for advances in this sort of 'crowd control' technology.

Almost everything has been fired at the protestors and residents of Bil'in: tear gas, sound grenades, clubs, rubber coated steel bullets, stun grenades, 'sponge' bullets,

an unidentified blue chemical mixture, stun bean bags
and live ammunition have all reportedly been deployed
by the Israeli forces at some stage since February 2005.
In the face of this provocation, the main body of protestors have reacted peacefully.

Sometimes though, local young people, in scenes reminiscent of old news footage from the first intifada,
eventually retaliate. They do so with an ancient weapon,
one that can be obtained without the help of an international arms dealer or a military superpower. The
ammunition for this biblical weapon is to be found
everywhere in the rocky, bone-dry West Bank. The stone
is always easy to hand in Palestine. And after a few
decades of practice, Palestinian youths can sling further
and more accurately than most.

Some protestors, particularly Israelis who attend Bil'in,
believe that stone throwing is wrong even if provoked by
military aggression. They argue that the stone throwing
undermines the peaceful nature of the event, while also
dissuading larger numbers of Israelis from attending.
Others say that the stone throwing is understandable. It
is a feeble, almost symbolic action by local young men
trying to defend their village. The stone has come to symbolise non-submission under conditions that leave little
means for powerful retaliation. Stone-throwing gives the
local teenagers a sense that they can provide some protection to their families and their community, when going
toe to toe with the military might of the region's superpower. However, this belief is, of course, illusory. In real
life, a slingshot is not enough to defeat Goliath.

*

Two hours after the first Israeli shots were directed at the
protestors, Bil'in was still under fire. Sporadic gunshots

blasted and bounced off the town's walls. The explosions of grenades erupted irregularly. The sharp taste of tear gas was still drifting in the air amid the sound of young Palestinian voices shouting angrily at the soldiers. My bones were weary and I was emotionally jaded.

Standing and watching Israeli soldiers fire at stone-throwers positioned amongst the olive growth and between local houses, I felt a little guilty. The Israeli and international attendees, including myself, would be leaving soon, leaving the people of Bil'in at the mercy of the army. Night raids by Israeli forces had reportedly become commonplace in Bil'in. Since the demonstrations began in February 2005, some local members of the protest organising committee had been taken from their homes by Israeli soldiers.

As I wearily watched the clashes continue, an American Palestinian and Bir Zeit student who also attended the protest called me over. He told me that he and his friend were getting a taxi now and making the long journey to visit the Dead Sea. I happily said that I would go along. In that moment I passed from being an 'embedded journalist' to becoming a tourist in the Holy Land – a choice unavailable to Bil'in's local inhabitants.

My nerves were shot through. I did not feel up to attending the post demonstration political discussion in the local town hall. We left Bil'in behind us, with gunshots and explosions still echoing through the streets. After negotiating a whole series of Israeli military checkpoints, we eventually arrived on the shore of the Dead Sea south of Jericho some hours later. Our journey was greatly facilitated by our international passports; a journey from Bil'in to the Dead Sea would be all but impossible for the villagers because they would not possess the documentation to travel required by the Israeli army. Even for those who had the relevant papers, the checkpoints would make such a journey so lengthy and hazardous as to be avoided.

Later I lay back in silence upon the lowest surface water on earth as it carried my whole body aloft. I gazed out east across the magical light twinkling on the water and then up towards the red Jordanian mountains. I began the day dodging bullets and swallowing tear gas. I ended it floating peacefully in the Dead Sea.

2

The Occupation from Behind a Gun

On his 21st birthday, Israeli solider Idan Goldberger was on foot patrol near the city of Nablus on the West Bank.

He was in position just outside the notoriously militant and impoverished Balata refugee camp. Occupying Israeli forces had clashed with local Palestinian gunmen regularly here in the past few years. A ring of Israeli steel made up of permanent military checkpoints surrounded the large urban centre. Since the outbreak of the second intifada, Nablus had become a central support base for the Islamic Palestinian organisation, Hamas.

With his birthday celebrations postponed, Idan carried out his work as an IDF solider. While on duty, Idan was oblivious to the disastrous path his patrol had taken. Unknowingly he had walked directly into the gun sights of an unseen local Palestinian. Suddenly a sniper's bullet ripped through his neck and throat. Idan collapsed and was rushed to undergo emergency medical treatment. Days like this would prove pivotal for many on the outskirts of Nablus.

Idan suffered massive injuries. A few centimetres up, and the Palestinian bullet would have made a direct hit to his head. Idan would have experienced his final birthday. Over two years of tough rehabilitation ensued, and having recovered impressively from his injuries, his military service was then at an end. Like most young Israelis who have finished their mandatory military service, he instantly left the country. He pulled on his backpack and took flight on a world tour holiday.

'I was in Ireland as well. I travelled across the island. It is a beautiful place.'

I had organised the interview through an Israeli friend, and waited for Idan at the Number 5 entrance to the massive Dizengoff Shopping Centre in central Tel Aviv.

Evening shopping had long since calmed down and the normally bustling area in the vicinity of the centre was serene.

As I waited, two painters were working in a shop across the road that had closed for the evening. A few minutes later, I noticed the two men kneel down and begin the familiar movements of the Muslim prayer. I had seen that prayer made in various locations while living in the West Bank the previous summer. The most politically poignant places were at the numerous Israeli army checkpoints that criss-crossed the occupied territories. Held up in the scorching heat for many hours, the sight of men forced to pray beside an Israeli army jeep, or under the watchful eye of Israeli troops is not uncommon. But seeing Muslim men in prayer, in a clothes store undergoing renovation smack-bang in the busiest commercial centre of a major Israeli city was, for my eyes at least, unique.

When I interviewed Idan in March 2006 he was a twenty-four-year-old university student who met me with a cheerful smile and led me to a local coffee shop. Save for some scarring, Idan seemed to have recovered fully from the injuries he had received in the West Bank three years previously.

He looked tired as I began to drink the beautiful Arabic coffee, here laced with a hint of alcohol. The interview began with general chatter about the usual preoccupations of student life familiar the world over. Study yet to be done, the cost of renting, lectures and, of course, the dreaded end-of-year exams. By the age of twenty-four, most Irish people have either finished university or have already completed several years of full employment. Due to the mandatory military service in Israel, most students like Idan do not complete their undergraduate studies until at least their mid-twenties. Almost everything in their personal life is postponed because of their military duty to the Jewish nation.

We sat outside a coffee shop at the junction of Dizengoff Street and Zamenhof in downtown Tel Aviv. A gentle sea breeze cooled us. The occupation seemed a world away, and in some ways, it was. Talkative, articulate and affable, Idan was ardent and convincing when describing his politics and philosophy.

'I am so busy at the moment. I have an exam in the morning, and with only ten days to go before the election, there is so much to be done.'

Considering what happened to Idan on the edge of the Balata refugee camp three years before, you could be forgiven for thinking that he would be working for one of the rightist parties preaching a message of 'no compromise' with the Palestinians. Idan, however, said that he despised political bigotry and expressed hope for an eventual peace between Israel and Palestine.

'I joined Meretz (a small left-wing Zionist party) before I was ever even in the army, and I was already against the occupation. However, and I know this sounds strange, but what happened to me on my twenty-first birthday made it even clearer to me how wrong the occupation is. Just look how much it costs us in Israel financially and also in terms of deaths and injuries. And look how much it costs the Palestinians as well.'

Idan was then chairman of the student wing of Meretz. A packed itinerary of school and party work was keeping him busy – too busy – for a young man with important exams looming in a matter of hours. It was clear at that moment that Idan deemed national politics more important than personal academic achievement. I was interviewing him on Saturday; in Israel, the working week begins on Sunday. He told me that he might have to leave an exam early the next morning because his party leader, Yossi Beilin, was visiting his campus. There was no doubting his level of commitment.

'It is a lot of work, yes. But I believe it is for something worthwhile. I think that everything in the end in Israel comes back to the occupation and that must be solved because we have so many other issues here. We have large numbers living in poverty and we have to look after our health and education system. The occupation costs us dear and prevents us from focusing on those issues. There was the big row last year when the [Jewish] settlers were taken from their homes in Gaza. There was a massive political controversy surrounding it, there was huge coverage in the media. But the reality is that many, many poor Israelis get evicted from their homes every year because they are unable to pay rent and cannot afford to stay. There is not as much discussion about that. We have got to get our priorities right here. And to be able to focus on all these problems, we need to find some solution to the occupation.'

Idan was justifiably proud that he had successfully fought for spoken Arabic to become a compulsory subject in Israeli schools, as part of the Meretz election manifesto. Israeli Jews can study classical Arabic in secondary school if they choose to. In reality, though, few can speak the language competently, because teachers ignore the requirements, choosing to focus on French or English instead. For Palestinians in Israel, on the other hand, learning Hebrew in school really is compulsory.

There are few economic or cultural incentives for Israeli Jewish schoolchildren to learn Arabic, but once in the army, basic Arabic is essential for Israeli soldiers. On a previous evening at a restaurant in Old Jaffa, sharing a meal of schnitzel and mash with some young Israelis who had just finished their mandatory army service, the issue of the language was raised. Out of three Israeli Jews at the table, two could remember distinctly only one sentence that they had been taught in Arabic: 'stop or I will shoot'. Their comprehension of the language did not go much further than that one brutal, but key sentence for a serving Israeli soldier. Idan believed that any chance of peace between Jews and Arabs depended upon a common linguistic base as well as a political one.

'People have to know how to speak Arabic because, if we want to go to Jaffa or to Nazareth [towns with large Arab populations in Israel] or wherever, we need to be able to talk and communicate with people in these towns. We also need to learn about Islam and Arabic culture in schools so we can know about our neighbours.'

As the darkness closed in on one of the Mediterranean's most troubled cities, the achingly hip Tel Aviv nightlife began to ignite around our coffee shop. The bars and clubs of the city start to fill up with secular Israeli Jews enjoying the final hours of their weekend.

'I have no time for people who say they do not care about the fate of the Palestinians,' he said earnestly.

'People say we should be strong, and I agree it is right that Israel is strong. However, people who say that they do not care about the Palestinians, it means they do not care about people who live so close. If they say that about our neighbours, how can they say that they care about people here in Israel? It is a lie if they say that. God made us all in his own image and I care about all people, including Israelis and Palestinians. Israelis say that we must be tough with the Palestinians. But when we are attacked and bombed we vote for the most right-wing, hard line security party. Why do we not think the Palestinians will react in the same way to being attacked by us?'

Young secular Jews have become increasingly disaffected from the main Israeli political parties in recent years. The demise of the peace process in the late 1990s and the explosion of the second intifada, has led to profound despondency with the political process. Many young adults in Tel Aviv display the same disdain and lack of interest in party politics as young people in much of the western world.

In the March 2006 elections, the small Green Leaf party who proposed to legalise cannabis, and the Pensioners Party, who stood on a platform of increasing state benefits for the elderly, won the support of large numbers of the secular youth in Tel Aviv. It became almost ironic and trendy for the youth to vote for the Pensioners Party, who secured a significant nine per cent of the vote in Tel Aviv, and joined the subsequent coalition government. But many young people from this sector did not even bother to vote. The set of politics held by Idan, arising from a concern about the major national issues undermining life in contemporary Israel, such as the occupation, holds little interest for many secular Israelis of his generation. Most young Israelis would rather tune out of the occupation and the conflict with the Palestinians, and focus on their personal lives in the bright, sparkly bubble that is Tel Aviv. In contrast young religious Jews have remained politically engaged and vote in large numbers for the right-wing Zionist parties.

'These issues, like the occupation, are still important. That is why I think people should be involved in politics. This is all our futures we are talking about,' said Idan.

The cool breeze drifted up the coastal streets. The late-night revellers started making their way to the large number of bars and clubs in Israel's seductive party capital.

*

Less than a hundred kilometres away, in a very different crowded troubled city, the day's final call to Muslim prayer was crying out across Nablus. There are no public sources of alcohol or Western-style nightlife on offer in the strongly religious city. Touring the West Bank's most populated city in July 2005 was rewarding for this curious visitor; walking along the market stalls (the souks) and streets of the city, which is home to over 130,000 Palestinians, the welcome for my English friend Ben and I, was generous and touching. Nablus was uncomfortably hot, heavy and sticky that summer, and the only thing more oppressive than the Israeli military's presence was the relentless sun.

The city was choked by an Israeli military checkpoint, and the high hills surrounding the clogged streets added to the sense of total imprisonment. Long queues formed along the roads in and out of Nablus of those Palestinians lucky enough to have the 'right' papers. Some waited for hours to be searched and questioned. Taxis cannot drive you from Nablus to the other cities or towns in the West Bank; they bring you only as far as the checkpoint, which you must negotiate by foot, and then you must catch another cab on the other side. The once proud economic hub of West Bank commercial life known for its soap factories and busy marketplaces, Nablus has suffered greatly as a result of military occupation.

One soap factory that Ben and I visited was more a stark testament to the waves of destructive Israeli incursions than a physical reminder of the importance of Nablus's chief export. The small building was almost empty, dishevelled, with only one worker inside. He did not seem all that busy as he slowly moved boxes from one end of the building towards the front entrance.

After some brief words with us, he lifted his t-shirt to reveal a torso seemingly potholed by bullet wounds. 'Israelis,' he said in English, pointing at his body.

In the massive re-invasion of the Palestinian cities of 2002, codenamed Operation Defensive Shield by the IDF, the soap factories of Nablus were practically destroyed. The IDF claimed that Palestinian fighters had taken up positions in them. Local political leaders believed that they were targeted because of their historic symbolic importance within the city's economy. Soap is made from olive oil in Nablus, and it has proved very popular in Palestine and beyond. Despite having little English, the man in the factory was able to tell us that this particular soap was good for many things, allegedly including virility. He handed Ben and I two large squares of soap for free and smiled at us mischievously.

The Balata refugee camp close to Nablus is the largest in the West Bank, with more than 20,000 registered refugees. The camp itself is desperately overcrowded, built on land only a couple of kilometres wide. It originally housed some of the refugees who fled Jaffa in 1948. The camp was very active during the first intifada, many of the refugees were killed and injured, and according to the United Nations numerous shelters were demolished by the Israeli army. During the second intifada the camp was again a centre for sometimes-violent resistance. Many Palestinian fighters and ordinary refugees lost their lives. Over 80 shelters in the camp have been damaged by the IDF since the start of the intifada until March 2004. According to the UN, there are 'serious sewage network problems' in the camp, and its roads and alleys are in desperate need of repair. The camp also has a reputation for militancy — even Palestinian friends I knew in Ramallah spoke in awe of its tough alleyways running through the densely-packed concrete buildings.

Few internationals now wander the streets of the embattled Palestinian city of Nablus or its neighbouring refugee camps. Gleeful locals dragged us into cafes and small restaurants, happy to see foreign faces arrive in Nablus. Equally, they were understandably hungry for the potential profit to be made from us. As we drank coffee and ate the super-sweet local cakes, we discussed politics and religion. When asked where we were from, the response to poor Ben's reply was universal.

'English, no. Tony Blair not a good man.'

This was said seriously by many Palestinians, but with no malice towards Ben as an individual.

'No. Blair, I do not support him,' Ben always replied good-humouredly.

However, with the constant highlighting of his country's then Prime Minister's record in the Middle East, Ben soon tired of this exchange. On a later trip to Jenin, he changed his tactics:

'Where you from?' he was asked by a man on the street outside Jenin's refugee camp.

'We are both from Ireland,' replied an exasperated Ben in a most distinctive English accent. I tried not to smile or mock this declaration of Irishness by an Englishman. I was unable to do either, and slagged him mercilessly.

*

Hamas flags and pictures of local *shahids* (martyrs) were displayed all along the tight market stalls of Nablus as we walked freely through the city centre.

It would come as no surprise to anyone who had visited Nablus that the city voted solidly for Hamas in the Palestinian parliamentary elections held in January 2006. The Palestinian Legislative Council in which Hamas won a majority of seats has little real power because of the continuing Israeli occupation, but the election results still indicated growing Hamas support. The reaction in Nablus to the occupation was different to that of Bil'in, however. The political and geographical isolation and resulting religious radicalisation of Nablus made joint Israeli-Arab political actions impossible. But like many living in Bil'in, the people of Nablus had also grown weary of the tactics deployed by the Palestinian leadership during the second intifada.

The January 2006 parliamentary election success for Hamas was mainly due to a substantial vote against the corruption of the ruling Fatah party, which was predominantly secular. The Islamic party, Hamas, represented clean politics and a stoic strength against the occupation. Hamas had eased back on suicide attacks within Israel for many months, so a vote for them did not represent a return to all-out conflict. Hamas's election victory was borne out of despair with the Palestinian leadership, the dreadfully-organised Fatah election campaign and a sort of defiance by the Palestinians themselves. A year previous, they had voted Mahmoud Abbas in as Palestinian President. An opponent of violence, he was also the preferred candidate of the Western governments. But in the months after his election, there had been no improvement on the ground for the occupied Palestinians, as the checkpoints remained and Israeli military attacks continued. Many thought, 'Why not now vote for Hamas? Voting for the favoured candidate in Washington or London had got us nothing before. Why not give Hamas a go?'

Despite the hysterical world reaction to Hamas's victory, their election was a democratic rejection of the Fatah administration by ordinary Palestinians themselves. The architects of the 'War on Terror' living many miles away in Washington and London had long said that the 'democratisation' of the Middle East was part of their plan. The Palestinians had held democratic elections, and yet the choice that they freely made would be thrown back in their collective face by the international community, who were unhappy with the Palestinians' choice.

Having briefly experienced the economic and political prison that the people of Nablus were living in, it was easy to see why resistance fighters were created there, fighters like the sniper who saw Idan in his rifle sights. Idan was just another casualty of the understandable bitterness fostered by the illegal occupation that he had been sent out to serve, and which he later campaigned against.

*

To describe the Israel Defence Force (IDF) as just the country's army is to seriously underestimate its crucial role within Israeli society. The army is not like an army of any other country, manned by professional soldiers trained to defend the state. Nor is it comparable to the armies of other countries which have compulsory military service. The IDF is simply the single most important institution in Israel. The force is the principal generator and creator of Jewish Israeli national consciousness.

Shared experience during your mandatory service while wearing the IDF uniform builds bonds within Israel. Indeed, the three years that every eighteen-year-old man and the two years that every woman must serve (plus the further period as a reservist later in life) are widely seen as not only fundamental to Israel's security, but also as crucial to building national identity. It is a symbol of shared sacrifice by the Israeli nation. Until recent times, it was almost unanimously regarded as a true people's army, where all Jewish citizens played their part in the defence of the state. The only Jewish exception is among conservative Orthodox Jews, the Haredim, who do not have to serve in the IDF, because of their religious obligation to attend the religious Yeshiva schools at the age of 18. Many secular Jews resent this practice. The majority of young Jews from diverse national, ethnic, linguistic and familial backgrounds are brought together in the barracks. Whether born in Haifa, Russia or North Africa, this is where a Jewish Israeliness is forged, sometimes while under fire, or often more likely, while doing the firing.

Palestinian Arabs who live within Israel and comprise one fifth of the population are exempt from army service. Members of some small religious communities like the Druze do serve, but in reality the experience of IDF service is almost solely that of the Jews of Israel. An army service record can have a hugely important influence on future career prospects. For example, a record with one of the elite brigades of the army can look very impressive on an Israeli CV. Networking takes place in army mess halls and within battalions, and friendships are made that can last for life.

In no other job market in Israel is military service more vital than that of politics. Most Israeli political leaders possess a sparkling army résumé before reaching the top of the militarised and muscular body politic. Israeli Prime Ministers have historically been former leading generals, or sometimes even former IDF Chiefs of

Staff. A strong military record impresses voters who think such politicians will be 'tough on terror' and very 'security conscious'. On the official webpage of the Israeli parliament, the Knesset, each member's military record is given prominence on their profile pages.

Some Israelis are concerned about the close identification between the military and the broader society. Social workers and psychologists have often highlighted unhappy experiences within the army as a contributing factor to wider social ills such as domestic violence, crime, mental illness and road rage.

Their concern is perhaps understandable, for so militarised are its people that the gun is a fundamental part of everyday life in Israel. The streets and transport systems are filled with rifle-carrying off-duty soldiers in uniform. The McDonald's at Jerusalem Central Bus Station regularly buzzes with noise as young male and female soldiers tuck into French fries with their weapons close at hand.

On my first trip into the walled Old City of Jerusalem I got lost within the labyrinth of streets and laneways. Completely perplexed by my useless map I stumbled into a small open square in the Jewish quarter. Approximately ten young children were kicking a football around happily. I looked on for a few moments and then spotted a number of adults standing around the perimeter. These adults, probably parents, were holding automatic machine guns, presumably to 'protect' their children.

Israelis born in Israel are called 'Sabras'. The sabra is a prickly pear, the fruit found on some cacti: hard and prickly on the outside, soft and sweet on the inside. This is how many Israelis view themselves. Their militarised existence and the occupation that has brutalised the Palestinians, and in the process hardened Israelis, have created a society that for the visitor can sometimes seem gruff and lacking general conversational pleasantries. However, when you get past the early cool introductions, most Israelis are friendly and welcoming individuals. While there is much surface machismo around, there is a softer interior beneath the prickly front, as their nickname suggests.

The IDF has fought wars during every decade since the foundation of the state in 1948. Its victories and fallen members are celebrated in song, books and official state memorial days, and Israelis regarded the army for many decades as displaying a high level of moral rectitude. In the face of threats from Arab neighbours, proud Israelis say that the IDF, particularly during the 1967 War, was a military force that was moral, brave and eventually victorious. It was viewed in Israeli society as a true people's army where all Israelis served to make the country strong, in the face of local Arab threats to its very existence. It is also a pivotal component of the 'new' Jewish identity created in Israel. The founders of the state wanted to create a 'new' Jew. Unlike the stereotypical Jewish person who lived in ghettoes across the world in the Diaspora who was seen as weak, compromising and afraid of anti-Semitic attacks, the new Jewish identity in Israel was to be of a hardy, independent, brave and powerful people. The IDF was, and is, central to this modern Israeli Jewish identity.

In contrast, Palestinian perceptions and experience of the IDF is of course fundamentally different to that of Israelis. For them, the army is their occupier, their

enemy, and is most certainly not the 'most moral army
in the world' as Israeli leaders consistently declare. It is
rather an instrument of oppression, an agent of occupation and a powerful body that is guilty of numerous
war crimes. Worried Israeli Jewish parents wave goodbye
to their beloved young children from their doorsteps as
they depart for their military service. They see their
cherished flesh and blood aged only 18, as moral and
loving. Once they are stationed in the occupied territories, the Palestinians do not see fresh-faced young innocent adults from the suburbs of Haifa or Tel Aviv.
Rather, they consider them to be the potential armed
killers of Palestinian children.

The army is still feted in contemporary Israel, but
decades of serving in the occupied territories have
changed its image somewhat. In previous wars, the army
was regarded as having fought 'normal' standing Arab
armies from Egypt, Syria and Jordan. But with the outbreak of the first intifada, many Israelis became uncomfortable with what they saw: soldiers shooting at
stone-throwing protestors. Becoming an occupying
force and dealing with a resistance insurgency was prov-
ing to be very different. During the second intifada, the
bulldozing of Palestinian homes, the manning of checkpoints and the occupation of a clearly resentful people
further damaged the myth of the purity of arms. Even
the most ardent supporters of the IDF would find it
difficult to defend this as a dignified, brave war. Unlike
previous battles, the occupation will inspire few rousing
IDF songs.

Significantly, a new, small but important phenomenon
emanated from within the IDF during the second
intifada. In late 2003, facing a planned resumption of

bloody bombing of the Gaza Strip, a group of over 25 reservist Israeli pilots signed a very public letter. The letter stated that this group of men would not follow orders if asked to bomb Palestinian urban areas. Following the deaths of many innocent Palestinians in Israeli bombing raids, the pilots said that they had had enough. While there had been refuseniks within the IDF before, these pilots were different; rather than coming from the hard left or the pacifist tradition, these men were mainstream Zionists, some even veterans with impressive military records. This letter caused a jolt within Israeli society, and the refuseniks were celebrated by some in the Israeli peace camp and became heroes in the global Palestinian solidarity and peace movements.

Covering the European Social Forum (ESF) in London in October 2004 for the Irish political magazine *The Village*, I met and briefly interviewed one of the leading pilot refuseniks. The ESF was a gathering of thousands of anti-war, global justice, charity and non-governmental organisation activists from across the world. Yonathan Shapira had been a member of the Israeli Air Force's crack 'Black Hawk' helicopter squadron. The squadron had been deployed over the skies of Gaza in the early months of the second intifada. Israeli Apache helicopters and fighter planes had uncontested control over the skies of the Palestinian territories and could undertake bombing raids with little fear of being shot down.

A series of operations by the IAF had led to numerous Palestinian fatalities in 2002 and 2003. Bombing raids and attacks on densely populated Palestinian urban slums had seen the blood of Palestinian women and children washed into the Gaza sewerage system.

Yonathan was feted and cheered by the thousands of attendees in the main hall of Alexandra Palace at the ESF meeting entitled 'What Future for Palestine'. He spoke of the innocents who had died in the occupied territories, and why he and his fellow refuseniks could no longer be part of it. He criticised the Israeli military, security and political leadership and outlined his personal vision for peace. He said he was not a pacifist and believed in defending Israel's borders – not in bombing innocent Palestinian civilians in the occupied territories. It was a very emotional meeting, with Palestinian activists and refugees also speaking from the floor. After his refusal to obey orders to attack civilian areas in Gaza, Yonathan had been dismissed from the army.

He faced a media scrum when he left the ESF stage. After a series of questions posed by other members of the assembled media on broad political developments in the Middle East, I got my spoke in eventually.

'Why are there not more of you?' I asked.

'It is just not that simple,' said Yonathan. 'You have to understand how difficult it is to take such a step back home. We are growing in number, but it is just not that easy for people to refuse, you have to understand that.'

But I did not understand. I could not understand why more Israelis did not refuse to serve, or at the very least refuse to serve in the occupied territories. There had been refuseniks in recent history, as in the United States Army during the Vietnam War. Many American citizens refused the draft, including celebrated high-profile objectors such as boxing heavyweight world champion Muhammad Ali. Why did not more Israelis do something similar in the face of their own country's military aggression? The feeling among the audience at the ESF was similar, and was reflected in the mood in the conference hall.

*

On a later visit to Israel in March 2006, a seventeen-year-old brother of an Israeli friend was driving me to my Old Jaffa hostel late one night, following a meal with his family in north Tel Aviv. He was set to start his service in the IDF very soon. Earlier, I had asked the family if they were worried and, of course, they were.

'Can you even refuse to serve in the territories, or state that you do not want to?' I asked.

'No, he can't do that, the army will not allow it,' said his father.

This seventeen-year-old boy was set to join the army at the same time as all his school friends the following year. If he had refused, he would almost certainly face jail time and be ostracised by all but his closest friends. Since success in later life is sometimes dependent on a good army record, such a decision at such a young age could have a devastating impact. He came from a left-wing Zionist family that opposed the occupation but did not believe in refusing to serve in the army.

Comparisons between contemporary Israel and America during the period of the Vietnam War are, of course, misleading. When US soldiers refused the draft, at least they had the support of a massive anti-war movement that numbered hundreds of thousands across the US. But if a young Israeli refuses, they can rely on no such support. The Israeli 'peace camp' is at an historically low ebb, barely existing on the very fringes of Israeli life. And even here, within the peace movement, the question of refusing to serve is a complex one. Many Israeli peace camp members argue that it is better to serve and try to use your influence from within the army.

So the decision to refuse for a seventeen-year-old is extremely difficult, and in truth, few would even contemplate it, having been brought up in a society where to serve in the army is regarded as an important duty for all Jewish citizens. Thus, the possibility of widespread refusal to serve in the occupied territories by Israeli soldiers remains remote in the medium term, even if the bloodshed in the territories continues or increases in scale.

The Israeli reserve pilots who signed the public refusal letter are exceptional people, both in their courage and in their number.

*

Idan Goldberger did not believe that refusing to serve was a good idea. Like many Israelis opposed to the occupation, he believes that he can influence things more from within, rather than from outside.

Now, he felt that he could make a difference from within the Israeli political process. Idan was involved in what many Israelis would regard as the front line of the peace movement in his work with Meretz, the political heart and soul of the 'peace camp' in Israel. (Beilin, the leader of Meretz, is most famous for his involvement on the Israeli side of the governmental Oslo Accords and the non-governmental Geneva Accord.)

Idan sees the general outline of any peace agreement between the Israelis and the Palestinians as being based on the Geneva Accord. The Accord is a detailed 'unofficial' blueprint for peace, sponsored by what was left of the Israeli and Palestinian peace camps in 2003. The Israeli side was represented by Beilin, but no one in the Israeli government has officially agreed to the Accord. The Israeli Prime Minister at the time of its publication, Ariel Sharon, rejected the Accord out of hand. Neither was it officially sanctioned by the Palestinian Authority, although close aides to then Palestinian President, Yasser Arafat, did take part in the discussions. Few Palestinians and even fewer Israelis saw the Geneva Accord as the basis of a potential deal; it was the international community that generated the most enthusiasm at the time of its publication to much fanfare in Switzerland in December 2003.

The Accord proposed a two-state solution: Israel and Palestine living beside each other. The Accord stipulated that only a limited and symbolic number of Palestinian refugees from the 1948 and 1967 wars would have a right of return to Israel proper, while others would receive compensation. Palestinian refugees who currently live in camps in Lebanon, Syria, and Jordan would be allowed to move to the new Palestinian state anchored in the West Bank and Gaza. Following the publication, however, there were varying interpretations of the aspects of the Accord that dealt with the refugees, which lead to worrying confusion and counterclaim.

Israel would dismantle the majority of the settlements on the West Bank, including substantial Jewish settlements such as Ariel. Many of the largest Jewish settlements, like Ma'aleh Adumim and others in east Jerusalem, would controversially remain part of Israel according to the Geneva Accord. The Israeli occupation would therefore end only partially, with some 'land swap' taking place between both Israel and Palestine, to compensate for the remaining settlements. Jerusalem would be divided administratively, though not physically, with the city becoming the capital for two states. Palestine would have administrative control over the Islamic holy sites, and a corridor between the West Bank and Gaza, currently divided, would be established 'under Israeli sovereignty and be permanently open'. Crucially, Israel would remain a Jewish state. It would not become a state of all its citizens as the tens of thousands of Arabs living within Israel have campaigned for.

Despite some initial media interest, bloody events in Israel and Palestine have consigned the Geneva Accord to the far edges of political discourse. Most objective observers see the Accord as containing the bare minimum of 'compromise' needed on the Israeli side for a workable two state solution to emerge. Yet most Israelis are currently voting for parties that do not propose anything close to the type of two-state solution outlined in the Geneva Accord.

Copies of the agreement were sent to every home in Israel. Idan was not concerned by their gathering dust in Israeli households as mainstream public opinion too ignores the Accord.

'No, not at all. I personally do not care if the settlements are dismantled as part of the Geneva Accord or under any other name. The name is not important to me. It is Israel recognising that there is a need to do this. Sharon himself said that the publication of the Accord was one of the reasons he was pushed into removing the settlers from Gaza (the Gaza Disengagement). So it has had a good effect already.'

Not all Israelis were so supportive. Predictably, the Zionist right within Israel angrily rejected the Accord, calling it a capitulation to Palestinian 'terrorism'. Even among the Zionist left, the Accord was not backed enthusiastically. On the Palestinian side, there was also much unease. Pro-Palestinian critics of the Accord argued that the unofficial agreement would still be a historic raw deal for the Palestinians. Israeli maintenance of the massive settlements such as Ma'aleh Adumim would make it almost impossible for a fledging Palestinian state to function, not to mention that all Israeli settlements in the West Bank are in fact illegal. The building of the settlements is illegal under the Geneva Convention because it states that an occupying force cannot alter the state of the land, cannot build any permanent structures and cannot forcibly plant or move people from its own state into an occupied territory. The Palestinian state envisioned in the Accord would be a 'non-militarised' one. A worthy vision of course, yet an enfeebled Palestine, utterly subservient to Israel militarily and completely economically reliant on its powerful neighbour worried many Palestinians. Left-wing Palestinian critics of the Accord saw within it a settlement desired by the rich in Israel: a future Palestinian state providing cheap labour to Israel's growing hi-tech economy, a neo-colony of its former occupier.

By 2006, even the vision outlined in the Geneva Accord seemed distant. With so much blood spilt on both sides, peace talks were not on the agenda. With Israel building its Wall and continually developing settlements, and Hamas's electoral victory in the territories, the possibility of a viable two-state solution seem increasingly remote.

'We have to still have hope. We need to hope that there still can be peace despite everything that has happened,' said Idan finally.

A few days after my interview with Idan, Meretz performed impressively in a mock ballot among the students in Tel Aviv University where he had been campaigning hard – but his delight was to be short lived. In the subsequent general election the party fared poorly, winning only 5 out of a possible 120 seats. This compared unfavourably with the far right-wing Yisrael Beiteinu (Israel is Our Home) party, for instance, which, among other controversial proposals, had called for the removal of Arabs from Israel. They won 11 seats.

In the March general election, many Israelis voted for the newly formed Kadima party, which won 29 seats and became the largest party in the resulting coalition government. The party established by Ariel Sharon in August 2005 was as a result of a split within the then governing right-wing Likud party. Likud had been wracked by heated internal divisions following Sharon's decision to remove Jewish settlers from the Gaza Strip. The ageing Sharon was left incapacitated by a major stroke in January 2006, and Ehud Olmert became Acting Prime Minister and leader of Kadima. The party was portrayed as 'centrist' in the Israeli and international media. It won support from both traditional left- and right-wing voting Israelis.

The Kadima TV election campaign broadcast for the March elections was instructive. In one advert, Ehud Olmert sat in front of a large photograph of Sharon. He was then joined by former hard-line military chief and Likud member Shaul Mofaz to emphasise the security element of the new party. In a separate advert, former Labour party leader and then Kadima's number two, Shimon Peres, spoke over grainy footage of Egyptian President Anwar Sadat and Israeli Prime Minister Menachem

Begin signing the famous peace treaty between those countries in 1979. This advert was an overt play for Labour voters or those who still believed, however faintly, in possible peace negotiations with the Palestinians in the future. The party's spin doctors were attempting to spread their potential vote-catching net thinly. Without large numbers of activists on the ground, the young party had no actual support base; it was a 'virtual party' as an Israeli academic friend told me. Almost all its campaigning was conducted through the medium of television.

When Kadima was victorious in the March elections, some of the international media coverage argued that Israeli politics had become more dovish. But in reality, the victory of the Kadima party and the collapse of the right-wing Likud's vote did not herald a period of better relations between Israel and the Palestinians.

The supposedly 'centrist and moderate' political philosophy espoused by Kadima does not stand up to much objective scrutiny as a blueprint for real peace and justice. What the majority of Israelis voted for when voting for Kadima's platform was to keep the major settlements in the West Bank and to continue the building of the Wall inside internationally recognised Palestinian territory. The vote also confirmed that the majority of Israelis were content with their government's behaviour in the occupied territories, with the assassinations of Palestinian militants and with the growing body count of 'ordinary' Palestinian civilians. This was Prime Minister Ehud Olmert's publicly stated plan for the territories, his so-called 'convergence' plan. Such a plan also included a unilateral declaration of Israel's borders with no consultation with the elected Palestinian Authority. Added to that, a compromise on partial Palestinian sovereignty of

Jerusalem, or the 'Right of Return' of the Palestinian refugees from the creation of Israel in 1948 and the 1967 War were not even on the agenda.

While there might have been some debate on the details, the Israeli political establishment and the majority of Israelis had essentially agreed on this agenda espoused by the 'centrist' Kadima party.

It was hard to see any basis for a long-term peace deal here.

Israeli everyday life, particularly in places like Tel Aviv, is in a bubble, removed from what is going on in the territories, as if hermetically sealed. Tel Aviv can be seen on the horizon by Palestinians living in some West Bank villages, a glistening skyscraper skyline. Despite the proximity, life for Israelis and Palestinians moves along in parallel, separate worlds that collide only in violent circumstances.

3

The Open-Air Prison

'Guys, just look slowly. There, at 9 o'clock,' Kevin whispered to us.

I carefully rolled my head left and stared at a nondescript cluster of rocks on the side of the road. I scanned the scenery surrounding them, not spotting anything unusual.

Then, like with a magic eye picture, the shape of an Israeli soldier wearing an olive green uniform morphed into view.

He was leaning over a large, sharp rock perched above the desolate roadside. My eyes quickly made sense of the outline of his image. The soldier seemed to be a sniper, less than ten metres or so away from us. He had his gun cocked up and balanced over the rock. The gun was pointing approximately at my head height. Only the top of the soldier's face and his helmet was visible as he peered intently through the sight of his gun. He was aiming his weapon straight at me and my two American companions, Tammer and Kevin.

We had just got out of our Palestinian taxi at the military 'flying checkpoint'. Another very tall solider, standing in the middle of the road had motioned to us three to walk towards him. He was positioned on his own, close to an armoured jeep parked sideward across the road almost fully blocking it. He seemed to realise that we were internationals as he had shouted over to us to come forward. At the same time, he told the three local Palestinians who were also in the taxi to get out and remain standing beside the vehicle. He wanted to talk to us separately.

As we walked towards him down the middle of the road, my two eyes were now focused on the sniper. It was the first time that I had, knowingly at least, been caught in the scope of a soldier's gun. I felt frightened and exposed. I was potentially in danger of being brutally violated and there was nothing I could do about it. I was powerless.

'Stop there. Passports now,' barked the soldier aggressively. We handed them over.

I concentrated on the soldier's hands as he meticulously studied our three international passports. Each was opened separately, page after page painstakingly inspected.

His facial expressions were diligent and dismissive in equal measure, as he looked at our photographs.

'What religion are you?' he said in what was a somewhat gruff Israeli accent.

'We are all Christian,' said Tammer, the American Palestinian, who was going to do all the talking for us.

'Are you sure?' said the six-foot plus, rock-jawed, broadly built soldier.

'Of course I'm sure,' answered Tammer brazenly.

Kevin and I kept our mouths shut. We were both silently hoping Tammer might cut back a little on the spiky attitude. We did not want to do anything to annoy this formidable, well-armed young man. The soldier raised his head and fixed a solid look on Tammer.

'You're Christian, yes?' he said deliberately. Tammer lied and nodded.

He looked back at Tammer's passport and then slowly back up again towards his face. And he stared intently again. He glanced towards the Palestinians standing at the taxi. Then he looked back again at Tammer.

I sneaked a look to my left. The whole situation was still proceeding under the watchful gaze of the Israeli shooter stationed beside the road. It may have been just my nervous imagination, but I could have sworn that the sniper's arm muscles tightened as he held the weapon. He was now leaning more heavily against the rock.

The three of us were standing somewhere between Ramallah and Jericho on an empty, barren road with desert stretching far away on either side.

Earlier, I had shared a taxi with Tammer, Kevin, two Palestinian young guys I did not know and the Palestinian driver. All Palestinian taxis are either purpose-built long, yellow Mercedes or mini buses, and ours had been a stretch Mercedes that could have carried six passengers in the back. The journey had been good-humoured, as Tammer used his rapidly-improving colloquial Arabic to talk to the three local lads. My poor Arabic, and Kevin's Egyptian Arabic, very different to the Palestinian dialect, proved to be a source of some linguistic amusement to all. On a long stretch of road through the desert, we had come across a small 'flying checkpoint'. These checkpoints are temporary, normally consisting of a few soldiers and maybe one or two military vehicles. They can be established and removed from the road-ways of the occupied territories by the Israeli military with great alacrity, making them difficult to avoid for travelling Palestinians even after significant planning. On this occasion, a solitary Israeli military jeep had been parked across the width of the road. We were the only other vehicle in the vicinity. The soldier standing in front of the jeep had clearly motioned to our taxi driver to stop.

'Who are these guys?' The soldier lazily motioned with his head towards the three Palestinians.

I looked away from the sniper and towards the three Palestinians. They were standing nervously jumping from one foot to the other at the front of the Mercedes. They looked meek and worried. In reality, I was not sure who they were.

'They are friends,' Tammer answered positively.

'Friends, how are they your friends?'

'We met them today in Ramallah.'

'Just today, hmm? Are they troublemakers?'

'No, of course they are not troublemakers,' said Tammer, smiling.

'What were you doing in Ramallah?'

'Having coffee, just hanging out. Nothing in partic-ular, really.'

'Hang … ing … out?' the soldier said slowly in his deliberate drawl.

'Yes. Hanging out,' said Tammer.

'I have been ... in Ramallah ... there is nothing to do ... in Ramallah,' the Israeli said, sarcastically, his upper lip slightly curled. His words were delivered with a healthy dollop of passive aggression through the ever-so-slow delivery of his questions.

The three of us stood silent. I am sure that each one of us went through a series of quick-fire internal questions and observations in our head such as,

'How were you in Ramallah?'

Israeli soldiers don't tend to be seen happily munching on a tasty falafel as they wander along the public streets, or sharing a laugh with locals over backgammon in the coffee shops.

'Was it during the bloody Israeli invasion of the city, three years earlier in 2002?'

'In fairness, you probably did not get to see some of the social highlights of the city or experience the full range of Ramallah's cultural and religious heritage when you were blowing up the shopping centre, driving tanks over cars and destroying its infrastructure.'

Thankfully, we all kept these musings cowardly internalised.

'Sure, there is plenty of stuff you can do in Ramallah,' said Tammer, eventually.

The soldier looked at Tammer with concentrated derision.

'You're American, yes?' he again questioned Tammer directly.

'Yes, I am. Have you ever been?' Tammer enquired.

'Yes, once,' the solider answered quickly, unused to having questions posed to him at a checkpoint.

'You ... are an ... American ... citizen?'

'Yes ...' Tammer sighed slightly in exasperation. 'Look. The story is both he and I are students in Bir Zeit University,' said Tammer pointing at me and then at himself.

'And this is my friend from Egypt who has just come here for the weekend. We are on a trip to Jericho just to show him the sights. We are all Christian, and he is a tourist,' said Tammer sensibly in a neat summation of most of the facts.

The soldier went quiet again.

He looked at us. He looked over our shoulders at the three Palestinians. He looked at the sniper. Then he looked at us again. He stared for ten, twenty, thirty seconds. There was a build-up of deadly desert silence. He gave our passports one final lazy scan. He then handed the three of them back.

'OK, back to the car and get into it ... Send the three of them over with their papers... Tell them to walk slowly. And you,' he barked while pointing at the three of us 'Walk slowly back to the car.'

We turned from the solider and walked towards the taxi. As we walked, I looked again at the sniper as he followed our every move. He then seemed to switch his focus quickly towards the Palestinians standing beside the taxi. It was only a short distance back to the car, but I felt every last step.

A horrific realisation swept over me. What if one of the Palestinian guys did make a 'wrong move'? I did not know them. What if the sniper misjudged one of our actions, say, if we dropped something or heated words were exchanged between the Palestinian taxi driver and the IDF solider? We were standing on an isolated spot deep inside the West Bank. A deadly incident here involving internationals would probably be most unwelcome for the Israeli authorities – but if something awful happened, would all the facts ever get out beyond the Wall? We were trapped at a checkpoint, literally staring down the barrel of a gun. Our immediate survival was in the hands of young, armed, tired, cranky and powerful Israelis.

This was essentially a tiny sample of daily life as experienced by the Palestinian people living within the occupied territories.

I looked away from the sniper and focused on the car's bright yellow door. I quickened my step. I opened the taxi door rapidly, happily falling into its red-hot interior. My exposed flesh was sucked onto the sticky leather seats which quickly clung to the sweat soaking my bare arms and neck. Tammer relayed the message from the Israeli soldier to our fellow travellers in Arabic. We watched as the three Palestinians were beckoned forward. We were full of relieved bravado in the car.

Tammer, a young Palestinian-American whose immediate family had left Palestine many decades before and now lived among the diaspora in the United States was calm throughout the incident. Indeed, with his straight talking, he had displayed some understated verbal resistance in the face of the menacing Israeli soldier. He had extended family that still lived in parts of the northern West Bank and had grown accustomed to the vicious wordplay exchanged at checkpoints when he visited his cousins, aunties and uncles.

'There is nothing to do in Ramallah, did you hear him?' Tammer said smiling. I should have said there was nothing to do in Tel Aviv, see what he would have said to that.

We all laughed, quietly. It was our passports that gave us limited freedom for straight talking with the solider. Local Palestinians would be so confrontational at their peril.

After 20 minutes or so, the Palestinians returned to the taxi following a much rougher and more direct line of questioning. We were allowed to drive on after a nonchalant wave by the thick-set soldier. But he would not move his jeep, so our taxi driver was forced to drive off the road and out onto a bit of the desert to pass. The laughing, joking and bad Arabic erupted again as we continued our journey to Jericho. Ours was just another checkpoint showdown in the West Bank under the red desert sun.

*

As of May 2008 there are 62 permanent checkpoints in the West Bank, with 16 more manned temporarily. There is a constantly changing and undefined number of flying mobile checkpoints erected across the West Bank. According to the United Nations, there were 85 such checkpoints in the final week of March 2008, while there was a weekly average of 69 in November 2007. The number of flying checkpoints is constantly in flux and sometimes can reach above an average of 140 per week.

Palestinians are denied or have restricted access to 24 roads that Jewish drivers can use freely. These roads cover a total of over 300 kilometres. And in March 2008, over 500 physical obstacles such as piles of dirt and large boulders were left on roads by the Israeli military to prevent Palestinian access.

The permanent checkpoint system divides the West Bank up into at least six geographical areas. This conscious partition by the Israelis means that Palestinian travellers must pass through an Israeli checkpoint before being allowed to leave their own immediate locality. Palestinian cars are searched fully, questions asked and papers called for. The whole process can be laborious, with Palestinians spending long hours just waiting. Often, the Israeli military denies access to young men between the ages of 16 and 35, citing broad security reasons for the policy.

Even if a Palestinian is lucky enough to possess a permit that allows them to enter East Jerusalem or the Gaza Strip, these passes are useless on 'comprehensive closure days'. On such days, the Israeli military will announce that no movement through the 26 established checkpoints built close to the Green Line is allowed. In 2005, there were 132 such 'comprehensive closure days'. In reality, recent years have witnessed the journey from the West Bank to the Gaza Strip being made almost impossible, leading to the enforced separation of Palestinian families, friends and the nation itself.

According to the Israeli military, checkpoints are erected for security reasons. They argue that it is the only possible way of slowing down and breaking up the Palestinian 'terror infrastructure', while gaining intelligence about them. Israeli forces at the checkpoints are the front line in the prevention of suicide attacks on the shopping high streets in Tel Aviv and Haifa. Critics counter saying that the checkpoints fulfil little security purpose; hardened militants and experienced young Palestinian activists have extensive local knowledge of the small laneways and roads off the beaten track and can circumnavigate checkpoints if necessary, although such journeys could take many hours longer.

This system of a maze of constantly changing military checkpoints seems to fulfil a much longer-term function in Israel's overall occupational policy towards Palestinian land. One thing is certain: they do make everyday life horrendously difficult for the local Palestinians. Travel and transport are essential to everyday life and commerce, but they are severely restricted by the Israeli military. Almost nothing can be sold, bought, imported, exported, exchanged or transported without Israeli permission. Almost everything in the West Bank, whether animate or inanimate, is counted, watched, logged, surveyed, searched, questioned and restricted by the Israeli authorities. This is despite the very limited administrative powers taken up by the Palestinian Authority since the signing of the Oslo Accords in the early 1990s.

Palestinians are becoming increasingly reluctant to make journeys to meet friends, family, political comrades and business acquaintances in other parts of the West Bank because the journeys are just too laborious and potentially dangerous. Just a short journey can become epic in scope. Even the US Central Intelligence Agency (CIA), hardly a leading supporter of the Palestinian cause, concludes that the recent degradation of the economy in the West Bank has largely been as a result of 'Israeli closure policies'. Such policies, the CIA says, have disrupted both labour and commodity market relationships. The West Bank is a small area and the real distance between locations, 'as the Jew drives' as local

Palestinian dark humour calls it, is quite short. But for
Palestinians, short distances become long and unman-
ageable.

Checkpoints have also become sites of numerous angry
clashes and killings between Palestinians and Israeli
security forces. Particularly deep inside the West Bank
and away from international attention, they are the
scenes of profound humiliation and oppression inflicted
on Palestinian civilians by occupation soldiers.

Tired, hot and angry Israeli soldiers are given almost unlimited power over a people that many of them believe
to be at least sympathetic to terrorists. The results are
predictably bad. Every Palestinian has a horror story
from a checkpoint. Some stories are impossible to verify,
and besides, who can the Palestinians report such incidents to? The Israeli Army is hardly going to keep a
reliable record, and few international or Israeli journalists live and work extensively within the territories. But
thanks to the work of some Palestinian, international
and indeed Israeli peace and justice groups, many incidents have been recorded and become public.

Living in the West Bank, you hear many such stories.
These include men forced to crawl on the ground in
front of laughing soldiers, women verbally abused,
young and elderly civilians kept in melting hot cars for
many hours by Israeli soldiers while queuing at a checkpoint, innocent people shot dead by trigger-happy
soldiers, and one story I was told of an elderly farmer
made to simulate sex with his donkeys in front of soldiers
before being allowed through. Other incidents, such as
Palestinian women giving birth on the side of the road
beside a checkpoint because they have not been allowed

through to access medical care, have been recorded by independent agencies. The UN reported in September 2005 that 60 Palestinian women had given birth at Israeli checkpoints since 2000. Horrifically, 36 of their babies had died as a result.

Israeli human rights agencies have also logged other incidents of human rights abuses that have taken place in the vicinity of army checkpoints, but most of these occurrences are out of sight and out of mind for ordinary Israelis and the international community. Their immediacy for Palestinians helps to further heat the boiling hatred within the hearts and minds of those on the receiving end of the occupation.

Sometimes, a story can escape from behind the Wall and shine a momentary light upon everyday humiliation in the territories. One such infamous incident in November 2004 pricked the consciences of some Israelis in a profound way. Video footage, subsequently aired on Israeli news, showed young Israeli soldiers stopping and questioning a 28-year-old Palestinian violinist, Wissam Tayrem, at a checkpoint. They forced him to play for them on his violin as they stood there preventing him from passing and attending his music lesson in Nablus. They then ordered the reluctant man to perform 'something sad' and began to laugh. It was a pathetic image of how easily they could abuse their power.

The broadcasting of the videotape proved poignant for many Jews. Stories of Jewish musicians forced to play instruments in front of laughing Nazi guards during the Second World War are seared into the collective memory of many Israelis. Although mild compared to many more bloody stories from the checkpoints, the symbolic power of this violin incident led many Israelis to question briefly how the occupation had 'transformed' Israeli soldiers. This navel-gazing is sometimes heard among Israelis from the left and right, concerned more about what the occupation has done to its own citizens and soldiers rather than the misery it has inflicted on the Palestinians. At its most extreme, it was articulated by former Israeli Prime Minister Golda Meir in her infamous observation 'We shall never forgive the Arabs for what they make us do to them'.

As international human rights law requires Israel to respect the right of residents of the occupied territories to move about freely, some groups make a point to keep a close eye on the checkpoints. These would include the women of Machsom Watch and the admirable people at B'Tselem. But those overseeing soldiers' behaviour at the checkpoints are mainly restricted to the checkpoints close to the Green Line. What goes on deep inside the West Bank or the Gaza Strip at unpredictable flying checkpoints is often kept hidden from the general Israeli public. Even when reports issued by Israeli and international human rights groups chronicle abuses by Israeli soldiers at checkpoints in the territories, their impact on the Israeli public is slight. Therefore, apart from fleeting moments of uproar, checkpoints remain an unchallenged application of military occupation on a whole people, a form of collective punishment.

The web of checkpoints, along with the geographical separation between the West Bank and the Gaza Strip combined with the construction of the Wall, has increased the pressure on the Palestinian territories. The policy of dividing the West Bank by checkpoints, settlements and military installations and preventing many locals from travelling within the territories makes many Palestinians question Israel's real intentions. Despite the stated policy of recent Israeli governments that they are in favour of the creation of a Palestinian state, their actions, argue Palestinian leaders, do not support this two-state rhetoric. Rather than creating a fully-functioning, viable, economically vibrant Palestinian state, some charge Israel with enforcing small, divided Arab cantons in the territories.

Palestinian leaders claim that Israel's policy is much like the former South African Apartheid government system of Bantustans. These were small, nominal independent black homelands formed by the racist regime wholly dependent both economically and politically on the Apartheid state. They were in no way independent nations. They fulfilled the ruling white minority's separation agenda by transferring a huge number of the majority black population away from the cities where whites lived, into isolated Bantustans. This policy also helped to divide the black population, thus weakening its political clout.

Other Palestinians say that the Israeli authorities would like to see the West Bank become something similar to a modern Native American reservation. Some political activists have speculated that the long-term aim of such a policy of restriction, partition, and prevention is to grind Palestinians down to such a level of despondency that they feel they are left with no other choice but to leave the Holy Land for good. The Israeli state would then have more space in which to continue its policy of colonisation in the West Bank.

In Bir Zeit University, a large number of young students I spoke to talked of nothing else but leaving the West

Bank to set up a new life abroad. Highly educated young people are even more trapped within the Israeli cage, than, say, the less educated elderly residents of refugee camps. Both are unable to move freely, and they live a restricted life, but the oppression is experienced differently by each. An educated youth in Bir Zeit is all too aware of the world outside. Probably multi-lingual, with conversational English, through internet, books and newspapers, he or she is familiar with the freedoms that exist beyond the Wall and beyond the Holy Land. For an elderly resident of a refugee camp, their imaginary and educational horizons are most probably much more restricted than that of a Bir Zeit graduate. In the atmosphere of deep disillusionment and despair that was widespread in the West Bank following five years of the second intifada, it is little wonder that many of the society's youngest and brightest wanted to leave.

But the checkpoint system may also have a more far-reaching and symbolic aim and result: nothing less than the attempted division and rupture of the Palestinian nation to such an extreme extent that Palestinian nationalism itself loses unity and collapses, with the Palestinian people purposely divided by the Israeli authorities into partitioned, localised enclaves. The growing division between the West Bank and the Gaza Strip is a clear example of this. Divided by Israel, both territories have developed separately in recent years. Gaza faces far more intensive poverty problems than the West Bank. Hamas and the Islamic parties have grown in strength much quicker than in the West Bank. Gaza residents often express their resentment at the better living conditions experienced by their brethren in the West Bank. By the beginning of 2008, two separate Palestinian administrations existed: one Islamic and Hamas-led on the Gaza

Strip, the other controlled by the more secular Fatah on the West Bank.

Modern Palestinian identity is one that already comprises fragmentation and an enforced diaspora. Palestinian refugees who fled their land from Israeli forces in 1948 and 1967 live mainly in refugee camps across the Arab world with their families and descendents. Other Palestinians have made lives for themselves in the Western world. There is a further gulf between Palestinians who live in Israel and those who reside in the occupied territories.

Before the late 1960s, most of the Arab world looked to Egyptian leader Gamal Abdel Nasser (1918–70) to lead the Arab armies to victory against Israel and return the Palestinians to their homeland. Since the defeat of his Pan-Arabism movement in the 1967 War when Israel crushed Egyptian, Jordanian and Syrian armies, a particular form of 'Palestinianism' has developed. This Palestinian nationalism primarily regarded its own people, rather than those of the neighbouring Arab states, as the agency of liberation. It was a specifically *Palestinian* nationalism that took into account the nation's historic past, but also its complex present composed of different religions, locations and political orientations that had been moulded since 1948. Israeli leaders have sometimes denied the very existence of the Palestinians as a people. Former Israeli PM Golda Meir once declared 'there were no such things as Palestinians'. Palestinians in the occupied territories have thus considered Israel's policy of partition, checkpoints and division as attempts to smash Palestinian identity into many pieces, weakening the people and making them easier to control. Such Israeli policies have not just bred resistance among Palestinians but also resentment and resignation.

While some, particularly the educated youth, speculate on breaking free and establishing a life for themselves in the relative freedom of exile, others cannot even contemplate such an option. For most in the West Bank watching the fading embers of the second intifada, life is about survival, making do with what little you have, hunkering down and getting on with it. As Yasser Arafat said during the most intensive moments of Israel's invasion of the West Bank in 2002, it's about 'just hanging on'.

*

In many ways, Abal el Rahman Isma'iel is a typical Palestinian politician on the West Bank. The mayor of the village of Deir Ballout, which is located a short distance north of Ramallah, is a hands-on political representative who waves at villagers while on his travels. He stops and chats cheerfully with the local shopkeeper and the farmer herding his goats through the village. He is a middle-aged, bearded man with gaunt features, and like most Palestinian men in almost all circumstances, he is rather formally dressed when we meet him on a warm afternoon, wearing a long-sleeved shirt, trousers and black shoes. The Middle Eastern summer weather naturally cries out for t-shirt, shorts and sandals, but such an outfit is hardly ever seen on the West Bank except on sporting occasions.

When an unattended decrepit-looking tractor blocks one of Deir Ballout's small, winding streets, the mayor goes over, jumps behind the ancient contraption's steering wheel and moves it out of the way himself. Equally typical for this part of the world, he has served time as a political prisoner in an Israeli jail. Almost every adult male you meet in the West Bank has spent some time incarcerated by the Israeli authorities.

Being the mayor of a town normally has a dramatic and exciting ring to it. One can almost picture classy champagne receptions with local businesspeople that need to be attended. Extended foreign trips to 'twinned' towns that have to be undertaken, and an element of power that the mayor can wield to shape his constituency how he wants. For the mayor of Deir Ballout, the reality of the job is significantly more gritty, stressful and powerless.

He has limited economic means and is thus severely restricted in what he can do. Much of his agenda is just about 'hanging on' to what little the people of Deir Ballout have, which is not much. The sleepy village is very small and rural, but its tranquil way of life was coming to an end as major construction on the Israeli Wall was planned for the area. Deir Ballout in the summer of 2005 was dying economically and was facing a dismal future, becoming a sad metaphor for Palestine's numerous difficulties.

'I am only the mayor for a short number of months, but during that time I have not been working on local issues such as roads or small things to do with the local people in the town,' he said through our translator.

'My whole time has been taken up by the Wall and the fight for our school.'

The translator struggled to keep pace with the speed of the Mayor's Arabic. He was infectiously welcoming and had already warmly greeted a small number of international students from Bir Zeit University on a day trip to the area. He met us in his mayoral office and quickly offered us delicious Arabic coffee. As we sipped, he left his office. He re-emerged loudly into the room again moments later with an unstable bundle of rolled maps tumbling from his arms. Some of the maps were huge and colourful, displaying the whole of the West Bank. Others were tightly detailed and much smaller, concentrating on the area directly surrounding his village. All the maps had one thing in common: they followed the route of the Wall.

'We have to get new maps all the time, because they keep on changing the route of the Wall. They do not inform us of what is happening. All this detail is important for our case. It is so hard to keep track of what they are doing, but we have to try,' he said while apologising as he finally dropped the maps in a chaotic heap on his desk.

The maps were then rolled out on his small table and on the ground. He pointed quickly to the route and the changes that had been made. His middle finger wound its way along a thin black line, with tiny writing in Hebrew and Arabic on either side. He spoke of the land owned by named local individuals where the Wall was due to go through, sections of the village that would be divided. It was difficult to follow his excited explanation of what was happening, not being familiar with the immediate geography of the place, but he was a man who had become consumed by this project. Rather than quietly hunkering down while the cement and concrete was piled high around his locality, the mayor had carefully watched every Israeli move. He had traced it in as much detail as he could. He followed each centimetre planned for the Wall.

He could clearly see the travesty facing his town and the slow chronicling of this tragedy by map-makers only seemed to spur him on to greater effort. Because of Deir Ballout's proximity to major West Bank Jewish settlements such as Ariel, the town was set to be completely encircled when the Wall was completed. As the mayor spoke to us, a large number of Israeli military helicopters could be heard buzzing overhead. Then Israeli Prime Minister Ariel Sharon was due that day to visit the massive Jewish settlement, Ariel, located a short distance away. I wondered if he looked down upon Deir Ballout while swooping low over the village in his final descent, as the route of the Wall was pointed out to him by one of his security advisors.

'The Wall will affect the whole of the West Bank and the Palestinians, but we are a special case. We are losing land, farmers have sold their animals because there is no land to keep them on anymore and people are leaving the town because of this. You cannot use the land that is near the route of the Wall. They do not allow this. When the Wall is completed there will be further restrictions on movement from the town. We really are a special case because we will have no way out. And this is no way to live properly.'

Deir Ballout, along with a small number of similarly affected West Bank villages and towns had taken their case to the Israeli courts. They tried to use the Israeli judicial system in an attempt to have the Wall re-routed and prevent the near fatal blow its construction would deliver to the residents of the village. Palestinians often use petitions to the Israeli Supreme Court in last-ditch attempts at achieving justice. The existence of the Supreme Court, and the fact that it sometimes rules in favour of Palestinian claimants is held up by many Israelis and international observers as proof positive of the relatively liberal nature of the military rule over the territories. Indeed, within Israel, the Supreme Court has an often thoroughly justified reputation for upholding the civil rights of Jewish citizens. It is heralded by many secular and left-wing Israeli Jews as a progressive body that defends individual freedoms. In contrast, it is hated by right-wing religious Zionists who believe it to be incurably liberal and activist in its rulings.

A closer study of the Court's role in relation to the Palestinians exposes other consequences. In reality, the clear majority of its rulings favour the Israeli government and military vis-à-vis Palestinians. The very fact that it delivers rulings on cases arising from within the occupied territories confers a certain legitimacy on that illegal occupation. In the case of Deir Ballout, it is understandable why the village and others, with the support of Israeli human rights groups have taken a petition to the Israeli Supreme Court. What other option do they have? But if their petition fails and the court rules in favour of the military and the Israeli government, what then? The Israeli government and supporters of the present route of the Wall can say, 'Look, you have had your day in court, a liberal court at that, and you have lost.' Such a decision would almost legitimise the route of a Wall that is being built on illegally occupied land and that has been condemned by the international community and all the leading human rights bodies, including Israeli ones.

But for mayor Abal el Rahman Isma'iel, such theoretical debates and the legitimising consequences of the writ of the Supreme Court in the West Bank were understandably not his central concern. He, along with the other villages and towns affected, employed a Jewish Israeli lawyer to

fight their case because he had to think of his con-
stituents, the farmers, workers, shop owners and
children of Deir Ballout.

When we left the mayor's office we drove south from
the town past small boys riding donkeys and old women
with their heads covered walking slowly. To say that the
pace of life in Deir Ballout was pedestrian does not capture the intensity of its sedateness. Like Palestinians
from all across the West Bank, locals accused Israeli
forces and Jewish settlers of attacking and ripping up
their olive trees to prevent their harvest. In Deir Ballout,
there was a nasty twist: Palestinian residents claimed that
Jewish settlers had purposely introduced wild boar to
the area. These animals could be seen running across
the main dirt road into the village, and residents said
that they gorged on and destroyed the local olive trees.

The destruction of Palestinian olive trees by Jewish settlers is well documented by human rights organisations
and by the Israeli media. It is an act not only of economic vandalism, but of hugely symbolic importance.
Olive trees are not only vital to the Palestinian rural
economy, but a symbol of historic ties to the land that
go back generations. Many of the radical settlers want to
uproot the olive trees in the same way that they would
like to uproot the Palestinians. The olives are crushed
into the ground by settlers, left to bleed into the dry
sand.

*

On the outskirts of the town, we passed the three-storey
shell of a building which was meant by that stage to be
a fully functioning primary school but was instead empty
and idle. The construction of the school was halted after

79

the Israeli military authorities claimed that it was built too close to the intended route of the Wall.

In the tortuous post-Oslo language deployed in the West Bank, part of the school was now designated to be 'Zone C', which meant that it was in an area deemed by the Israeli military to be under their full control. The 1993 Oslo Accords were signed by Palestine Liberation Organization (PLO) leader, Yasser Arafat, and Israeli Prime Minister Yitzhak Rabin and Foreign Minister Shimon Peres. For years, the Israeli government had refused to meet or talk to the PLO, and the Accord were seen as historic, bringing to an end the first intifada. The Accords led to the formation in 1994 of the very limited self-governing PA in Gaza and in small urban pockets of the West Bank.

Most Palestinians I spoke to regard the Oslo Accords as an appalling deal in retrospect. While it was the first time that Israel recognised the PLO as the legitimate representative of the Palestinian people, according to many, there were few other positive results. The Accords say nothing about settlement construction in the occupied territories, and the national aspirations of the Palestinian people are ignored. There is nothing in the agreement about an eventual Palestinian state, the issues of Jerusalem or the refugees.

Many Palestinian critics see the principal reason for Arafat's support for the agreement as politically selfish. The PLO had since the late 1960s existed in wretched exile in Jordan, then Lebanon and finally Tunisia. When sitting in North Africa, Arafat and the PLO leadership watched the spontaneous outbreak of the first intifada in the occupied territories on television, far from the violent

Palestinian streets. The uprising took place in the territories beyond the control and largely independent of the PLO leadership. Many critics say that Arafat worried that his organisation's power in the occupied territories was on the wane; he wanted to get back to Palestine at any cost to reassert his hegemony, and Oslo served as a vehicle for his return to power. As part of the agreement, Israel allowed Arafat return to a rapturous reception in Gaza in July 1994. Palestinian supporters wept as their leader returned to guide them to a future state. In contrast, his Palestinian critics saw Arafat and his political and military supporters as having compromised so much with the Israelis that they were now little more than petty collaborators in the occupation.

Following the signing of the Oslo Accords, the West Bank and the Gaza Strip had been broken up into zones. Zone A covered the Palestinian urban centres such as Ramallah, Nablus and Jericho where the Palestinian security forces were meant to wield civil and military control. In Zone B, including towns such as Bir Zeit, the IDF was to have military control, while the Palestinians would oversee civil matters. In Zone C, the Israeli's would have complete control. Zone C made up 60 per cent of the West Bank. Israeli incursions into Zone A were frequent, and real Palestinian power was slight. Despite the language in the agreement, Israel still controlled the land, skies, exit and entrance points to the West Bank and Gaza Strip. Also, the Israeli authorities tended to unilaterally designate areas as being in Zone C when it suited them. Sadly for the people of Deir Ballout, this included the area around their planned school.

'This was to be a great school, with full access for children with disabilities and great facilities,' said the mayor with obvious pride in his voice as he stood on the flat roof of the empty building.

'We wanted to have the school just outside the town centre, so there would be more space for the children to play and to get them away from the centre of the town. It was a perfect location, everyone thought so … and then this happened,' he said sadly.

From the roof of the empty Deir Ballout school, if you squint hard, you can make out the high-rise skyline of Tel Aviv. Tel Aviv is one of the Israeli cities that the Wall is intended to protect from suicide bombers.

'This is not about security – this Wall could not stop a rocket being fired into Israel. It is about taking our land and our village. That is the real issue here,' said the mayor.

Just over two years after meeting the mayor of Deir Ballout and the protest in Bil'in, the Israeli Supreme Court made a number of rulings on the Wall.

In the case of Bil'in, in September 2007, the court ordered the Israeli government to redraw the path of the Wall. It concluded that the route of the Wall was 'highly prejudicial' to the residents of Bil'in. On the following day, the same court legalised the Jewish settlement of Mattiyahu East, which had been built on a disputed portion of Bil'in land. The judgement ordering the re-routing of part of the Wall near Bil'in was welcomed by Palestinian and Israeli peace activists. But the Bil'in committee who organised the weekly demonstrations continue the regular protests. They say that the demonstrations will continue until the implementation of the court's ruling for the Wall to be pushed westward away from Bil'in. It has yet to be moved by the Israeli military.

*

The Jewish-German philosopher Theodore Adorno wrote darkly about modern capitalist society having become 'a totally administered world'. Formulating his philosophy in the years directly following the Second World War, his view of a nightmarish dystopian present had much to recommend it. Conscious of writing under the shadow of the Hiroshima mushroom cloud and in the wake of the horrors of the Holocaust, Adorno deployed his Marxism in an attempt to explain why the socialist utopian revolution had not emerged in the first half of the twentieth century as many on the political left had hoped. Adorno saw western popular culture in the 1950s and 1960s as playing a crucial role in homogenising society and diluting dissent. In Adorno's thinking, the modern developed state was frightening, distant, inhuman and unassailably powerful. Despite much talk of 'freedom' and 'democracy', in reality, modern living was one of restricted choice, suffocating oppression by powerful and centralised elites. He bemoaned the 'open-air prison that the world is becoming'. I thought of Adorno on my most recent visit to the West Bank security crossing at Kalandia in May 2008.

The Kalandia checkpoint is the major thoroughfare between Israel and the West Bank and is located on the outskirts of East Jerusalem. In 2005, Kalandia was a chaotic commercial hub; fleeting market stalls sprung up and quickly melted away again, screams from Arab taxi drivers filled the air and a formless mass of bodies squeezed their way unhappily through narrow Israeli army security gates. Israeli military jeeps sped up and down the roadway that ran through the checkpoint. A lone concrete look-out tower stood high above, ominously overseeing the general commotion. The look-out was splattered with paint thrown at it by protestors. A tattered Israeli flag hung from the small narrow slits at the top. Israeli soldiers poked their guns out of the tower, aiming down on the Palestinians queuing below them. Soldiers physically moved Palestinian men into queues. Arguments started, with the men remonstrating loudly against the armed guards. Young, pretty female IDF soldiers laughed among themselves, giggling and messing with each other like any normal teenage girls. But once the friendly banter between them was over, they turned to face their duty, questioning, ordering and searching hundreds of Palestinian women, some of them their elders by many decades.

Kalandia was an overall nexus of tense militarised disorder. Seemingly random gun shots were fired into the air, soldiers shouted and sweated and Palestinians waited and sweated some more. Israeli soldiers searched for would-be suicide bombers while Palestinians waited to be allowed to continue on with their lives.

Next to all of this, the construction of a new 'processing centre' for the Palestinians was underway. The building work continued all summer long in 2005. By May 2008, the centre was open and the shapeless chaos of three summers previous was replaced by a more orderly and quieter Kalandia. The Wall was now completed in the adjoining area and it linked up with the new concrete processing centre. On the surface, Kalandia had become

more placid. The tattered, limp Israeli flag had been replaced with a brand new, well-ironed, bright, blue and
white flag. The Star of David flew with confidence over
the checkpoint. The market stalls were gone and even
taxi drivers were more serene. Yet the atmosphere created
was, if anything, more sinister and dehumanising for the
Palestinians who had to go through it.

I had left Ramallah ten minutes before and was being
driven towards the checkpoint in an East Jerusalem-
registered, green-and-white mini bus. There had been a
major demonstration earlier that day in central Ramallah
marking the anniversary of the creation of the State of
Israel and the resulting Palestinian exodus in 1948.
Because of this, there seemed to be even more tension
than usual in the built-up area between the city and
Kalandia. Israeli helicopters could be seen in the clear
sky, and in the distance the thuds of what sounded like
grenades could be heard.

As we approached the checkpoint, large numbers of
young Palestinian children and teenagers were running
in and out of the neighbouring Kalandia refugee camp.
Some were rolling burning tyres in front of them as they
ran towards the main road that approached the checkpoint. Others carried large rocks and rubble and flung
them onto the road. It was clear that they were trying to
block the main road into the refugee camp.

As our mini bus got closer to the large group of Palestinian youths, it became apparent that something else
was going on. In the background, through the dark
smoke produced by the smouldering tyres, I could see
more than ten Israeli army jeeps parked across the main
road. Some 30 or 40 Israeli soldiers were now standing

across the centre of the road in front of the checkpoint. They were starting to advance towards the youngsters.

Then there followed the shattering explosion of a number of stun grenades fired simultaneously by the Israeli soldiers towards the refugee camp entrance. For some reason, our mini bus driver started to speed up towards the rocks and rubble that the Palestinian youths had piled onto the road. The bus was packed with 12 or so passengers and the Arab women in particular were arguing loudly in Arabic with the driver.

As he headed at great speed towards the road block, we could only watch as the Palestinians began to fling stones at the Israeli lines, and then scamper back into the adjacent camp. Our driver reached the burning tyres and braked hard. The youths made space for our bus, but continued to throw stones at the advancing soldiers. With some admirable skill, our driver negotiated the rocks on the road, and continued driving towards the Israeli soldiers. At this point, some of the passengers were clearly distressed. Israeli soldiers fired tear gas canisters past the side of the bus towards the Palestinians, while rocks sailed over us the other way. The driver swung to the right and drove rapidly past the line of soldiers who were now shooting plastic bullets in the direction of the Palestinian youths. He braked suddenly when he got to the car park connected to the Kalandia checkpoint.

We eventually alighted, a little shook up, but happy that no bullets or rocks had shattered the bus window, as they so easily could have. We made our way towards the 'processing centre' to leave the West Bank and continue our journey towards East Jerusalem.

More than 30 minutes later, I was still queuing at the checkpoint in the oppressive heat. The Palestinian men, women and children waiting at Kalandia checkpoint were starting to get a little restless. It was not even the time when most Palestinians had finished work yet, but the number of people who had the relevant pass and were waiting to leave the West Bank to enter East Jerusalem was increasing rapidly.

Where we stood around a turnstile there was no clearly defined queue. People were forced to crush forward to try to force their way into the narrow opening that only allowed through one person at a time. The turnstile was controlled remotely by the unseen Israeli guards on the other side of the centre. People would enter the turnstile, and then half-way around, the Israeli guard would stop it randomly, catching them between its hard metal bars, stuck there until the soldier decided to unlock the gate.

Each person had to come through the intensive security checkpoint one by one, and it was painfully slow. Think about the exasperation that has engulfed the Western world over the increased waiting times and security checks that passengers must deal with in airports in recent years. Now imagine having to deal with that every day in horrible heat rather than in an air-conditioned airport, questioned by armed soldiers who regard you as a potential bomber – and all this, not for a holiday, but just for your daily commute home. Each Palestinian has to wait his or her turn to be called forward by an unseen Israeli soldier heard only through a loudspeaker. Papers are checked, and sometimes people can get through fairly rapidly. At other times, Palestinians are held for longer periods and the whole checkpoint 'system' grinds to a weary halt. These delays continue despite an increase in personnel on the ground. The number of armed soldiers in 2008 seemed to have also increased from the 2005 levels, but now they are kept behind the safety of large concrete walls and thick, bullet-proof reinforced plastic.

I waited for an hour before making it to the front of the queue. In the background we could hear the tear gas, gunfire and sound grenades in the continuing battle between the Israeli army and the youths from the local Kalandia refugee camp. This wicked noise added to the tension and pressure of the wait. Finally, after seeing mothers pushing and shoving their way in, elderly men crushed at the front trying to reach the turnstile, and young students desperately attempting to lift their school bag and equipment above their heads, I forced my way into the turnstile. This is not an edifying procedure because if you do not push yourself forward, skipping others in the anarchic queue, it will be ages before you reach the turnstile. Sometimes, Palestinians caught up in the heave forward understandably snap and argue among themselves.

When I got through, I placed my bag in the metal detector. I walked over to the glass window to present my passport. On the other side of the glass sat the two guards who had been overseeing this upsettingly slow process. They had been checking each Palestinian ID at a snail's pace.

Both the guards were female. Neither could have been more than 20 years old. Inside their protected office, one guard looked lazily at my passport and nodded for me to continue on. The other guard sat back swinging on her chair, with her two feet up on the table. She had a magazine balanced on her knees which she seemed to be reading in a languid way. She never once lifted her eyes to look at me.

Kalandia checkpoint is the main gateway into the West Bank from East Jerusalem. Prior to 2006, with much of the Wall still incomplete, it was a heaving commercial centre, an unexpected creation of the Israeli occupation. Israeli troops questioned Palestinians one-on-one while a general sense of uncontrolled madness surrounded the area. By 2008, it was different. The massive Kalandia checkpoint was now completed with the imposing wall fully formed on both sides. No Israeli soldier interacted directly with Palestinians, but rather through bullet-proof plastic and shouting orders through loudspeakers.

The sensation you get while standing waiting your turn is a threatening one, and the experience of the whole process leaves you feeling like an animal. The checkpoint itself is large and imposing, with the constant banging of metal as gates open and close. The checkpoint is like the overall experience of the Israeli military occupation for the Palestinians, frightening, disconnected, inhuman and unassailably powerful.

There are some chinks in the checkpoint and the Wall's construction. Graffiti, much of it written rapidly in Arabic under the threat of gunfire, is hastily drawn all over the Wall near Kalandia. More 'professional' artwork, such as that of the secretive British 'guerrilla' artist Banksy, brightens up the dull surroundings somewhat. One of his creations depicts a hole in the wall with a calm beachfront in the distance. Another has a ladder going over the Wall and a young girl holding a bunch of balloons that float her towards the top.

*

Qalqiliya, a city in the north-west of the West Bank, has
it worse than most. When you visit, it becomes clear
very quickly that the 44,000-plus people who live there
are essentially imprisoned. In the west of the city, there
is an imposing eight-metre-high wall. In the north, south
and east there is a fence which includes patrol roads for
Israeli military vehicles and trenches. There is only one
checkpoint from which you can exit to the west, and
that checkpoint is located on a narrow and extremely
busy road with long tail-backs. It has been reported that
up to ten per cent of the city's population has had to
leave their homes because of the construction of the
Wall, which has led to the closure of the city market and
hurt the local economy. Over 35,000 of Qalqiliya's inhabitants are registered as refugees, and unemployment
levels are 76 per cent, compared to just 20 per cent before the start of the intifada in 2000.

In July 2004, the International Court of Justice made its
landmark judgment on the Wall. The court ruled against
Israel by 14 votes to one. Part of the advisory ruling read:

> 'The construction of the wall being built by
> Israel, the occupying power, in the Occupied
> Palestinian Territory, including in and around
> East Jerusalem, and its associated regime, are
> contrary to international law ... All states are
> under an obligation not to recognise the illegal
> situation resulting from the construction of the
> wall and not to render aid or assistance in
> maintaining the situation created by such con-
> struction'

In its defence, the Israeli government says the barrier is
not a permanent border, rather a 'temporary defensive

measure' against suicide bombers from the West Bank. It argues that the route was not chosen as part of a land grab, rather based on 'security needs and topological considerations'. 'Death is permanent. It is irreversible. The inconvenience caused to the Palestinians by the security fence is temporary and reversible, once terrorism stops and peace is achieved', claims the Israeli government website.

By November 2007, 409 kilometres of the Wall had been completed with a further 66 kilometres under construction. Once complete, the Wall will run 723 kilometres long. By anyone's reckoning, this is a large-scale 'temporary measure' to dismantle when a peace deal is signed. Since the Gaza Disengagement in 2005 when Israel removed its settlers from the Gaza Strip, international pressure on Israel to cease construction of the Wall has all but ended. The silent death of any future viable Palestinian state is taking place while the Wall develops and the checkpoint system intensifies within the territories. While the world still pays lip-service to a two-state solution, the facts on the ground make such a solution all but impossible.

*

The mayor of Deir Ballout brought us to meet a friend of his who lives in the neighouring village of Mas'ha. Hani Aamer lives in his family home with his wife and children. His modest house resembles more an ugly threatened militarised bunker than a home for raising a young family. When we approached his front garden we were confronted by a lone Israeli soldier. He was standing by the tall metal gate that blocks the entrance to the small area of land in front of the Aamer home. A large sign on the gate had 'mortal danger' written on it in

Hebrew, English and Arabic. Behind the solider, the middle-aged Hani Aamer came from his front door and wandered down to the gate.

He spoke to the soldier for a couple of seconds, who eventually turned around to us.

'You have five minutes,' he said loudly.

Hani Aamer opened a gate for us and brought us up the short laneway to his extraordinary home. His house, which was once located on the edge of good farming land, is now totally enclosed. On one side, a Jewish settlement backs onto the house, and on the other stands the eight-metre-plus concrete Wall. The remaining two sides are surrounded by a tall gate erected by the Israeli army who constanly patrol it.

Hani claims he had been offered money by the Israeli authorities to move, but he and his family had refused, despite their isolation and the danger in which their choice placed them. He simply said that this was his family home and he did not want to leave; admirable personal stubbornness had fused with Palestinian nationalist aspirations to stiffen his family's resolve to stay put.

'It does not matter how much we are offered. They want to take the house and build the Wall or settlement on it,' he told us, as his wife brought us homemade lemonade while we sat in their front room.

The front door was open and all you could see was the massive Wall just a few metres from the house. It blocked out the sunlight, leaving the sitting room consumed by a deep, dark shadow.

'We have been on the media and many groups know about our position here now. I think that is the reason we have not been forcibly moved by the Israelis,' he said through a translator.

Understandably the Aamer family home has become a celebrated case for international and Palestinian peace groups who oppose the Wall. It is a Kafkaesque story that has attracted international media including Al-Jazeera Television to the Aamer home. Hani Aamer said that rocks are sometimes hurled at his family from the adjoining settlement. His wife and children must pass through the gates in the large fence around their property to get to and from school. The army does not always allow immediate entry or exit, arguing that the family home is in fact a militarised zone. Thus they might have to wait in their own front garden for long periods before being allowed out to live their lives.

As Hani relayed his family's extraordinary story to us in his living room, we were suddenly addressed from outside by the Israeli military.

'Please leave the house now. This is a military zone,' a solider roared at us in English through a loudhailer.

When we got up and walked out the front door, seven Israeli soldiers had taken up positions within the front garden. Some were standing around while others hunched down in firing positions in the garden. An army jeep had arrived at the scene as well. The soldiers had 'invaded' and now occupied all sections of the garden. We were brought to the fence by Hani and passed through the gate using the only key the Israeli army had given the Aamer family. This was the only gate that the family was able to pass through out of their own front garden, and even that was on a restricted basis.

The soldiers followed our every move as we sat down on a road outside the gate and Hani spoke to us for a period. While he told us his life story and the difficulties caused by the Wall's arrival to his doorstep in 2004, constant volleys of gun shots could be heard not too far in the distance.

We eventually left the Aamer family and returned with the Mayor to Deir Ballout. We left him to face his increasingly difficult task of preventing the Wall's on-ward construction. After a day-long excursion to Deir Ballout and its neighbouring villages, we bid the Mayor farewell and the ten international students and our Palestinian interpreter, teacher and driver set out on our journey back to Bir Zeit in our mini bus.

Just outside the village we were stopped at a permanent checkpoint. We waited for 30 minutes before being called forward. All of our passports were taken away and checked by the Israeli soldiers. This took a further 15 minutes or so. We were then waved on through. We drove on for maybe 30 seconds and we were waved down by another two soldiers standing in the road. They walked up and down the side of the mini bus. They beckoned for our windows to be opened. They asked for our passports. They were taken away and checked again. This took a further 20 minutes. Eventually our passports were returned and handed back to us. We set off again. We drove on ten feet and took a right at the crossroads. A lone solider was standing in the road and motioned to the driver to stop.

We all started roaring laughing. We stopped again, and the soldier saw us laughing. His eyes looked lazily inside the mini bus. He looked stoned, like a significant number of Israeli soldiers I had encountered across the West Bank. He smiled and was pleasant, partly because he could surely also see the madness of the whole thing. Regardless, he checked our passports, which took a further ten minutes or so.

Imagine this every day for a resident of Deir Ballout, when the mood would not be one of general mirth and the response of the soldiers most likely not as benign. Why would you ever leave your own village if such restrictions were put in place? Towards the end of my summer-long stay in the occupied West Bank I noticed that I travelled less to Jerusalem, or even to Ramallah, just outside Bir Zeit. The journeys were so difficult to plan because of the checkpoints and the long delays, and sitting in a sweltering hot taxi or private car for any length of time in the Holy Land is not pleasant. It became easier to spend time in the town, the university and on the Internet. I felt like that after only one summer there – Palestinians live with it 24/7, all year long. The will to travel, to move, to exist beyond your own small area is squeezed out of you as the geographical parameters of your existence become smaller and smaller within ever-decreasing checkpoint circles.

You are doing time, collectively as a people, in the open-air prison that your reality has become.

4

Dancing in Ramallah

I left the Institute of Women's Studies building, which is isolated on the far edge of Bir Zeit University campus. It was only a few weeks into my stay in the occupied territories. The Palestinian heat was still toasting my pale Irish skin mercilessly.

I started to stroll along the downhill walkway towards the college canteen to get some falafel and salad for lunch. I looked to either side of the path at the rolling, desperately dry hills of the West Bank, almost barren except for a small number of olive trees. I watched an Israeli military helicopter buzzing, at a low altitude a kilometre or so away. It was hovering, menacingly, over what looked like a cluster of white-walled two-storey Palestinian homes.

As I approached the canteen, I could clearly hear an angry speech being made in unintelligible yet exuberant

Arabic. The sound of excited clapping and irregular noisy cheers from many young voices followed and filled the momentary lull in the speaker's delivery. Deliberate and consistent chanting began, among what sounded to my eager ears like many hundreds of youthful, enthusiastic demonstrators.

When I finally reached the canteen and walked around to the building's west side, I eventually saw the protest. It was smaller than it sounded – maybe fewer than a hundred young Palestinian students stood together, some holding flags from the different political factions, others chatting on their mobile phones and talking to friends in tight private conversational knots. The crowd was mixed, with young men and women standing together dressed in jeans, the men wearing bright modern shirts and many women dressed in Western style tops. The majority of female students was wearing some form of head-dress, although the veils were often colourful and wrapped in a way that obviously corresponded as much to local contemporary fashion as ancient religious tradition. To one side of the protest close to the front, there was a group of female students wearing more modest, sombre head-dresses that showed the whole face, but included full-length dark shawls. These were supporters of the Islamic student political movement on campus.

Around the perimeter of the protest, other more disinterested-looking students sat on the steps leading into the Science and Administrative buildings. They were lying back stretching their legs laughing and joking, enjoying the break from lectures and the simmering heat of the high sun. These were clearly the cool kids. Their languid laziness combined with obvious apathy towards

the protest contrasted sharply with the studious serious-
ness of the students directly involved. Beyond the students sitting on the steps, I noticed that the door to the
university's Registration building was chained shut from
the outside, with a large lock swinging below the handle.

A young male speaker had now seized the microphone,
connected to the super-loud sound system. He took in
an overtly deep breath and began to deliver one of the
angriest, most passionate speeches I had ever witnessed
at a demonstration. Although I could not understand a
word of it, I was taken in by the pure, visceral emotion
that this animated student was so obviously feeling. The
protestors listened intently to his every utterance as
shown by their concentrated stares; they, too, empathised
completely with his loudly-stated stance. Getting
whipped up by the heavy cadences of the speaker, the
atmosphere at the protest was one of controlled but
determined anger. Yet some of the other students sitting
around soaking in the rays on the university steps
seemed much less interested in the growing excitement
among the standing protestors and were largely
unmoved by the intoxicating ire of the speaker. Some
clapped politely, and others did not bother to acknowledge the speaker at all.

Holding the Palestinian national flag in one hand and
the microphone in the other, the speaker shouted,
roared, spoke slowly and then rapidly. He got the protestors to chant back in unison to his calls. I could only
guess at what he was saying. One of the reasons that I
had enrolled in Bir Zeit was because I knew that the
university had long been regarded as a significant forum
for debate and political discussion within the Palestinian
political process.

The annual student union elections are seen by local and international commentators as pivotal events that give some indication of wider political processes at work in the territories. For decades, the secular groupings, Yasser Arafat's Fatah and the leftist PFLP held sway on campus with many of the leaders of both major political parties filling leading posts in the student body. In recent years, the Islamic student group, essentially Hamas, has grown in popularity in Bir Zeit, formerly a bastion of Fatah student power. Such a political change on campus foresaw the rise of the Islamic factions and the corresponding demise of the leftist and secular groups within wider Palestinian society.

Was this rally a show of strength by Hamas on campus with the elections for the PLC just months away? Maybe I could get talking to one of the student leaders to try to organise an interview. I was told that student politicians were often wary of granting interviews or speaking to foreign journalists. Israeli undercover spies were a real and constant threat to many Palestinian activists young and old in the West Bank. Maybe if I got talking to one of the leaders of the Islamic student body at this protest, I could begin to build up a rapport and gain their trust.

Despite my then total ignorance of Arabic, I began to suspect that the speaker was directing his sharply politicised bile at the 'Zionist entity', promising that the younger generation of Palestinians would free Jerusalem from Israeli occupation, or pleading with West Bank residents never to forget those who live in exile in the refugee camps. Perhaps the angry rally had been organised in reaction to a localised Israeli raid or an attack on Bir Zeit town or university that I had not yet heard about. All I was certain of was that I was attending my first authentic political rally in the occupied territories against the Israeli military.

I spotted Mohammad, one of the many young former students with frighteningly fluent English who were employed on a part-time basis by the university to help international students.

'What is he saying?' I said pointing at the speaker. 'Is this rally organised because of some Israeli military attack? What political faction is he from? Are these all Hamas students?' I asked quickly.

'One moment, David, let me just hear.' He went quiet and listened to the young speaker as he reached an impressive crescendo of noise and gestures, waving the Palestinian flag over his head while shouting individual Arabic words into the microphone.

'He is Hamas, OK,' said Mohammad.

'Right. Is he saying anything about Fatah? Or criticising the ceasefire or the talks with Ariel Sharon?' I said, developing a hook from which a decent article about contemporary internal Palestinian politics could easily be hung.

'No, nothing like that,' he said, not looking at me but still staring and listening to the speaker.

'Well, what then?' I said bewildered.

'He is calling for a student strike because the registration fees have increased this term.'

'What?'

'This protest was called by all the political groups, I think, to support a campaign against the increase in the registration fee. He is the Hamas spokesperson who is backing the strike and attacking the college authorities for the increase in the fee.'

'That's all? It's only a student protest over registration fees?' I said incredulously.

I was disappointed. I had attended many rallies over student issues while studying in the National University of Ireland, Maynooth. I did not have to make the difficult journey all the way to occupied Palestine to witness one of these. I had naively believed that all rallies in Palestine would be about marching to freedom in Jerusalem rather than slashing the fees and doubling the grant.

'Afraid so, David. Were you expecting something a little more exciting?' he asked, smiling playfully.

'Well, not this, anyway,' I said sourly, finding it impossible to hide my rather pathetic disappointment.

'You see, you will come to realise something important while you live here. Life goes on sort of normally, in an extraordinary sort of way.'

*

Bir Zeit University is an institution despised by some Israelis as the educational 'breeding ground' for many of the leading lights in the Palestinian resistance movement. It is an institution feted in Palestinian circles for the very same reason. The university's alumni include such high-profile figures as Marwan Barghouti, the leading Fatah politician and an heroic political prisoner for the Palestinians, and many of the territories' leading academics, politicians and administrators. The university has an excellent academic tradition, and by Middle Eastern standards is a very liberal college, with over half the student body comprised of women. The university is located on the edge of the town, positioned on a hill overlooking the main road to Ramallah.

The town itself had a mixed population of some 5,000 Palestinian Christian and Muslim residents. Historically, it is predominantly a Christian area, but this was to change following the creation of the State of Israel and the resulting exodus of hundreds of thousands of refugees. Many Muslim Palestinians, particularly from the area of Al Ramla (now located within Israel), were forced out by Israeli soldiers and fled to camps close to Bir Zeit. The local Jalazone refugee camp is a legacy of the *Nakba*, and it now hosts more than the population of Bir Zeit, with 9,000-plus refugees.

Bir Zeit would be regarded as a religiously moderate and politically left-wing town under the influence of a small number of important and established local families. The town's population has decreased since the 1967 War when Israel occupied the West Bank. Many young Bir Zeit residents went in search of a more peaceful and prosperous life elsewhere. The Israeli authorities have often granted permission for Palestinians to leave, but make it extremely difficult for them to return. Some estimates say the number of people living across the globe in exile from the small town of Bir Zeit runs into the thousands.

Spread out along the side of a series of rolling hills, the town survives by providing a service economy to the local student population, combined with the more tra-ditional Palestinian reliance on olive harvesting. Few other vestiges of rural life remain in the modern town, like the small number of farmers who walk their noisy, anarchic herds of goats through the town each evening.

Thanks to the university and the proximity to the West Bank's commercial epicentre in Ramallah, Bir Zeit is more prosperous than the vast majority of similarly-sized Palestinian towns in the occupied territories. However, an economic downturn in recent years and the constant raids and attacks by the Israeli military have made life increasingly tough for locals. Bir Zeit was located within Zone B on the West Bank, which means the Israeli army essentially had free rein in the town. Night-time raids, arrests of students, clashes with armed Israeli forces, stone-throwing youths and checkpoints are all part of life. Apache helicopters swoop overhead while unpiloted drones buzz faintly in the skies above Bir Zeit and across the West Bank, an ominous airborne presence. Despite these difficulties, Bir Zeit sustains a number of shops, restaurants and internet cafes. The town itself is made up of just a small number of streets that link together in a tight central square. Standing in this square provides a panoramic view over the sweeping olive trees in the valley, a Palestinian refugee camp and a Jewish settlement high in the middle distance.

Among the fig trees at the highest point in the town there are extensive ruins, said locally to date from the Roman Empire. There remain a large number of impressive ancient columns and other structures scattered around the site. Locals claim that Israeli archaeologists, with Israeli army support, arrived many years ago and undertook work at the site, removing some artefacts. The Roman artefacts and buildings serve as a physical reminder that all empires and occupations, particularly in the blood-soaked Holy Land, see their once mighty rule come to an end. A potential tourist attraction and very valuable archaeological site, the ruins are left to the rapidly growing weeds. The local residents find themselves more concerned with the current dangerous and unstable situation than with ancient history.

On the opposite side of the town from the Roman ruins, is the local community sports centre. It is regarded by many locals as one of the best facilities in the territories, although by Western standards it is very poor. The facility has one basketball court, a small concrete football area in dangerous disrepair and inside, a room for table tennis. This is a favourite hang-out for teenage boys, a place where music can be played, fun can be had and the occupation and the difficulties of societal restrictions in such a 'traditional' society as Palestine are forgotten for a few hours.

The table tennis matches take place under the rebellious watchful eye of the socialist revolutionary leader Che Guevara. His iconic face is painted proudly on the internal wall. His steely, determined eyes appear in graffiti anywhere that people have been oppressed, from Beirut to Belfast. But here in Bir Zeit, he looks over the local Palestinian youth with a paternal eye from under a keffiyeh; the iconic black and white scarf worn by members and supporters of the Palestinian insurgency for decades, even when the temperatures are devilishly hot.

If you are religious, the town provides a wide selection of locations for worship. A growing number of mosques serve the Muslim population, but there are also Catholic and Orthodox churches. Bir Zeit translates as 'oil well' in English. With this sort of name, you might cynically expect to see occupying American soldiers patrolling its narrow street, but the oil in question is not of the black, crude and expensive kind, but rather the much less lucrative olive variety.

Because of the location of the university, Bir Zeit is a town where knowledge and intelligence is particularly prized. Young children consistently try out their English on foreigners. 'Hellohowareyouwhat'syourname?' is shouted at you in squeaky, excitable voices from all corners. Cute and funny at the beginning, it can become tiresome after a few weeks. On the walls of the town there are some pictures of dead *shahids*, but not as many as in other towns and villages in the West Bank. *Shahids* are Palestinian civilians who died as a result of Israeli attacks or militants who died during missions in Israel, including suicide bombing. One poster that was everywhere in Bir Zeit was a photograph of the late Palestinian-American intellectual and writer Edward Said. The first day I walked around Bir Zeit with a group of other students, I mentioned that I was impressed at the sight of so many posters of a leading cultural thinker plastered on the walls.

'That is something you would not see back home, or in the UK or the US I suppose – an intellectual as a poster boy,' I said.

'In the US it is almost illegal to be an intellectual at the moment,' quipped Will from Texas, a fellow Bir Zeit student.

Bir Zeit University is a critical part of civic society in Palestine, an aspect of life in the territories that has been largely suffocated by the Israeli occupation and ignored by a PA seemingly more interested in the establishment of a dizzying variety of security organisations than in supporting important civic institutions. The university began life as a primary school in 1924, when education facilities for Arabs were very poor. Within a decade, it had already developed into a co-educational secondary school. Despite the Israeli occupation after the 1967 War, the school's governing authorities made plans to transform the school into a third-level institution. The Israeli authorities frequently closed the university by military order, arbitrary closures which often lasted for extraordinarily long periods. In 1976, the first BA degree in Bir Zeit was conferred in an historic ceremony. Following the signing of the Oslo Accords in the early 1990s, there was rapid expansion in both campus buildings, facilities and in the development of courses. Foreign money from rich donors in other Arab states helped fund the expansion.

The university, faculties and students very much conceived of themselves as playing a crucial role in the creation of a future viable Palestinian state. Palestinian universities like Bir Zeit would provide the engineers, politicians, planners, medical experts and the young visionaries who would fill pivotal roles in the early difficult years of any future Palestinian state on the West Bank and Gaza Strip. Since the creation of the State of Israel in 1948, hundreds of thousands of Palestinians living in exile across the Arab world have proved themselves to be among the most creative, intelligent and innovative people in the region. Despite the constant pressure of working under occupation and the lack of regular financial resources, Bir Zeit University hopes to encourage its Palestinian graduates to ignore the understandable lure of permanent emigration and to remain in the territories and deploy their talents for the benefit of a Palestinian homeland.

In April 1992, the University was reopened after 51 months of forced closure by the Israelis. Students had been studying at home, in the houses of university lecturers and anywhere else they could. Under such a system of enforced 'underground' education, some students took over a decade to finish their degrees. In recent years, a highly-developed intranet system has allowed students to continue to study online. While this form of lecturing and study is still not perfect, and Internet access is far from universal in the occupied territories, it does allow some courses to continue despite Israeli closures, or closures due to up-turns in violence in the region.

Since the late 1990s, international students have begun to enrol in the university in increasing numbers. They come to study in the Arabic and social sciences programmes, to experience at first hand what life is like under military occupation, or to support a Palestinian educational institution under fire. In the early months of the second intifada, the numbers of international students attending the university predictably collapsed as scenes of violence flashed across the global news. But by the summer of 2005, the numbers of internationals enrolling in the university courses had climbed up again.

In the semester that I attended, over 50 students from across the globe studied at Bir Zeit, despite the Israeli occupation and fears of violence. The class was an eclectic range of both undergraduate and mature students from across the world. Those who attended included a significant number of American students who had been studying Arabic at home, a middle-aged American Christian theological teacher, young Europeans inspired by both academic concerns and a wish to express solidarity with the Palestinians, pure-and-simple adventurers, amateur film-makers, Palestinians who were now citizens of the West who wanted to come home even for a semester, Hebrew-speaking Germans, an Iranian student, a Liverpudlian history lecturer, Canadian backpackers, a Swiss activist who had previously lived with the Zapatistas in the Mexican jungle, a Quebec nationalist and me, an Irish journalist. I lived in a sparse but perfectly adequate apartment with four other international students, located on the road to the neighbouring town, Jifna.

With the intensification of the bloodshed on the West Bank since the beginning of the second intifada, the University's circumstances have further deteriorated. Since the occupation began, at least 15 university students have been killed, many while partaking in street demonstrations called in opposition to the occupation, and a huge number of students and teachers have been arrested and detained by the Israeli military.

The military often mount checkpoints at the university gates to check your papers while you wait to attend your morning lectures. Flying checkpoints are also established on the road between Ramallah and Bir Zeit, as many students must travel this road to get to the university, and the checkpoints massively increase journey time, with students often missing lectures or sometimes even graduation ceremonies. Academics complain that checkpoints on the road to Ramallah are often erected for extra-long periods of time on important university occasions, such as graduation ceremonies, registration days or during the crucial opening days of term. Because of travel restrictions, students from the Gaza Strip often miss whole semesters or full academic terms at Bir Zeit because the Israelis will not grant them permission to travel between their home and the West Bank. One lecturer who taught me Arabic had close family living in the Gaza Strip, but because he had not been granted travel permission he had not seen them for many years.

The constant violence, economic problems, arrests and harassment of students, and uncertainty about the future make the succesful university that is Bir Zeit all the more thrilling to witness first-hand. For all its problems, Bir Zeit University continues to operate at a high level of academic excellence in the occupied West Bank. A location of debate, development and research, the university represents all that is best, complex, tragic and inspiring about the Palestinian people living under occupation, and their collective struggle for freedom.

*

Two months on from the January 2006 victory by Hamas in the Palestinian elections, and Ramallah looks much like it did the previous summer.

On the outskirts of the city, a somewhat chaotic and irregular building boom continues, with ugly multi-storey white apartment blocks and offices springing up on top of the isolated rolling hills. One tall building is left unfinished on the Bir Zeit road, completely empty inside. A hollow shell of white, with no fitted windows or doors, it looks like an abandoned over-sized piece of dusty Lego. Adjacent to that site, construction workers are busy laying the foundations of another building. This could also be left idle, half built.

On the narrow, cluttered streets of Ramallah's city centre, some private cars and many more public taxis clog the city's arteries. The road system within Ramallah is permanently on the verge of a disastrous cardiac arrest. Hot and sweaty taxi drivers shout at each other in far from classical Arabic. Soldiers and traffic police man the area as best they can, trying to impose some sort of order.

Some 'incident' or other is always happening in Ramallah, thus further contributing to the chaos. Examples of these unscheduled incidents would include a Hamas economic strike calling on shops to close because of a bombing in the Gaza Strip, minor scuffles and clashes between rival factions in the city, or, most problematically, Israeli invasions into the heart of Ramallah.

During one such incident that I witnessed in the main square, the Manara, there was a small explosion from a car. It made everyone jump and fear the worst. Palestinian security men ran from the vicinity of the car ordering people to move away from the bomb threat. I dutifully moved as far away from the potential explosion as possible, watching many of Ramallah's citizens running past me towards the incident. Thankfully there was no further explosion, but the disarray added to the madness on the streets.

Public taxis, called *sheruts* in Israel and by some Palestinians, are the only form of transport available to the vast majority of Palestinians. You will not find a developed public bus, tram or train system here, as the Israeli occupation makes the construction of such a system impossible in the territories. There are absolutely no road markings and only a handful of traffic lights. Following the signing of the Oslo Accords, Ramallah was located in Zone A, which meant that the PA had nominal control, with Israeli forces controlling all roads into the city and making some incursions.

Young men hang around the Manara in large, idle groups, a physical manifestation of the chronic unemployment in the territories. Armed guards in multicoloured uniforms, members of the endless number of PA security institutions, walk around slowly in the sweltering heat, swinging their machine guns over their arms, stopping to talk to friends or to have a cigarette whilst leaning against a wall. They look like they have little to keep them busy, but at least they have a job, unlike many of their male contemporaries.

While there is a consistent energy to the place, it is nervous rather than creative. The city is dusty and ugly, particularly in the centre. Its dishevelment makes the contrast with and longing for Jerusalem all the more pronounced among local Palestinians. Only a few short miles down the road, al-Quds, as it is known in Arabic, stands magnificent on a hill. The location of the crucifixion of Jesus Christ, the Dome of the Rock, the third-holiest site in Islam and the sacred Jewish Western Wall, Jerusalem has been occupied by Israel since 1967. Many from the West Bank are denied access to the city they crave as their capital. While all mainstream Israeli parties have opposed any real Palestinian sovereignty over the city in any future peace deal, Jerusalem, already fundamental to Palestinian identity for cultural, political and religious reasons, has become idealised by those living with the shoddy reality of Ramallah.

Despite being the economic hub of the West Bank, Ramallah is not an easy place to do business. After spending the summer becoming slowly addicted to the argileh, I had decided to purchase one before my departure. My German flatmate, Toby, pointed me in the direction of a store just off the Manara. The small shop was packed solid with a wide range of different coloured water pipes with elaborately decorated glass bowls, tubes and ash trays. Business was slow, but I was still tip-toeing around the store because of all the glass on the shelves and on the ground.

After I had chosen my pipe, I wandered up to the counter to begin the haggling. The store owner sat slumped over the table with a cigarette hanging from his mouth. His demeanour was one of perfected surliness. After asking me where I was from, he got talking a little about his own background. He said he had been awarded a business degree in a Boston University in the United States twenty years previously. Business in Ramallah was hard, and the formulas he had studied in the text books then were of little help now.

'What do you think of this place? What do you think of the people?' he asked me.

My answer was swift, polite and clichéd.

'It's a wonderful, beautiful country and I have really liked the people I have met,' I said smiling.

He looked into my face. He then looked out his shop window at the bumper to bumper traffic, the broken pedestrian walkways and the potholed road. He looked back at me with a sneer.

'You are joking, yes? This is not a beautiful place. This is an ugly place – a very ugly place. And the people here … the people are as dumb as asses.'

Selling argileh in Ramallah was one thing, but surely there was no more difficult business than running 'the first Irish pub in Palestine', as it brashly branded itself. In June of 2005, the new Irish Pub took out an advertisement in *This Week in Palestine*. With the occupation, an economic downturn and growing support for Islamist parties not known for their alcohol consumption, this was a risky venture, to say the least.

The pub advert was interesting. Next to the large sign reading 'Irish Pub', there was a graphic of a blue cocktail glass, not the type of tipple you would generally associate with the authentic Irish pub experience. 'Happy Hour' was set between 6pm and 8pm, which would perhaps be popular along the liquid streets of Dublin, but in Ramallah? People falling out of a bar with a few drinks on them before 8pm would not be common in the West Bank. The advert also promised 'Free Fish and Chips dinner. After your fourth drink'. The owner was obviously extremely optimistic in changing, and increasing the drinking habits of the local population.

The pub was located in a district some distance away from downtown Ramallah, a taxi ride from the centre of town, which also made the owners' task all the more problematic. I wanted to experience at least one pint of stout on the West Bank, so I went to the pub one night with my friends, Englishman Ben and Swiss Gergey. When we got there, the room downstairs was open-plan and empty except for two young men playing backgammon at a table. When we knocked at the door, the guy with his back to us swung around. He looked astonished to see anyone arrive. He waved us in and brought us upstairs to the bar.

It was a nicely lit, warm, small bar with a pool table. We stood at the bar and I asked for a pint of Guinness. The young man who had ushered us upstairs had now gone behind the bar and looked at me strangely when I made my order. After a few minutes of linguistic fumbling, misunderstandings and orders getting mixed up, we eventually got three bottles of the local Taybeh beer. It was not clear if the Irish bar had any stout at all, not to mention fish and chips.

After spending a pleasant hour playing pool, the manager arrived. He introduced himself, and after we said we were going back into the centre of Ramallah he said he would give us a lift.

'It is hard. We are open only a short number of weeks, but we have been not very busy,' said the manager while looking back at us from the driver's seat.

'It is a bit outside Ramallah ... not easy for people to find,' said Ben.

'Yes, but we want to get people to know about it. There are business people and many foreigners in Ramallah who would come if they knew about it. We need to make it well known. Maybe we could organise something for you and the other students in Bir Zeit?'

Whatever about organising something for the students of Bir Zeit, the manager was correct about the high number of westerners living in or travelling through Ramallah. Any of the diplomats, charity workers, journalists and people involved in the non-governmental organisations might be partial to spending a night in an Irish bar in Ramallah, but it was hard not to be pessimistic about the new pub's long-term chances of survival.

'Where are you all from?' asked the manager, who had just turned the ignition on.

'I'm from England, he's from Switzerland, and he's from Ireland,' Ben said quickly, pointing at each of us in turn.

With that the manager turned his engine off and swung around to face us again.

'Ireland! You are from Ireland! That is so great – and you came to our pub! Thank you,' he said excitedly. I was a bit embarrassed by his obvious delight, while the other lads started to laugh a little.

'You ... you ... like, you know that Irish thing?' he said while pointing towards me.

'I do not know the English word, but you look like it.'

He then held his hands a little distance apart.

'You know that small Irish person?' he asked me, smiling.

I now knew what he was trying to say; he had obviously noticed my somewhat diminutive stature in the pub earlier.

'A leprechaun!' shouted Gergey helpfully.

'Yes! Yes! An Irish leprechaun,' the manager roared back and clapped his hands together. At this stage both Ben and Gergey had almost passed out laughing in the backseat of the car. He then turned around and started the car again and drove us to the Manara Square.

As we departed, I wished the manager of the 'first Irish Pub in Palestine' all the best. He would need it.

*

The Ramallah coffee shops are packed with men smoking the argileh, debating loudly and watching either Arab news or the local music stations on television. Rumour had it that one of Hamas's first planned moves in office was to ban the Arab music channels in Palestinian coffee shops, ending the constant supply of videos from Middle Eastern versions of Britney Spears.

Two months on from Hamas's victory in the elections and despite the rumours, Lebanese pop singer Nancy Ajram and many others were still being shown. The undeniably beautiful Nancy had beguiled and transfixed the imaginations of many young Palestinian men I had met the previous summer. Her sexy posters could be purchased in the souks in the Muslim quarter, in Jerusalem's Old City and also from many stores in Ramallah.One could be deep in conversation about the intifada, or playing an intensive and serious game of backgammon, but if Nancy came on the noisy TV screen in the corner, everyone went quiet. Her devastating hip movements, seductive eyes and racy videos were played over the musical backdrop of her modern, danceable interpretations of traditional Arabic sounds. Think a Middle Eastern Christina Aguilera, but more modestly dressed.

If there was to be a major conservative social and cultural sea change within Palestinian life following the Hamas victory, it would hit not just Palestinian Nancy Ajram fans, but the wider Ramallah nightlife. For despite some Israeli reports to the contrary, there is more than just one nightclub on the West Bank. Indeed, Ramallah is relatively well served when it comes to nightlife. OK, it is hardly London, New York, Dublin or indeed Tel Aviv, but there are some pubs, cafes and restaurants and a small number of clubs that entertain the small indigenous Ramallah social set and the foreign arrivals working in the diplomatic corps and for the non-governmental organisations. Places like Stones and Sangrias provided an evening refuge where internationals and Palestinians could have a drink and forget momentarily about the occupation and imprisonment within the West Bank. During the summer of 2005, high on a hill overlooking Ramallah, Snowbar nightclub was open. It had few customers, with just the odd international and some Palestinians attending the slightly run-down poolside bar.

The surreal experience of late night partying in Ramallah, was exposed one night that summer. Some tracer fire from gun shots fired over Ramallah could be seen in the distance from the Snowbar dance floor. No one knew who had fired the shots or for what purpose. It could well have been to mark the suicide attack earlier that day in the coastal Israeli city of Netanya, an attack in a shopping mall which had killed 5 Israelis, including

4 women, and injured 90 more. Or, it could have been just random shots from some gun-loving local. Either way, it was a rather unusual and disconcerting sight when you are sipping a beer.

The knowledge that you are drinking and enjoying yourself in an occupied military zone where people are constantly being killed and battles fought feeds both a sense of excitement and feelings of deep guilt. Such nocturnal freedom and social expression are non-existent in most of the West Bank.

The social scene in Ramallah is not like that of the West, and Palestinian women unaccompanied by men are rarely seen in nightclubs, restaurants or bars, whereas walking around the streets of Ramallah on a weekend night one is struck by the groups of young men hanging around. Also, there is no openly gay, lesbian or bisexual social scene in Ramallah – and certainly nowhere else in the territories – obviously because the society is far more socially conservative than many. What's more, a number of Palestinians mentioned to me that there was a fear that homosexuals could be Israeli spies. This strange theory seems to originate from the first intifada, when the Israeli security services allegedly blackmailed gay Palestinians into becoming spies by threatening to 'out' them to their parents and communities. Life for Palestinian homosexuals under occupation is an even greater burden than it is for the rest of their compatriots.

Compromising photographs, video tapes or cash are used by the Israeli secret police to help to 'turn' Palestinians and recruit them as spies. Like most occupying armies, spies and informants are a central component of the Israeli anti-insurgency strategy. Shadowy informants are often the sources of information for the Israeli security services before it carries out 'targeted assassinations' on those Israel suspect to be Palestinian militants. This information is often compromised, incomplete or just plain wrong, and many innocents have died alongside the militants targeted in these attacks, not to mention the legality or morality of a state purposely murdering a 'suspected' militant before they are charged, tried or found guilty of anything.

Despite these social constraints, Ramallah, unlike Nablus, Jenin, Gaza or Hebron, is relatively liberal, with alcohol freely sold (although public displays of drunkenness are not appreciated), Western music widely available and a sense of irony among the young that can reveal itself in acidic comments about other Palestinian towns. Like young people from all self-consciously urbane cities, Ramallah's youth consider themselves to be much cooler then their brethren living elsewhere.

Ramallah also has a strong cultural scene, with some sort of arts festival taking place almost every month. The magnificent 700-seater Ramallah Cultural Palace was opened in 2004 with funding from the Japanese government, a stunning facility that is unique in the territories. It plays host to a variety of musicians, theatre groups and films from Palestine and across the world. I went to see high-profile and popular Palestinian hip-hop act, Dam Rap, one evening – though the dates got mixed up and it turned out to be a night of Italian music.

On my return to Ramallah in March 2006, I wandered down to a café I had frequented quite often the previous summer. While enjoying the thick, strong Arabic coffee I was called over to a table by the friendly waiter, who – I think– remembered me from the previous year. I had made his coffee shop at the bottom of a main street east of the Manara my regular spot to smoke argileh and play backgammon, or *shesh besh* in Arabic.

When I walked over to his table, the waiter left and came back moments later with a generous helping of free, scrumptious *maqluba* ('turnover') to be shared between one other customer and me. The other man at my table, whom I had never met, was a burly moustachioed man, probably in his late 50s. His English was good.

The very substantial maqluba was dropped in front of us in a wide-rimmed metal dish. The dish had been up-turned to reveal glistening tomatoes, which had absorbed the juices from the succulent lamb beneath an aubergine and rice casserole. The lamb was covered in a lively and eclectic range of contrasting spices which defied easy categorisation. Pitta bread was piled high on separate plates beside each of us. The eating process was a physical, communal and somewhat competitive affair. Each of us ripped the thick, hard pitta apart and delved into the shared dish of maqluba. The pitta bread was twirled around the dish to soak in the sauces and pick up the food. There was relatively little lamb com-pared to the rest of the ingredients, but it was delicious. We led our pitta quickly through the messy rice and sauce in search of a lump of meat to grip, lift out and up into our grateful mouths before our eating compan-ion found the precious meat themselves.

Between the lamb searching and maqluba munching, the conversation quickly went past the usual topics – where I was from, why I was in Palestine – and then moved on to the central focus of most conversations with Pales-tinians.

'Where are you and your family originally from?' I asked.

'Jaffa,' he said sombrely.

'Jaffa – yeah, it's a really beautiful place. I stayed there a while back,' I said, smiling. I instantly realised that I had made a stupid and offensive mistake.

'I have not been there ... my home ... for many years,' he said after a pause.

This was not the first time this had happened. I had met young people in a refugee camp close to Bir Zeit whose families were originally from the Haifa area. They had been forced out in the 1948 War by the Israeli forces, but spoke as if they thoroughly knew the area that was now situated in northern Israel. In a way, they did know it through family stories passed down through the generations. They spoke of Haifa and its former Arab neighbourhoods not only in the past tense, but in the future tense, too, as a place that they would eventually be allowed to return. They had never visited Haifa – but I had. It was always a horrible moment when this came up in conversation. A trip to Haifa for me meant relatively little, but to some young Palestinians, it was the centre of their individual and familial narrative, their history and identity. There were other Palestinians who yearned to visit Jerusalem for the same reasons, and while they did not have permission, for me the constant trips to that religious city from Bir Zeit had grown somewhat tiresome.

As we ate, I tried to ignore the large dollops of meat and dark sauces pouring from the sides of the man's great cheeks. I quickly moved the conversation away from Jaffa and on to politics. He spoke honestly and freely about his own political development and views, and was not nearly as cagey and careful as many Palestinians when you speak to them first. He had spent time in prison and been a member of the PLO in exile in many places in the Arab world. He had returned to Palestine with the wave of PLO exiles that came home with Arafat following the signing of the Oslo Accords more than a decade ago. He was not really involved in politics anymore, he said, and was just doing a 'normal job', one that he would not specify.

'Many people I speak to in Bir Zeit and other places are very critical of the Oslo Accords,' I said.

'Tut.' The man swung his head back sharply and made the noise again. Tut. This was a lazy and concise way that Palestinians often register their disapproval.

'So you would disagree? You think Oslo was a good agreement?' I asked, hoping to initiate a more developed and detailed response this time.

He swung his head back again, this time with his mouth full.

'Tut,' he said again, this time with some difficulty.

'I don't understand. What do you think of Oslo?'

He looked straight into my eyes, and continued to chew deliberately. The movement in his mouth was loud, but rhythmic. The waiter had joined us and was sitting to my left and to the other man's right. He dipped his hand, covered in a pitta bread glove, into the maqluba and swirled it around to soak up the lamb juice. I do not think his English was good enough to follow our conversation, but he smiled and nodded while we spoke and ate anyway.

'My friend, you like this, yes?' said the café owner in broken English.

'It is gorgeous, *zachki kitirr* (really delicious), *shukran kitiir* (thanks very much),' I said, smiling.

I looked back at the PLO man and he had stopped chewing. He was still staring at me.

'What you must understand, Mr Irish Writer is that the best and only good thing about Oslo is that it brought us back. Abu Ammar [Yasser Arafat] and the others were able to get back. But not including that, your intellectual friends in Bir Zeit are right. Oslo was a disaster, because it was the end of dreams for the Palestinians living here,' he said while pointing his index finger south towards the table.

'When the PLO was away, in Jordan, in Lebanon, in Tunis, Palestinians here could dream that life would be better, much better, if those in exile were allowed return and run things. But when we came back, things did not get better. There was more violence, deaths, the Israelis are still here, and the situation is not good. He shook his head. It was never real peace, we were never able to run things anyway, the Israelis, they are still in charge, still powerful. The people here have no more dreams anymore. There is no one, no saviour in a foreign country anymore who we can call back to make things better. It is just us here, trying to do the best we can. I really think we should dump the PA. Get rid of it, it has no real control anyway. The weak PA and the powerful Israeli is the reality. There are no more dreams, there is just this reality,' he concluded.

He then picked up one whole pitta bread from his side plate and delved it into the dish, and continued munching.

The political conversation had ended.

The café owner looked at both of us.

'*Shesh besh!*' he said, banging his hands against the table.

'*Iwa* (Yes),' said the dispirited ex-PLO man.

*

Rami was a middle-aged Bir Zeit restaurant owner who kept international students and local residents fed while holding court on hot local topics as diverse as Hamas and hummus.

He looked more like the classic Italian proprietor of a busy New York pizzeria rather than the head man in a mid-priced, tasty but struggling restaurant in a small town in the occupied West Bank. Rami was often slightly unshaven, wore the top of his shirt wide open, and made Latin-like exasperated gestures when conducting animated conversation. His restaurant provided much-needed employment as waiters and chefs to local Palestinian students trying to pay their way through university.

Rami was the ultimate host, providing a quick and affordable menu from a mixture of Palestinian and international cuisine. He played a range of music over his CD system: ancient and modern patriotic Arab songs, Lebanese female vocalists, and evocative instrumental music from the local ancient instrument of choice, the oud, were all particular favourites. With the seasonal influx of international students and the already Westernized musical tastes of many young Palestinians, the Middle Eastern CDs were often interspersed with contemporary rap and rock.

One night, a small group of international students took refuge inside the restaurant. Heavy, sustained and at times very violent clashes between local Palestinian youths and Israeli troops were taking place outside in central Bir Zeit. We closed the restaurant door and observed the street battles from the windows. Israeli soldiers were attacked by stone-throwing men as they tried to make arrests and carry out house raids in the town. Heavily armed soldiers disembarked from their fortified jeeps and fired deafening stun grenades and tear gas at the locals.

Soldiers took up positions outside a nearby fruit and vegetable shop, guns propped and ready to fire in the direction of the stone throwers and the restaurant. As the madness continued for close to an hour, the tension within the restaurant was finally broken when Rami decided to play the Tracy Chapman song *Talking about a Revolution* at the highest volume. As we watched scenes reminiscent of the first intifada, the street clashes in Bir Zeit took place to Chapman singing her heart out into the West Bank night air. It was truly surreal, and darkly comical.

Rami was also always on hand to provide crucial linguistic help to international students learning Arabic. He was politically liberal and worldly, a Christian with little faith, and a proud Palestinian who could criticise his own people while remaining sympathetic. Running a successful restaurant is widely regarded as one of the toughest professions around, even in wealthy cities like New York, London and now Dublin. Bir Zeit was far from those brightly-lit, economically buzzing Western metropolises. Rami's restaurant had suffered directly under the Israeli military onslaught since the beginning of the second intifada. Profits were difficult to engineer in a land marked by curfews, checkpoints, arrests and military attacks on the one side, and a resistance insurgency on the other. Fewer Palestinians ventured out for evening meals or late-night coffees, and it was easy to understand why; Rami's battered kitchen bore the scars of previous Israeli raids, while the windows at the front were cracked and shattered in parts following military attacks.

The open-plan front of the restaurant provided a comprehensive view over central Bir Zeit and its neighbouring rolling arid hills and smooth valleys. Volleys of sporadic gunshots could be heard regularly out of the dark from an unspecified distance. It was simply impossible to ascertain whether this was a local letting off of steam, a Jewish settler, a gun battle between Palestinians and Israeli soldiers, or just one of the many weddings that took place in the West Bank in the summer of 2005. The firing of guns wildly into the air took place at many outdoor Palestinian wedding celebrations. The young Palestinians sitting in the restaurant would argue long and hard over which model of gun could be heard while devouring their warm fresh pitta bread generously dipped in tangy hummus.

The restaurant was a perfect place to spend the dark humid evenings, sipping Taybeh and discussing the central topics of Palestinian concern with the local clientele and Rami himself. Dislocation, loss, families in exile, time spent in jail, anger at local, Israeli and international authorities, the difficulties of travel, bitter and caustic re-evaluations of recent political history, sombre predictions for the medium-term political future, religion, women (for almost all my late night social conversations were with Palestinian men), children, helplessness and national pride. These themes, both international and West-Bank-specific, fuelled the endless conversation over coffee, beer or sharp, tasty homemade lemonade.

Rami was an unconventional thinker for anyone who comes to the Holy Land expecting Palestinians to be abstract political stereotypes. He was sympathetic to the most left-wing of the Palestinian factions, but was trying to make a living as a small-time capitalist restaurant owner. He had a strong sense of himself as a Christian Palestinian, yet seemed to posses what many would regard as a modern, Western scepticism towards religious belief. He defended Palestinian identity as inclusive of Christians, Muslims and others, but did admit some concerns about the cultural and social impact that the Hamas-led government could have on life for Christian Palestinians in the territories (particularly for restaurant owners who sold alcohol). Like many critics of the Palestinian leadership, he articulated no clear thinking about any strategic alternative that should be pursued by the national movement.

'But the left and the secular parties are on the wane here, surely,' I said to him one evening during a long, drawn-out but lively discussion about the late Yasser Arafat's leadership and legacy.

'That's the way it looks at the moment. But you have to understand, David, these things do not always stay the same,' he said.

'But nobody can stop the rise of Hamas now, really.'

'Look, what does a person do when they are really in trouble? If that individual's life is going completely wrong and they can do nothing to improve it what do they do? Even if that person is not religious, he will in his most desperate, hopeless moment cry out, "Oh God, please help me." He will look to the skies, heaven and religion to come to his rescue. The Palestinians are such desperate people; we seem to have no hope. There seems to be nothing here on the ground that can save us. That is why many have turned to God, looked to the skies, and gone to Hamas.'

Rami delivered this opinion while his constantly moving hand finally came to rest, cupping the top of his shaven head.

'But how will that change in the future? Look, I am not here all that long, but for me, I find it difficult to see any change.'

'I don't know, but it will change. I cannot predict when or how. How can anyone predict such things, David? But things always do change. And the Palestinian people will

come back, they will eventually move away from those religious parties after a time and come back and support
the non-religious groups, like the PFLP and others.'

Supporters of the left-wing Palestinian groups, such as
the PFLP, expressed similarly fatalistic attitudes when I
spoke to them in the West Bank. The leftist groups, once
the major opposition to the leading Fatah party, had
watched their support dwindle over the past decade as
the Islamic resistance organisations gained ground among
Palestinians living in the occupied territories. In the
Palestinian refugee camps in other Arab countries and
across the Palestinian diaspora the rise of the Islamic
groups had been far less meteoric, and there, organisations such as the PFLP still maintained considerable support.

The PFLP was founded in 1967 by the late George
Habash, a Palestinian Christian and intellectual. In the
1970s and 1980s, the PFLP and its splinter organisation,
the Democratic Front of the Liberation of Palestine
(DFLP) provided most of the poster-boys and girls of
the Palestinian resistance so feared by Israelis. A series of
spectacular hijackings of aeroplanes and high-profile
international missions undertaken by the leftists groups
resulted in both military and civilian deaths, but also put
the Palestinian issue at the front and centre of world
political opinion and media. Since its decline in membership and supporters in the territories, the PFLP maintains
its shrunken base in mainly Christian, intellectual and student circles. In towns with high numbers of Christian
residents, such as Ramallah and Bir Zeit, the organisation's graffiti, slogans and flags are still quite prominent.
But in cities with a higher concentration of Muslims, such
as Nablus or Hebron you will rarely see the PFLP's

distinctive logo, a logo that emphasises the 'Right of Return' of the 1948 and 1967 Palestinian refugees. This is because so many Palestinian Muslims have in recent years turned to Hamas.

But in Rami's restaurant, you tended to meet secular and left-wing Palestinians. One twenty-something Palestinian, Amin, was a lively character. An ex-Bir Zeit student, he worked locally with young people and had plans to return to his studies. His worldview was a strange mix of Marxism plus religion, sprinkled with phraseology from black American ghettoes via Tupac, Ice Cube and other rap artists. I got to know Amin a little bit. He was a much-politicised young man who could provide interesting critical analysis of post-Oslo Palestine. He was also warm-hearted, but very depressed about his country's future. Yet he did talk about his hopes and dreams for travelling outside the region.

One night following a long debate focussed on the mistakes made during the second intifada, Amin was regurgitating the PFLP party line against Fatah. I asked him a question that was consistently raised among the international students in Bir Zeit.

'Do you regard the second intifada as *over*, or is it still continuing?' I asked.

'When the PA have members of the resistance and revolutionary movements in jail then you know it is over. We have reached that point,' said Amin sadly.

(Leading members of the PFLP and other factions had been jailed by the Palestinian authorities.)

'You seem very downbeat about the future, then,' I commented.

'Yeah, it's hard to be anything else,' said Amin.

He went silent but then looked up and started to get more personal.

'I have two phrases in life that I live by,' he said.

I expected him to quote a Palestinian national poet, a leading figure from the PFLP or perhaps some Socialist axiom or nationalistic call to arms.

'The phrases I live by are "Fuck the World" and "Shit Happens".'

He laughed a little bit, but he was in fact deadly serious. There was no easy propaganda here. This was the voice of disillusionment felt by many Palestinian young people in the West Bank, almost four years since the outbreak of the second intifada. Many believed that they had watched their brave uprising fail, and by the end of it, victorious Israel was building a Wall on their land and continued to occupy it.

The anger, pessimism and fatalism contained in Amin's two phrases captured a general mood that I encountered across the Palestinian territories in the summer of 2005, in the wake of Arafat's death. Even the Hamas supporters I spoke to were hardly brimming with exitable confidence. Young Hamas supporters in the universities and elsewhere did not speak in sweeping victorious statements or messianic Islamic slogans. They knew that their own party was on the rise, but they were also painfully aware that the overall prospects for Palestine as a nation had probably never been worse.

There was still stoical resistance, of course, and a belief that by simply existing Palestinians were taking a stance against Israeli occupation. But the heights of activist passion inflamed by the first and second intifada had dissipated. What remained was seething bitterness and hatred that was somewhat sullen, for now. Many of the leftist Palestinians I spoke to spent most of their time criticising the way Fatah had handled the recent uprising, and there was little in the way of discussion about positive ways forward. Nobody I met called for a return to a widespread uprising, even supporters of the Islamic parties like Hamas. There was a desire, particularly among the more secular Palestinians, to huddle down and make do with the present circumstances as best you could, while holding on to the belief that a third intifada will come at some unspecified point in the future.

'Of course we will rise again, and the PA and the other spies will not stop us. Where there is injustice there is resistance, simple as that. And Palestine is that simple,' said Amin.

*

On one of the final nights of our stay in Bir Zeit, myself and a couple of my flatmates left Rami's restaurant after a meal. Our flat was only a five-minute walk away. As we wandered home in the dark, we could see across the valley of olive trees: armoured Israeli jeeps had entered from the Ramallah side of Bir Zeit. I wanted to get home quickly, as meeting armed Israeli soldiers at night in the West Bank is unpleasant to say the least. As we reached our flat, a car approached us slowly. The Palestinian driver stopped and opened his window.

'Heh! You should be careful – there is a checkpoint just down the road, and a few soldiers walking the Jifna Road are coming up here,' he said in perfect English.

I looked down the pitch-black road but could see nothing. We thanked him and continued. We reached our building, but it was clear that something was brewing in Bir Zeit that night.

An hour or so later I was in bed and was woken by what sounded like a smothered explosion from the centre of Bir Zeit. I leapt from my slumber and looked out of my window. From my third-storey bedroom I could see most of central Bir Zeit. A series of Israeli army jeeps and what looked like larger troop-carriers were driving quickly up and down the streets of the town. It was after 1.30am and the roads of Bir Zeit were otherwise deserted.

A massive searchlight was fixed on top of one of the jeeps and was being shone onto various buildings and into people's homes. A military helicopter could be heard in the sky. One of my flatmates, Ben, was still up, and came to look out of my window. The two of us watched what looked like a series of night raids on properties, which continued for over an hour. We got tired, and decided that we had watched enough. There was little that we could do anyway.

But just before I closed the blinds, two of the jeeps started to speed down the road towards our isolated building on the Jifna Road. We watched as the search light was shone onto our building and up its exterior wall. We both ducked as the powerful light hit my window and briefly drowned my bedroom in a bright beam. The two military jeeps stopped directly outside our building. We decided it was best to go back to our rooms and stop watching from the window.

For the next half hour I lay awake frightened, worried and gripped by a feeling of absolute helplessness as I listened to what was clearly the noises of Israeli soldiers raiding flats above and below ours; the large thuds of boots running up and down the stairwell; the door being opened by Israelis, followed by muffled Palestinian shouts; the sound of furniture being flung about violently. I resigned myself to the fact that the soldiers would eventually break into our flat. I had visions of being confronted by an armed soldier in my bedroom, shining a torch in my face and speaking rapidly in Hebrew as I desperately fumbled for my passport. The feeling was one of overall violation.

The next day, Ben told me he had heard the noise as well. We had no one to call for help – it wasn't like a break-in back home, where you could ring the authorities. Here the Israeli soldiers *are* the authorities, and you are their occupied enemy.

You are not even safe from the occupying forces while asleep in your bed. This creates a chilling psychological effect of consistent, internalised, uneasy fear. The Israelis have total control over the Palestinians, even with the so-called powers of the PA. Their writ over an entire people is complete and it is suffocating.

In the end, thankfully, Israeli soldiers never smashed into our flat during the raid on the building. But the potential violation of our personal space, and our inability to do anything about it, was terrifying. Bir Zeit had suffered a series of raids, arrests and attacks on property that night. Some local Palestinian students had been 'picked up' by the Israeli military. By most standards in the occupied territories it was nothing, likely not enough to merit a mention in local media. But I was leaving the West Bank in less than a week; the tension had been cumulative, and by that stage I really needed a break from the omnipotent occupation.

5

More Than One Wall

The door to Bir Zeit University's Internet room was large and clunky due to the reinforced glass and the heavy, metal handle. The door sprang back immediately on its creaky hinges once you released the handle.

The narrowness of the door meant that it was always a little difficult to negotiate. This was especially true during a busy period like lunch time or in the morning before lectures began, when students gathered to check their email or to surf the 'net. Only one person could comfortably enter the Internet room at a time.

On this occasion I grabbed the handle of the door with my left hand and pushed hard to prevent it from springing back. Just as I placed my right foot forward, a young female student wearing a dark hijab and long grey shawl came towards me, trying to exit the computer lab quickly. She held a folder close to her chest with both her hands. She did not raise her eyes, and looked towards the floor as she walked.

My immediate reaction was to step back, and to lean against the door to hold it open, allowing her pass. It was an unconscious movement of a learned Irish chivalry that came naturally, one that was not made to impress.

When she reached the open door, she lifted her head and looked at me as I held the door wide for her to exit. Her expression erupted into complete shock. She gasped and stopped dead in her stride. Clearly, a man holding a door open for a woman was not all that usual here, or at least not for this student. With me in my summer hat, still sporting my milky white Irish skin, it was obvious to her that I was a foreign student.

I instantly panicked, unsure at what I'd done to make her look so aghast. I accidentally let go of the metal handle. The door sprung back forcefully and whacked my foot, dangerously exposed in my sandal. I let out a fierce yelp and swore, Christian-style. I lifted my foot and grabbed it with my right hand, rubbing my rapidly-bruising toe. The sweat was just cascading down my cheeks and back in the morning heat, and now my face went even redder.

After a few seconds of feeling truly sorry for myself, I peered through the glass on the door at the young student who remained standing there. She looked at me with an increasingly incredulous expression. I grabbed the handle again, and in my weakened state limply opened the door again, while attempting to stand on my one good foot. I held the door open and motioned with my head for her to walk through. She stood stationary. After a few more embarrassingly elongated seconds, it finally dawned on my melting mind that this was now a fully fledged cultural misunderstanding.

I hopped on my right foot through the door and limped past the student. It was impossible to make my way into the room like this while also holding the door. So I finally let go of the door and it slammed shut again with an awful clatter. I struggled over to the nearest chair and sat down, caressing my toe.

The young student looked at me once more. There was a trace of pity in her eyes and then the faintest of smiles. She contemplated me silently. She looked like she was thinking that I must have been some sort of a bumbling alien being who had somehow landed in Bir Zeit, unable to undertake even the most basic of human actions, like opening a door and walking through it. Eventually, she turned on her heels and finally exited the building.

Less a clash of civilisations, perhaps, than an interaction of idiocy.

My awkwardness in that situation was not just a product of my own ungainly ways, although that most certainly played a role. Rather, I was already edgy about any inter-action with Palestinian women, no matter how basic. Part of that was confronting the unknown: I was planning to spend the summer living in an Arab country that is by Western standards relatively conservative, and the majority of whose inhabitants are Muslim. I did not want to offend.

During the orientation day for all the international stu-dents at Bir Zeit University, our course co-ordinators gave us a few helpful pointers. There were all the usual parts of an orientation, such as a map of the town, basic contact information, health and safety issues regarding food and drink, and an academic timetable. Female international students were told that it would be best for them to dress conservatively in the West Bank. That did not mean having to wear a hijab, but it also meant not wearing a miniskirt. Experiences of life in the West Bank were very different for female international students compared to their male counterparts.

The vast majority of Palestinian men are very respectful towards women. Foreign women can walk the streets, travel around the territories and go to bars and restaurants in the evening without having to worry. What's more, the problems that Western women deal with in some Arab countries with unwanted advances and public declarations of undying love are much less of a problem in Palestine. That being said, some of the female students on my course were to have uncomfortable interactions with local men over the summer.

On the orientation day there were also pointers that were particularly directed towards the male international students. The men were warned that starting a potential relationship, no matter how innocent, with a local Palestinian woman was fraught with difficulties. A public relationship between a female Palestinian student and an international male would apparently set local tongues wagging. Palestinian families are concerned about honour and public perception, particularly when it comes to their daughters. A foreign male student and a local girl started to go out with each other a few years previous, and it caused a minor sensation on campus. Palestinian family life is conservative and marriages are often arranged in more rural areas and small villages, but this is less likely to happen in big towns and cities like Ramallah. Sex outside marriage, like everywhere else, happens. But as with Ireland until recent decades, it is viewed in a negative light. In the tight communities in the West Bank close bonds have been forged because of years of struggle under occupation, as well as a conservative inheritance passed on through generations of strong family life. Like anywhere in the world, this tight community and family life can be suffocating for the young, particularly for teenagers. It must also be said that such familial structure has helped maintain cohesion within Palestinian society despite years of war, exodus, poverty and occupation.

Our course co-coordinator was refreshingly honest when outlining the social minefield that lay in the path of any international student planning to deploy his charms locally. She warned that just because a Palestinian woman did not wear a hijab, wore makeup or 'Western-style' clothing did not necessarily mean that she was more liberal than the average Muslim student. Indeed, we were told that a Palestinian woman wearing a hijab, could well have a much more advanced feminist perspective than a more Western-looking student. Also, in the few nightclubs in Ramallah, local women who attended were likely to be chaperoned by male relatives. If they were on their own, you were urged to be more careful in your interactions with them. Any action could be misconstrued, and, it was claimed, lead to her speed-dialling all of her brothers, uncles and her father, and things could get somewhat messy.

Such advice is not typical during an orientation day in a Western third-level institution. However, the course organisers were erring on the side of caution, and it certainly produced the desired effect on me and most of the other students on the course. I did not spark up conversations with local women in shared taxis or on campus, and I only spoke when spoken to. Sometimes this did happen – a student with dark eyes beneath her hijab would be sitting silently beside you in a taxi, when suddenly you would jump with fright when she began to speak to you. Palestinian students often wanted to use their English and to learn something about the foreign arrivals, like where you were from and why you came to Bir Zeit. It was different, of course, with the female lecturers and the staff in the international students' office, or equally with the female students who had actually been born or educated in the West, like the Palestinian Americans on campus.

But the hints and tips during orientation didn't play that big a role in my experience, as any meaningful conversations with Palestinian women on a day-to-day basis would have been quite difficult. Social life is divided by gender. In the cafes in Bir Zeit and Ramallah where we sipped coffee and beer, the vast majority of the clientele were male, and the cafes where argileh was smoked and backgammon played were an exclusively male preserve.

On campus it is not unusual to spot two young male students linking arms as they walked. This is an Arab display of male friendship, purely platonic. However, public displays of affection between the sexes are rarer; although you sometimes see young couples holding hands in places like Ramallah, you almost never would in more religious cities like Nablus. Yet at political rallies the audience is mixed, and more female students attend Bir Zeit University than male students. Palestinian women have played a vital, and often high-profile, role, in their country's fight for freedom.

If you are to judge a society solely by the number of women wearing hijabs or the shortness of the skirts local women can wear, then Palestine is much more conservative than Western Europe, but more liberal than Saudi Arabia. But to ascertain the level of freedom in a society purely on this narrow basis would be a mistake. When it comes to sexual politics, Palestine, like everywhere else, is a complex place. The role of women in Palestinian society cannot be summed up with a simple reference to headscarves and hemlines.

*

To those accustomed to Western media portrayals of Middle Eastern women as being subordinate, submissive, silent and deferential, Muna Giacaman destroys that Orientalist stereotype the moment she opens her mouth.

Since 1998, the West-Bank-born academic held the post of coordinator of the Palestine and Arabic Studies course for international students at Bir Zeit University. In that capacity, she has had to undertake the sometimes-difficult task of easing international, mainly Western, students into everyday life in occupied Palestine. Born in Bethlehem, she began her education in Palestine, but later spent a long period of her life working, teaching and living along the west coast of the United States.

Irreverent, intelligent and politically astute, she can speak comfortably with both Western and Palestinian students. She has bridged a cultural, political and sometimes religious divide that some of the most pessimistic of theorists and politicians have described as impossibly vast. When I returned to Palestine in March 2006 to cover the Israeli general election Muna was top on my list of interviewees.

The international community was still in deep shock two months after the surprising Hamas victory in the scrupulously fair PLC elections. In reaction to the outcome of the Palestinian vote, the United States and the European Union set about mounting devastating economic sanctions on the democratically-elected Hamas-led administration. This further increased the hardship faced by the Palestinian populace, particularly in the desperate Gaza Strip. With so many Palestinian workers in Gaza employed by the PA, the boycott had an immediate impact: if you were lucky enough to get paid for your work, you certainly did not get paid on time. Anger and growing radicalism enflamed the Palestinian street as the occupied territories seemed more internationally isolated than ever.

Western commentators and journalists spoke darkly of the growing power of Islamic extremism in the Middle East, which clumsily included the election victory by Hamas. The defeat of the mainly secular Fatah party, many commentators warned, would lead to huge attacks on personal freedoms, particularly those of Palestinian women living in the occupied territories. On a social level, they said, Hamas would impose a strict public policy on personal morality for all Palestinians. No less frighteningly, on a military level, the victorious extremists in Hamas would bide their time before unleashing a renewed terrorist war on Israel. They would send terrifying waves of young suicide bombers who dreamt of a paradise in the afterlife, into Israel to kill more innocent citizens until the Jewish state was destroyed. Such a vision of near-apocalyptic disaster for the region gripped world leaders, pro-Israeli bloggers and conservative Western print and television media alike.

If Islamic extremists had now taken control of the territories, surely the Christian Palestinians often ignored by Western media would pack their bags en masse and flee Palestine in fear of the radical Hamas government? If someone was to worry about this deeply disturbing prospect, it would be Muna Giacaman. A Palestinian feminist she would surely be intensely concerned at the measures Hamas was now to take against women. I wanted to include her take on Palestine under its new Hamas-controlled parliament in my report.

When I met Muna in her office in Bir Zeit, she seemed hassled, alright, but it wasn't because of the imminent appointment of the new Hamas Prime Minister Ismail Haniyeh that had her worried – it was the long line of Palestinian and international students at her door with their never-ending queries. She was pulled this way and that by young students vying for her attention. When I finally began my interview, she apologised for the delay and welcomed me back to Bir Zeit. She looked stressed, and I was concerned that discussing the Hamas victory wouldn't help.

'We were surprised, yes, at their election victory,' said Muna, as her face relaxed. She was obviously not unduly worried about the elections, and she easily launched into a nuanced, balanced analysis of the Hamas breakthrough, an analysis thoroughly lacking in much of the Western media coverage and in the political reaction to the victory.

'Even Hamas were surprised by their own victory. Everyone knew that they would do well in the election, but to win it outright was a bit of a shock. Nobody is sure exactly how things will change but so far since the election, nothing on the ground, as you say, has changed,' she said confidently.

The overwhelming reaction in the West to the Hamas election victory was to characterise it as just another element of the supposedly endless rise of Islamic fundamentalism, and part of an inevitable and potentially cataclysmic clash of civilisations between East and West. But these nightmarish concerns were not shared, in the early months at least, by liberals in the West Bank.

'From talking to people before and since the election, it was clear that many Palestinians just wanted Fatah, the former ruling party, out. And that was mainly because of corruption in the PA. That is what people in the West have to understand: at the heart of this vote was a vote against corruption and waste within the PA. It was not about religion and fundamentalism, it was a protest against the way the PA was being run and people wanted to see drastic action taken,' said Muna.

'But in terms of changes since they got in?' I asked.

'Nothing has changed since January. Of course there are and were concerns that Hamas might make internal moves to make this a more conservative society but, for the moment at least, they are more interested in trying to form a government. To be fair to them, they have been making very reassuring noises about Palestinian society as a whole, saying that they do not want to impose Sharia law. In fact, much of our law is based on Islamic law already, and if you are Christian, it is based on Church law.'

When asked whether the Hamas victory would lead to tensions between Palestinian Christians and Muslims, Muna smiled and maintained that this is a specifically Western obsession.

'Again, this is something that the West cannot understand. Religion has never been an issue within Palestine. It is the West that goes on about the clash between Islam and Christianity, but in Palestine that has never been a problem. The occupation does not distinguish between Muslims and Christians. We have all suffered during our history since 1948. We know from some early polls that have been done in Christian villages that a percentage of Christian Palestinians voted for Hamas. Now that shows you that the vote was very much a political vote, principally against corruption, and not one based on religion. Some in the West have their motives for talking about and focusing on so-called Islamic fundamentalism and tensions with Christianity. But in Palestine it is not an important issue for us.'

Muna added that because corruption was such a focus of the Palestinian parliamentary election, the political issues surrounding the Israeli occupation were not clearly defined in the campaign.

'Already since taking power, Hamas has exposed corruption that had been going on, and the robbery that was taking place of public money in Palestine. That is what people wanted when they voted for them, to clean up the whole structure of the PA. That is the promise they made to the electorate and they will have to fulfil that. Because they stood so much on the corruption issue they never said anything about where they stood on the so-called 'Road Map'. Nor have they had to say anything about what they think about eventual negotiations with the Israelis. So we knew that when we voted for them. So in some ways, we have helped create what the West call the 'crisis', with no negotiations taking place between the Palestinians and Israel.'

But I wanted to force the interview towards the important subject of women's rights. The changing role that women would play in Palestinian life under the new Hamas-led government had been and would continue to be monitored closely within the territories as well as abroad. The rights of women and the wearing of the veil have become touchstone issues in much of the coverage given to Islam in the West.

The situation of women in contemporary Palestinian society is a hugely intricate one, influenced by tradition, culture, religion, class, politics and patriarchy. It can be said that generally, women in Palestine enjoy more freedoms than those in many other Arab countries. However, that has to be qualified in terms of regions within the territories. As discussed, life for a young woman in strongly religious Nablus is starkly different to that in the more liberal Ramallah. The life of the Christian teenage daughter of a West Bank urban intellectual will contrast hugely to the experience of the young daughter of a Muslim small farmer living on the outskirts of rural Jenin. The lifestyles of Palestinian women in Israel and those in the occupied territories are again very different.

Yet despite the contrasts in women's lives in the area, it must be noted that in terms of life in the territories, it is still the Israeli occupation that has the most impact. From mothers stopped at Israeli army checkpoints, to families forced to get by without their men, either incarcerated in

Israeli prisons or killed by soldiers, to young female university students prevented from getting to class, the occupation permeates all sectors of life here. Despite that the changing role of women in Palestinian society since the Hamas victory has been debated in the territories with added vigour.

The March 2006 edition of *This Week in Palestine* (which is, despite the name, a monthly publication) concentrated on the role of women in Palestinian history and society. I picked up a free copy in a Ramallah café when passing through on my way to Bir Zeit. The edition coincided with International Women's Day, but that this publication focussed on such a topic so soon after the Hamas victory was interesting. Various articles looked at the significant contribution women had made to the national struggle, while defending some of the gains that women had made socially in recent decades.

An editorial written by Tony Khoury was measured in tone and did not express any overt fears that Hamas would impose restrictive laws upon women. Pointing to the fact that Hamas has many female members, albeit not in the leading ranks, the editorial struck an optimistic note in the shadow of the election victory: 'The new Hamas-dominated council also has its share of women deputies. Spring is already in the air. If nothing else, the promise of the warmer weather to come should put us in better mood. Go out, smell, inhale and enjoy,' Khoury wrote cheerfully.

Muna Giacaman was quite sanguine about Palestinian women's collective futures.

'We have no fears at the moment that there are going to be any major changes to women's rights here. We do not see Hamas making dramatic moves like turning Palestine into Afghanistan or even Iran. We do not see something like that happening,' she said optimistically.

'In fact they could well use the teachings of Islam to improve the lot of people economically and socially, including for women. That could indeed be one result.'

Female students are the majority at Bir Zeit University, and in March 2006 the university helped organise a film festival focusing on women's issues.

In the PLC elections, a record number of women were elected under the new quota system. Sixteen women, including six from Hamas, won seats, compared to just five women elected in the 1996 elections. Just 16 female members in a parliament of 132 is of course far from proportional, but at 12 per cent it does not lag far behind the 13.3 per cent of female TDs who sit in Dáil Éireann in Dublin.

Some of the newly-elected female Hamas PLC members argued openly for an interpretation of Islam that pushed a more progressive view of women's role in society. Jamila Shanti, a philosophy professor at the Islamic University, who headed the list of Hamas female candidates, told the *Guardian* shortly after the election that women needed to tackle discrimination.

> Our first job is to correct this because this is not Islam. We are going to show that women are not secondary, they are equal to men. Discrimination is not from Islam, it is from tradition. It may not be easy. Men may not agree.

Also writing in the March 2006 edition of *This Week in Palestine*, Rima Tarazi from the General Union of Palestinian Women (GUPW), celebrated the role that women had played in the local elections in 2005 and in the national January 2006 parliamentary elections in Palestine.

> As the years 2005 and 2006 can be truly called 'the years of elections and democracy' in Palestinian history, the GUPW succeeded in leaving its imprint on those elections and on the democratic process. Together with several sister groups, it held training sessions for women in the various areas and locations and led a campaign for enhancing and expanding women's participation in the municipal and legislative councils, with some success. As a result, three women were elected as mayors for the first time in Palestinian history and almost 20 per cent of the elected municipal and local council members are now women.

Despite earlier speculation that hijabs would become compulsory attire for female members of the PLC, Hamas leaders denied early on that this was to be the case. Things were very far from perfect for women, and as with any patriarchal, conservative society, the problems faced by women in Palestine as a result of structured inequality between the sexes are many, varied and deep. Issues dealing with differing employment opportunities, pay scales, violence towards Palestinian women and lack of health facilities for women in the territories have all been rightly raised by activists. They are chronicled and studied by academics. Palestinian women are under-represented at political, judicial levels and in other sectors of the economy and society.

In March 2005, Amnesty International published a detailed report on women living in the occupied territories. It criticised both the Israeli government and the PA in its conclusions, maintaining that Palestinian women suffered under both the occupation and discriminatory Palestinian laws and customs. The report concluded that Palestinian women faced what it called a 'triple challenge':

> 'Living under Israeli military occupation which controls almost every aspect of their lives, as women living in a society governed by patriarchal customs, and as unequal members of society subject to discriminatory laws.'

The Western media would suggest that it is because some women in Palestine wear the hijab that they live a life inherently more culturally and socially iniquitous than that of their Western counterparts. Yet the reasons that some women in Palestine wear the hijab are many, and it is not always a result of oppression. Some wear it for religious reasons, or to conform to social norms, peer or parental pressure, and others wear it on semi-political grounds, to express their solidarity with the Palestinian cause or with Muslims internationally.

Islam is obviously crucially important in Palestinian and wider Arab life. The language of the Holy Koran, classical Arabic and its colloquial offshoots, are spoken by or is familiar to all Arabs, whether they are Muslims, Christians, Jews, Druzes or practice other religions. Islam provides the wide historical base on which the culture and society of the region is built, much like many argue that a broadly Judeo-Christian tradition forms the basis of Western society.

While most Western commentators are aware that the Judeo-Christian soil of Western civilisation has sprouted beautiful and diverse flowers and a similar number of poisonous weeds, the Arab world is often not perceived in such an expansive and diverse manner. The Muslim world is often shown to restrict growth, with the dark branches of Islamic extremism supposedly dominating the contemporary landscape.

Despite the sweeping generalisations of Orientalists and those who foresee a violent East-West schism, the Muslim world and its history is one of complexity, nuance, colour, diversity and heterogeneity. It is one that does not conform to the ridiculous, reductive and sometimes downright racist representations of a non-existent homogenised Islamic world in the Middle East, one that some claim is increasingly radical, dangerously extreme and seduced by terrorism.

Even in a part of the Arab world so geographically small as the West Bank, differences, discontinuity, debate and flux permeate life in terms of class, region, sex, religion, politics, family and tradition. I have drunk beer with Palestinian middle-class intellectuals in Ramallah and met a Palestinian Bedouin family living in a cave on the outskirts of Hebron. The Middle Eastern world is as diffuse and complicated a world as our own Western civilisation. It cannot and should not be easily reduced to digestible political and religious sound bites that are used to frighten, provoke anger, feed global division and eventually fan the increasingly hot flames of war, Western conquest and imperialistic domination from Gaza to Kabul.

Hamas is an extremely different organisation to Al-Qaeda, for instance. The Palestinian group has launched horrific suicide attacks in Israel that have killed many civilians, and as an organisation it has also deployed nauseating and highly offensive anti-Semitic language. On the other hand, the organisation is also one with a wide community base providing social care, health and education facilities and programmes to the desperately poor, particularly in the Gaza Strip. Refugee camps and towns where Hamas has significant support in the occupied territories, tend to have well-organised social safety nets. The homeless, beggars, and the clearly destitute are rarer than they are, say, in my own city of Dublin, despite the consant economic crisis in Palestine and the economic boom that Ireland has been living through. The violent aspect of Hamas's existence represents only a part of what is a sweeping social movement that contains within it many factors and components. Even on the military front, Hamas has in recent years stopped its horrific suicide bombing campaign in Israel, albeit for tactical rather than moral motives. Suicide attacks on Israeli civilian targets by Hamas militants have dropped dramatically since 2004 despite the continuation of Israeli military raids and bombings of the occupied territories which have at times reached fiercely bloody levels. Hamas leaders have also offered Israel a decade-long ceasefire if Israel were to retreat to the Green Line (as it is required to do under international law) and allow a Palestinian state to be declared covering the whole of the West Bank and Gaza. The offer has been rejected by the Israeli authorities and generated little coverage in the international media. Since its election victory, Hamas has been engulfed in an internal debate between 'moderates' and 'hawks' over the best political and military strategy open to them.

The language of Hamas spokespeople can indeed be described as bellicose. The organisation's military wing still carries out some violent operations and lobs home-made rockets into civilian areas of southern Israel. Yet one does not have to be a social scientist of much note to see that Hamas is displaying many of the same indicators shown by other revolutionary movements who took up the reigns of power while moderating their message. Such similar changes have been evident in other anti-imperialist and anti-colonial organisations the world over, from the IRA in Northern Ireland and the Republic to the Sandinistas in Nicaragua. It is of course understandable that Israeli civilians should be less likely to see Hamas as moderate or evolving, but would instead view them as the killers of their children and the potential agents of Israeli destruction, but the international community can harbour no such excuses. Placing a blockade on the Hamas-led government has only served to bolster the more militaristic strands within the organisation, while also rejecting the Palestinian democratic decision.

In the months since the election, Hamas has had to deal with a series of almost hourly crises: harsh Israeli attacks, particularly on the Gaza Strip, clashes with Fatah supporters unhappy with the new regime and finally the crippling international economic blockade. Hamas seized control on the streets of Gaza in June 2007, following a short, violent civil war between Hamas and Fatah militants. When the gunfire stopped, Hamas controlled Gaza, while Fatah controlled the West Bank. The two separated areas of the occupied territories have never been so politically apart. Peace talks between both sides continue. In reality, since the elections, the Hamas leadership would not have been able to concentrate on influencing internal Palestinian social and cultural life even if it had wanted to. Basic survival for the party and its supporters has been top of the agenda.

Following my interview with Muna, I wandered into the computer lab. I wanted to see if an Internet connection was free so that I could file my copy with the Belfast offices of *Daily Ireland*. The room was half empty with plenty of computers available. As I walked up and down between the rows of PCs, the screensavers that had become familiar to me during the previous summer flickered. Photographs of the Brazilian footballer Ronaldo in a Real Madrid FC shirt or Ronaldinho in a Barcelona FC shirt were very popular, as both Spanish clubs were supported by thousands of Palestinians. Other monitors displayed pictures from a Hamas political rally or soft-focus promo shots of one of the hot new Lebanese pop sensations.

In that room, through unregulated and uncensored Internet access, young Palestinians have an electronic escape route over the Wall and into the wider world. With such access to unlimited information it is difficult to see how Hamas or any other Islamic organisation could impose widespread Sharia law. There are a variety of competing currents of political and social thinking in Palestinian society including secularism, socialism, Pan-Arabism, feminism, traditionalism, nationalism, a range of religious politics and, most significantly, democracy. Even with the growing support for the Islamic parties in the territories, it is hard to believe in the medium term that Palestine could adopt some of the strictest interpretations of Islamic law on personal behaviour, and do so in a democratic manner.

In the early months following the election, despite the almost hysterical reaction in the West to the Hamas victory and the rise of the Islamist organisations, the women's movement internally within the territories seemed generally optimistic that the 2006 vote did not necessarily herald a negative period in Palestinian women's rights. However in a region of sustained flux the future is never easily predicted.

*

It was difficult to look at the Yasser Arafat look-alike and not feel profoundly sad. The Arafat double took pride of place on the stage during the Nakba demonstration in Ramallah's Manara Square in May 2008. He wore the distinctive olive green uniform with a keffiyeh hung over his shoulder, carefully folded into the shape of Palestine, just like Arafat had done. He had the mandatory few days' worth of greying stubble and he waved his two fingers up and down in a victory salute, just as the PLO chairman had done at countless marches and political rallies. From even a short distance away, it was as if Palestine's most important political leader had risen up from his grave. For a second it seemed that his death in late 2004 had been some sort of elaborate hoax, concocted perhaps by some shadowy international secret service.

Tens of thousands of Palestinians packed the central Ramallah square. Some had negotiated checkpoints and travelled from across the West Bank, but most of the attendees were from the city itself or its neighbouring suburbs. People stood on the roofs of adjacent buildings to get a better view of the stage. Other people hung out from the window of the nearby 'Stars and Bucks' coffee shop, straining to hear the speeches. The majority of the attendees were young, born decades after the Nakba. The demonstration lasted for many hours and included numerous political speeches interspersed with live performances by Palestinian musicians and singers.

The two MCs for the event were a young Palestinian man and a striking young woman wearing a red and white Palestinian scarf around her neck. Her lungpower was not in question as she bellowed at high pitch into the microphone in incessant Arabic. Her passionate brown eyes were full of nationalistic pride and ardent belief. She controlled the numerous speakers and led each one to the microphone with instructions whispered into their ears.

The long, long list of speakers included representatives of various sections and parties of the Palestinian liberation movement. Although predominantly male, there were a number of female speakers. In the audience the gender balance was, if anything, tipped towards women. The young men gathered closer to the front and bounced up and down, clapping wildly during the musical interludes. Patriotic songs chronicling the Palestinian struggle and celebrating the continued resistance roused the young men into deafening chants. Swaying supporters waved the flags of different parties from side to side.

Towards the back of the crowd, young women were wearing a specially-produced commemorative T-shirt. The T-shirt showed a key, representing the key to the door of the Palestinians' former homes. A declaration in Arabic and English read 'Our homes are not for sale', with the year 1948 printed in red on the back. Over 20,000 black balloons were dramatically released into the sky above the West Bank, each one representing one day since the foundation of Israel. For a few short moments, they blocked the sun over the streets of Ramallah, creating an eerie, ominous cloud over the city.

At political or anti-war protests in Dublin and elsewhere the audience usually gets restless by the third or fourth speaker. People shuffle from one foot to the other, wondering aloud why each party and organisation involved has to have a separate speaker on the platform, after the crowd has already marched. They check the sky, knowing full well that it could start bucketing rain at any moment. Exasperation grows, and by the time the fifth speaker gets up to make similar points as the previous four, many start to sneak off to the nearest pub to continue discussions in a more sociable setting. Others drift off to do some weekend shopping or to catch the second half of the big match on TV.

Nobody was leaving the Nakba protest in Ramallah, and no one seemed all that concerned at the inordinate length of proceedings. If anything, the young people were enjoying it. It was a day out, a chance to gather in a public place with many hundreds of their peers. Of course the messages and speeches during the demonstration were serious, but life in the West Bank for a young Palestinian can be stifling. A major event with music and dance and chanting provided an important release. It was an opportunity to express your own personal identity as well as your national one.

The female MC was well able to control the stage. When a boisterous young man at the front jumped up onto the platform and started to dance excitedly to the music, she deftly signalled to a nearby security officer. The officer came over and gently pushed the male back down into the audience. As anywhere, there's always one. In this case, the one who was going to cause a few problems on stage was the Yasser Arafat impersonator.

The lookalike had clearly begun to enjoy his pivotal role in the proceedings. He moved himself to the centre of the stage and stood in front of the speakers. As he waved to the audience, they cheered loudly. Eventually he started to chant, and the crowd chanted back. He reached for the microphone and took it from the male MC. The MC tried to pull it back, but after some quick whispering and negotiating, 'Arafat' got his hands on the microphone. The Arafat impersonator then started to give a speech, which was received with rapturous excitement. Earlier that day a taped message from the present head of the PA and PLO, Mahmoud Abbas had been played to the Ramallah audience. It had not garnered such a welcome.

The crowd started to chant again in unison with the Arafat double. He was clearly fancying himself in the role as the father of the Palestinian movement, even if it was only for a brief moment. He was enjoying it a little too much as far as the organisers were concerned. The male MC again attempted to reef the microphone back from Arafat's grip. Just before it was pulled back off him, the Arafat double began another chant and this also echoed across the Manara Square. The MC thanked him, and Arafat drifted to the back of the stage where he continued to wave his patented victory salute. But he would deliver no more speeches.

The sense of loss felt by the Palestinian people since the death in Paris in November 2004 of their former leader is still immense. Even his Palestinian critics, and there were many who bitterly opposed Arafat within the movement, admired his fortitude and resilience over the decades. The man dubbed 'Mr Palestine', has left a gaping hole in Palestinian life which has not been filled. Neither the leadership of Ismail Haniyeh and Hamas nor Mahmoud Abbas and Fatah have the widespread support or personalities big enough to take over Arafat's central role at the fulcrum of the Palestinian nation.

His historic legacy is understandably contested. Israelis did not weep when he died, as most were convinced that he was a terrorist mastermind and a roadblock to peace. They concluded that the Oslo Accords that Arafat signed with them in the early 1990s provided but a momentary lull in the violence. He was their implacable foe, always intent on Israel's destruction. The Bush administration had declared him a pariah before he died. Even within more moderate international political circles, he is judged harshly, judgements sometimes prompted by well-founded accusations of corruption and human rights violations by the PA under his watch. Some Palestinians are vicious in their criticism of him, but even his most negative nemeses had mixed feelings. As one strong supporter of the PFLP once told me, 'When I think of him, I get so angry because I hate so much about him. But at the same time I can't hate him, because he was Palestine for so long.' The majority of Palestinians adored him and continue to mourn his passing.

Strangely, it was not Arafat's participation in and coordination of violent acts or corruption that made the majority of Western leaders turn on him and decry his legacy. It was rather his supposed rejection of the 'best chance for peace' provided to Palestine by the Camp David talks in 2000.

At the time, President Bill Clinton was facing the final months of his presidency and he was thinking legacy – his own legacy. Despite pleadings from Arafat that the timing was not right, Clinton organised a summit to conclude a comprehensive peace deal in the Middle East. Clinton promised the PLO leader that if the summit failed, there would be no public proportioning of blame.

The talks between Clinton, Israeli Prime Minister Ehud Barak and Arafat continued on and off throughout the later half of 2000. It is now common knowledge in Israel and the United States that in 2000, Barak made Arafat an offer that had never been and will never be bettered. Arafat's ultimate rejection of 'Barak's Generous Offer' has entered modern history and lore as the act of a stubborn man unwilling to accept a compromise and unable to lead his people to peace. It was the final proof of the Palestinians' supposed ability 'never to miss an opportunity to miss an opportunity'. The violence that followed with the intensification of the second intifada was therefore considered to be Arafat's fault. In Israel, both the Zionist left and right concluded that Arafat did not want peace, and hopes for a two-state solution died while he was alive.

Clinton, despite his earlier private assurances, publicly blamed Arafat for the collapse of the talks, thus helping to reinforce the international image of Arafat as the belligerent barrier to peace. In a telling story in his subsequent autobiography Clinton recounts how Arafat rang the Oval Office in his final days in office and thanked the outgoing US President for the efforts he made for peace.

'You are a great man,' Arafat said.
'I am not a great man. I am a failure and you made me one,' Clinton replied.

Firstly, the courtesy that Arafat had shown in calling this departing leader was thrown back in his face. Secondly, the failure to make peace is not seen by Clinton as a tragedy that millions of Jews and Arabs must live with in the Middle East, but as a missed opportunity for Clinton to build his legacy and propel himself into the league of great presidents.

But the 'generous offer' was never anything of the sort. Arafat's refusal to sign despite extraordinary pressure from the White House, the Israeli government and world opinion was the only decision he could make if he wanted to remain true to his people's cause and their search for real freedom.

Prior to the 2000 talks, the Palestinian leadership had accepted their future state would only exist on the West Bank and the Gaza Strip, areas which make up only 22 per cent of historical Palestine. Israel would keep 78 per cent. This already showed extraordinary generosity by the Palestinians. In the 2000 talks, Barak wanted to keep almost 70 settlements in the West Bank which would be annexed by Israel, thus taking a further ten per cent of the remaining Palestinian land.

The road network between these settlements would also remain, criss-crossing the future Palestinian state. Barak also wanted Israel to retain 'temporary control' over a further large chunk of what the Palestinians would be left with. This land included more Jewish settlements that would remain 'temporary' for an indefinite amount of time. Some Israeli bypass roads and checkpoints would remain in the West Bank as well. These are but a few of the deficiencies of the generous offer, on top of which, the new Palestinian state would not have East Jerusalem proper as its capital city, but a small number of villages to the east of Jerusalem, and the refugee issue would not be dealt with in a comprehensive manner either.

Arafat did not sign it because he could not. The Palestinians had compromised enough, if he had signed the agreement, it would have been rejected by Palestinians and his position would have become untenable. It must also be said that if the agreement had been signed, a majority of the Israeli public would almost certainly have rejected it. The Israeli public and political mood was not ready for a deal in late 2000. Barak's multi-party coalition government would have split if any deal had been signed, with the more right-wing parties jumping ship first. The Likud opposition led by Ariel Sharon would then have organised a massive and most probably successful movement against any agreement signed by Barak. So even if Arafat had signed, there is no reason to believe that Israel would have also done so.

Has there been a more difficult modern national liberation movement to lead than the Palestinian one? They are the victims of history's most high-profile victims, an unenviable position from which to make a case for nationhood globally. They had to mount a military struggle from exile, leading a people who are spread in a diaspora of millions across many nations from refugee camps in northern Lebanon, to Jordan, to the crowded city of Gaza. Their own cause has been used and abused by neighbouring despotic Arab governments, been wrapped up in Cold War politics and is now sadly subsumed into the so-called 'War on Terror'. They are trying to fight and to reason with the region's superpower that has the unquestioning support of the world's superpower. And their very legitimacy as a people and as a nation is openly questioned by many.

Yes, Arafat made tremendous strategic mistakes, was far from a perfect leader of the Palestinian Authority and used violence, rhetoric and doublespeak to further his aims. The leadership he headed eventually started to see the interests of their own caste as more important than those of the great mass of Palestinians. In this it followed the well-trodden path of most national liberation movements, where the elite and wealthy within the movement are represented by the more conservative wing. He was certainly not the clean-cut hero of a vanquished nation, but the problematic icon of a desperate national liberation movement which was often barely clinging onto life.

Despite his failures, history should be kind to the man who, through his very existence and his will to survive, epitomised the collective experience of the people he led. Whether in the bombed-out shelters in Beirut in the 1980s, in his compound in Ramallah in 2002 working by candlelight while surrounded by Israeli tanks or by his refusal to be forced into signing one compromise too far at Camp David in 2000, Arafat represented the steadfastness, complexity and indestructibility of an uprooted people and a oppressed nation. The flawed father of a nation perhaps, but the father nonetheless.

The Arafat impersonator on stage in the rally started to move to the front again. He had grown tired of being relegated to the background and reached for the microphone from the female MC. She turned around and looked sternly at him and said something angrily. He backed away slowly. She was in charge now.

*

On one of the daytrips organised by the University, we visited a community centre located somewhere between the villages of Mas'ha and Deir Ballout.

We were served up a magnificent feast of local Palestinian cuisine by a group of ten or so women. After we finished our meal, we sat in a circle with the women, some of whom were former political prisoners while others had lost close relatives in the struggle. All had some horrific tale to tell.

For a few hours we listened to engrossing stories of life under occupation. One former political prisoner, who looked to be in her later 40s, told us of her many years spent in Israeli incarceration. She spoke of mental and physical torture. Our translator, an American student with perfect Arabic, broke down in tears many times during the meeting. We asked questions in English.

'What kept you going when you were in prison?'
'The dream of the Palestinian flag flying over the Al-Aqsa Mosque,' she said simply.
She then asked us where we were all from. When I said Ireland, she spoke rapidly to our interpreter.
'Ireland! Your struggle is our struggle. I wrote to Irish prisoners when I was in prison myself,' she said.

I was embarrassed, as I had little 'struggle' to face growing up in suburban Dublin. But it was clear that this former prisoner felt connection between the Republican movement in the North of Ireland and her own fight for freedom.

After a few gruelling hours of first-hand testimony of checkpoint nightmares, prison time and lost loved ones, it was time to depart.

We later visited a local all-girls primary school. Our small group of international students was greeted with squealing, screaming children excited by the strange arrivals. After forcing our way through the swirling mass of happy youngsters, we reached an empty classroom. We sat down and were greeted by the older female principal and two younger female teachers.

Through our translator, we were able to follow the debate and discussion that took place between the female members of staff at the school, those from the University and a few of the female international students. Chris, an English guy finishing his thesis in a Canadian university, and myself were the only men there. The verbal jousting focused mainly on the women's struggle in Palestine. All the members of staff that we met wore hijabs, and it seemed to be a religious school, yet the views expressed were classically feminist. The teachers saw their role as preparing the young girls to play a full part in Palestinian life and to achieve the best academic qualifications possible. The teacher who contributed most to the debate wore a jet-black shawl that covered her head and draped all the way down to her feet. The headscarf above her head did not just sit on her scalp; rather it rose in a triangular shape above it. I was not sure if this change from the norm was to signify her position within the staff structure, or if it carried some cultural or religious significance.

After the fascinating debate, the young teacher in the black shawl told our interpreter that some of the school children were to perform a Palestinian song and dance routine for us. She and another teacher left the room and returned a few moments later. There then followed what was obviously an awkward conversation in Arabic between all the teachers and some of the Bir Zeit staff who had come with us. After a few moments, our interpreter turned around to Chris and I.

'They said that only the women can go out and watch the children perform. They are so sorry about this. Some of the girls are not wearing headscarves and they don't want to perform in front of men without them. I think they are a little embarrassed,' our interpreter added.

Chris and I said it was no problem, and we were not concerned that we would have to wait in the room while the performance took place outside. As the teachers left, the young woman in the black shawl looked at us.

'I am very sorry,' she said sadly.

'Don't worry about it,' I said quickly.

Ibtisal, one of the female staff from the Bir Zeit office got up to leave the room to watch the children's performance outside. As she walked past Chris and I, she turned to us.

'You see, there is more than one wall here,' she whispered while smiling.

6

Loitering on the Margins

An elderly woman standing beside me began to weep softly as she watched the taped interviews with survivors, painfully recalling their experiences. A few feet away a younger woman with red, puffy eyes held a rolled-up handkerchief tight to her closed mouth. The visitors who passed the various installations were from different generations and locations. They included Israeli parents with their young children, foreign tourists studying guide books closely, older gentlemen on their own and teenagers on school trips. All the visitors slowly wandered through the sombre building, some whispering furtively to each other, while others walked in gloomy silence.

A trip to the Holocaust museum in Jerusalem, Yad Vashem, is a difficult day's journey. The detailed, chronological, multi-media museum brings you step by step from the early years of Adolf Hitler's Third Reich.

Beginning with the initial attacks on political rivals and German Jews, and then developing the nightmarish narrative through the official classification of Jews, *Kristallnacht*, the oppression and the eventual removal of the Jews from the ghettoes and their transfer to the concentration camps. The names of those iconic places have now become shorthand for 20th-century inhumanity; Auschwitz, Dachau and the other camps are brought to life by the testimony of survivors. The brave resistance and eventual failure of the Warsaw Ghetto Uprising in 1943 is highlighted, followed by the methodical implementation of the 'Final Solution' with the concluding, incomprehensible body count of six million murdered Jews.

Through photographs, scale models of the camps, videos, interactive computer touch-screens, newspaper articles, music and harrowing accounts from Holocaust survivors played over a sound system, visitors are emotionally exhausted by the conclusion of the visit. The massive building, with its dark, eerie interior is an extraordinarily elaborate and fitting tribute to the millions who were murdered during what the Jews call the *Shoah*.

It is the only museum I have ever walked through where visitors around me wept openly. There were no kids running around noisily, or people chatting loudly on mobile phones, as in many other museums. The atmosphere inside was one of respect for the past and real contemporary grief. Most Israeli families, certainly those of European descent (Ashkenazi Jews), had relatives murdered in the death camps during Hitler's reign. Some survivors still live in Israel.

In the early years of the Israeli state there was a reluctance to commemorate or focus on the experience of the Holocaust. The history of millions of Jews as victims of a state-backed slaughter was not compatible with the Zionist notion of the new Jewish Israeli who was hardy, war-like, strong and almost indestructible. The Zionist relationship with the Shoah has changed in recent decades, and indeed, the Holocaust has been subsumed into the official Zionist timeline, one that is reflected in the very layout of Yad Vashem.

Walking through each chronological section inside the museum, you are brought closer and closer to a dazzling light that peers in from the end of the building. Following pictorial displays of the liberated camps and the desperately few survivors, the final historical installation is grainy, black and white video footage of Israel's first Prime Minister, David Ben-Gurion, reading the Declaration of Israeli Independence in May 1948. After watching the video, you walk towards the welcoming light, and out through a large concrete door. You then find yourself standing on a balcony, overlooking a spectacular panoramic view of the rolling empty hills west of Jerusalem. After spending many hours in the desperate dark, concentrating on the horrific detail from the most appalling period in Jewish history and humanity's lowest moment, you cannot help but be relieved to be out in the sunlight and free from the oppressive misery.

The journey within Yad Vashem is essentially that of the modern Zionist story. The Jewish people suffered unimaginable horrors in 'civilised' Europe during Hitler's reign: an attempt to exterminate them as a people took place under the watch of supposedly enlightened and democratic nations. Because of this, the only way to ensure the survival of the Jewish people was to create their own state, here in the barren, undulating hills of Palestine.

It is a story that provides the core of Israeli Jewish identity, one of collective death followed by eventual renewal and rebirth in Zion. It maintains that even after the darkest period in modern history there can be a form of Jewish national redemption. The presentation in the museum can be a very convincing one, sweeping you along with visceral, raw emotion.

Significantly, the museum's final timeline completely ignores the Arab population of Palestine, a people totally innocent of any act or part in the horrors of the Holocaust. Even the panoramic view from the balcony at the end of the visit is symbolic. Here are the empty, rolling hills of Palestine. It is there in front of you, the early Zionist mantra of a 'land without a people, for a people without a land'. More than 750,000 terrorised Palestinians forced to flee their homes to Lebanon, Jordan, Syria, the West Bank and Gaza are invisible. Those who even today continue to live in exile in refugee camps are absent. The Arab Palestine that existed before 1948 is nowhere to be seen. Today's Arab citizens of Israel, who comprise a significant minority of the population, are also wholly absent from the official Zionist story of how and why the state was created. The Palestinian Nakba and the hundreds of thousands of Palestinians who would lose their homes, land and nation as a result of Ben-Gurion's declaration of Israeli statehood go unmentioned.

*

Zionism, the idea of creating a Jewish nation state, had a complex history that predates the Holocaust. The concept of a 'return' for all Jews to the land of Jerusalem or Zion had for centuries played an important role in Judaism. The Almighty's promise to Abraham that the Holy Land was to be the land for the Jewish people was recorded in the Torah, or equally, in the early books in the Christian Bible. The defeat of the 'Great Jewish Revolt', and the destruction of the Second Temple in Jerusalem by the Romans in AD 70, followed by the defeat of a further Jewish revolt in AD 132–5 with the resulting dispersal of Jews away from the Holy Land are pivotal events in Jewish history. At Passover every year, Jewish families the world over toast 'next year in Jerusalem'.

But the idea of a return was not principally a political one, but rather a more symbolic aspiration in the spiritual and cultural life of Jews in the diaspora. The return would not be carried out by Jews themselves, but, rather more spectacularly, with divine intervention by the arrival of the Messiah. The desire to create an actual Jewish nation state, with borders, an army, a standing government, civil service and a capital city – the wish list of political Zionism – did not take the form of a defined programme of diplomatic and military action until the late nineteenth and early twentieth centuries. Even then, it was not until after the Holocaust that political Zionism won the support of more than a minority of world Jewry.

The vision of an avowedly Jewish state was constructed in the minds of a series of nineteenth century Zionist writers, most famously the Budapest-born journalist Theodore Herzl (1860–1904). Contemplating the increase in anti-Semitism across nineteenth-century Europe and the collective experience of centuries of religious persecution, Herzl eventually proposed that only a Jewish state could provide protection for the Jewish people.

The first Zionist Congress met in Basel in Switzerland in 1897. Over 200 delegates attended. While looking towards

Palestine as the most likely location for any future Jewish state (despite the Arab population already living there) some Zionists were willing to contemplate other possible sites for their 'homeland'. In the coming years, the Congress would openly discuss tracts of land in Africa as possible locations for the state. However, despite the Congress being a predominantly secular affair, it was felt that the religious and spiritual connections between Judaism and the Holy Land, and Jerusalem (referred to as Zion in the Torah and other ancient texts) in particular, made it by far the best location.

It must be noted that other political currents, particularly socialism, won significant support from Jews across the world in the early 20th century. The left-wing Jewish Bund, for instance, was profoundly anti-Zionist, arguing that working-class Jews had more in common with their Gentile brothers and sisters than with capitalist Jews. The Bund said that Jewish workers should fight for their rights through domestic trade union struggles. This, the Bund argued, was the way to combat anti-Semitism on a national level rather than through a policy of non-assimilation and the creation of a separate Jewish state. Jews led socialist revolutionary movements and mass trade unions in Russia and across Europe in the early 1900s. Many Orthodox Jews were also very hostile to the secular beliefs of the Zionists and some saw the plan to create a Jewish state in Israel prior to the arrival of the Messiah as sinful and sure to rightly anger God.

While adherents of Zionism at the turn of the 19th and 20th centuries were still few in number, Jews had been arriving in the Holy Land in waves of immigration called *aliyah* ('ascent' in Hebrew) since the 1880s. Many such immigrants were Zionists who believed that they had arrived in the Holy Land to help to build a future Jewish homeland, establishing among other things the first small Jewish kibbutz as early as 1910. This pre-state Jewish society, the *Yishuv*, was the womb from which the eventual state of Israel would violently emerge. This society was celebrated as a rugged rural paradise by early Zionists.

Other immigrants who came in the aliyah included many Jews from Europe and beyond who were forced to move themselves and their families to avoid anti-Semitism and persecution. Others still were economic immigrants, propelled by financial necessity that had fuelled centuries of migration across the globe. For many, it was a combination of economics and ideology. Still, the numbers of immigrants involved was but a tiny fraction of the world's Jewish population. In the 1920s, one quarter of Jewish immigrants who had arrived would eventually leave Palestine. When the numbers involved in aliyah in the 1920s were at their height, they were still relatively small compared to the global Jewish population. One figure says that only four out of every one thousand Jews in the world came to Palestine in the 1920s, with the United States a far more popular destination until it restricted its immigration policy.

Prior to the First World War (1914-18), Palestine was part of the Ottoman Empire, as it had been since the 16th century. As the War began, Jews were still a small minority of the population in Palestine, despite the best efforts of the Zionist movement to promote *aliyah*. The small community of Palestinian Jews who had already been living in the Holy Land for generations were often uneasy about and openly hostile to the Zionists and their movement.

The Holy Land was held up by Zionist propaganda as a 'land without a people for a people without a land'. Immigrants were often surprised to arrive and find an Arab population very much alive and farming in Palestine. At the very least, hundreds of thousands of Arabs lived in the area of modern Israel and what is now known as the occupied territories when the first aliyah began in the 1880s.

The existence of thousands of Arabs in the Holy Land was always going to present a difficulty for the Zionist project. Early pronouncements from leading Zionists like David Ben-Gurion promised compromise with Palestine's Arab farmers. For instance, in 1926 he said that 'the Arab population is an organic, insoluble part of Palestine. It is rooted here, it works here and it will stay here'. This reasonable rhetoric was understandable, considering that secular Zionists viewed their political beliefs as part of the broad sweep of enlightenment and modern political nationalism. There was not as much open talk of 'population removal' or 'ethnic cleansing' as there is in today's language.

But other right-wing Zionist leaders were, as hindsight would prove, more honest in outlining the brutal consequences that the creation of a Jewish state would have for the indigenous Arabs.

> 'We cannot give any compensation for Palestine, neither to the Palestinians nor to other Arabs. Therefore, a voluntary agreement is inconceivable. All colonization, even the most restricted, must continue in defiance of the will of the native population.'

So wrote leading Zionist Vladimir Jabotinsky in 1923.

The logic inherent in the development of Zionism ran like this: the Zionist movement incorporated important cultural aspects such as the revival of Hebrew as a living language (albeit with the consequential fading of Yiddish and Ladino as spoken dialects among European and Sephardic Jews). It also provided an 'answer' to perennial Jewish fears of discrimination and exploitation with a 'last refuge' if needed. As the day of Israel's establishment came closer, the rhetoric hardened from both the left and right wings of the Zionist movement and military actions followed.

In practice, Zionism was the physical imposition of a narrow ethno-nationalist vision onto an indigenous Arab population of hundreds of thousands. If there was going to be a Jewish state in the Holy Land, the vast bulk of Palestinian Arabs could simply not remain where they had been living for centuries. In essence, Zionism was a colonizing project like most others, and the Palestinian Arabs were its colonial victims. In the creation of a settler state for one of history's most persecuted peoples, another nation and people would be uprooted, dispersed and driven from their homes in their thousands. They would become the refugees of the refugees.

*

Tight streets meander through ugly breeze block buildings, rubbish is strewn across laneways, layers of thick exposed electrical wires link across houses; this is not a sight new to anyone acquainted with modern Lebanon. The black, green and red bunting is draped over the crowded narrow alleyways. The Palestinian national flag, ragged and torn, has seen better days as it hangs humbly from a pole. Pictures of Yasser Arafat beam down over his people. A single, massive photograph displays the dead spiritual leader of Hamas, Sheikh Ahmed Yassin, who smiles benevolently through his beard. Both men look like proud grandparents, overseeing their children and grandchildren as they trundle on with their lives in the refugee camp below, far away from home.

Some 10,000 Palestinians live in the camp founded in 1948. Most live in concrete block shelters, many built by the refugees themselves. The UN has been unable to assist in maintenance work on these shelters because of a ban on the entry of building material imposed by the Lebanese government. Only 60 per cent of the camp's shelters are connected to the sewerage system. The rest of the camp dwellers must use latrines.

You can circumnavigate the Al-Bass Palestinian refugee camp in Tyre in southern Lebanon without knowing it is even there. Walk down Rue Abu Deeb alongside the major archaeological site, towards the Mediterranean Sea, through the busy Shiite neighbourhood with its Hezbollah flags, into the sleepy Christian quarter and past the fishing port and back out onto the main road to Sidon – and you won't see it. There were no international tourists in southern Lebanon in early 2007, so the pathways and corniche are empty and the leisurely walk takes approximately an hour. As tourist trails go, it gives you a comprehensive sense of the troubled city's centre while also allowing you view the impressive remnants of the Roman hippodrome.

But take this route through the city and you will know nothing of the thousands of Palestinians who live on top of one another in the narrow confines of the Al-Bass camp, hidden tight within Tyre's centre. Wary

Lebanese Army soldiers guard the main entrance to the camp close to the central taxi stop. A long-standing political arrangement ensures that the Lebanese Army does not enter the camps, and they are run by the Palestinians themselves.

Life for a Palestinian in Al-Bass and the 11 other refugee camps across Lebanon is grim. Typical refugees, their parents, grandparents or great-grandparents fled north into Lebanon in 1948 from towns, villages and farms. Their initial hopes of an early return to their homes waned as Israel grew stronger. Living in Lebanon, their ability to work, study and travel outside the camps is severely restricted. Their lives and identities depend on the micro-universe of the poverty-polluted camps. They call themselves Palestinian but, if younger than middle-aged, they have almost certainly never been to Palestine. Their whole identity is forged by a desire to return to a country that no longer exists, and their plight is increasingly ignored by international leaders, including their own. So they sit, sullen and angry in a tiny desperate island of exiled Palestine, surrounded by a country that is not their own, dreaming of a place that they cannot visit.

Outside the camp the tumultuous world of sectarian Lebanese politics and society carries on. On many occasions, the circumstance of the Palestinian refugee has had a violent impact on this country of complex, religious politics. Following Black September in 1970 when the Jordanian army crushed the Palestinian militants and forced them out of Jordan's refugee camps, the leadership of the PLO made its home in southern Lebanon and Beirut.

In the coming decade it would engage in attacks on northern Israel but also embroiled itself in the bloody Lebanese civil war. In the early 1980s, Israel invaded and occupied Lebanon in an attempt to destroy the PLO and quell the cross-border attacks. It also wanted to create what was essentially to be a vassal state on its northern borders. The PLO under Arafat was expelled from Lebanon in 1982, leaving the refugees leaderless. The Sabra and Chatila massacres quickly followed: over 1,000 Palestinian civilians were butchered in the streets by Christian Falangists, the Lebanese allies of Israel. A subsequent Israeli investigating commission would declare that Defence Minister Ariel Sharon bore 'personal responsibility' for the massacre and recommended that he be dismissed from his ministry. Sharon would be elected Prime Minister of Israel in 2001.

Though the Lebanese civil war period is rightly seen as a disastrous one for the Palestinians, at least the refugees and their plight was at centre-stage. Since the mid 1980s, the Palestinian refugees in Lebanon have become a forgotten people. Their impact on society, culture or the economy outside the camps is negligible. Hezbollah, the major Lebanese Shiite force, is anti-Israeli and is concerned, at least in rhetoric, about the conditions of the Palestinian refugees. But in the end, even Hezbollah is more interested in internal Lebanese affairs than in the Palestinian cause.

While in the country I interviewed Professor Hilal Khashan, a leading Lebanese political scientist. We spoke on the sumptuously lush campus of the American University of Beirut (AUB). A tranquil, academic Eden in the centre of the bustling city, the campus is certainly a seductive spot. AUB is located only a few minutes' taxi ride from some of the largest Palestinian refugee camps in southern Beirut. Following a series of questions about the unstable internal political situation in Lebanon, I asked Prof Khashan to speak more broadly about the political position of the Palestinians in the country.

'The Palestinians here have been repeatedly pounded and defeated. Most Palestinians, if they can get the chance to work elsewhere, leave the country. This country is the most inhospitable to Palestinians. The Palestinians are treated like pariahs in Lebanon,' he said rapidly in English as he tried to fix the stuttering electrical fan in his office.

'Since the departure of the PLO in 1982, the Palestinians have been in a state of gloom and despair here. They are a broken and defeated people and they have been thoroughly marginalised. Particularly since 1982, Palestinians can't own land, they can't inherit property, they can't work, they can't do anything. Living conditions are miserable. And I don't really think politics is a real issue for most Palestinians now. Their ultimate aim is to be able to survive physically. I mean, the only thing that brings the Lebanese together is their hostility for Palestinians.'

Prof Khashan's analysis of the Palestinian's plight within Lebanon was so darkly bleak, yet so clearly correct that the sheer force of his depressing logic made my head hurt.

Dispersed across nations, disjointed Palestinian identity is a creation of vanquished valour. The PLO, once the organisation that held together the many threads of Palestinian life from the refugee camps across the Arab world to those living under Israeli occupation has lost its centrality. The Palestinian Authority is now the focus, and all eyes are on those who reside under occupation in Gaza and the West Bank. Those who sit in the poverty of the peripheral refugee camps with their dreams of return have been forgotten, the living left-overs of an historical crime, loitering on the margins of their people's misery.

It is at grass roots and sometimes individual levels that some hope can be found. Charity, the United Nations and individual workers and volunteers attempt to alleviate some of the problems in the camps. Sara, an English-Palestinian friend, is a young woman who seems comfortable with her East-West identity. With a father from Jerusalem who has spent many years working in medicine, Sara was brought up in the English midlands. Despite her distinctive English accent, Sara can launch into very good colloquial Arabic. While Sara was studying the language at the American University in Beirut, I met her and her friend at an excellent restaurant just off Rue Hamra in west Beirut one balmy night. During the conversation, Sara mentioned that she travels into the refugee camps of Sabra and Chatila to teach English to Palestinians living there. Even this small example is an attempt to weave together the isolated threads of the Palestinian diaspora in the west and the refugees living in the Arab world.

I mention to her that some Lebanese we had met while travelling in the country had displayed hostility to the Palestinians living in their midst. I asked her how she as a Palestinian felt about such anger.

'Well, I can understand some of it. The PLO may have been part of some of the trouble here over the years.

But you cannot blame the ordinary Palestinians for that. How can you blame refugees for that? They never asked to be here,' concluded Sara.

And they continually ask for their right to return, to be recognised. That is a request that may seem so simple and just, but has caused so much pain and death and will not be acceded to anytime soon, if ever.

According to a major 2003 survey of the Palestinian refugees, a huge majority wanted their right to return to be recognised both internationally and by the Israeli state. But only ten per cent said that they wanted to return to what is now Israel, to live in the Jewish state. Just over 30 per cent said that they would like to live in a new Palestinian state if it were founded in the West Bank and Gaza, and some 17 per cent said that they would accept fair compensation and stay where they were while also receiving Palestinian citizenship. Just over 20 per cent said that they would accept Palestinian citizenship and return to designated areas inside Israel which would be swapped later on for Palestinian areas as part of a peace agreement. Only 13 per cent said they would refuse all options.

Considering the economically brutal and socially barren reality for Palestinian refugees it is no wonder that pre-1948 Palestine has become a vision of idyllic harmony for them. Indeed, within the modern Palestinian nationalist narrative, Palestinian land before the creation of Israel is viewed as an almost prelapsarian paradise, free from disputes. The more desperate the contemporary situation has become for the Palestinians, the more perfect the past is perceived as being. Even the most hard-nosed and cynical of Palestinians that I met became misty-eyed when contemplating pre-1948 Palestine.

Sa'd Nimr, my lecturer in Middle Eastern and Palestinian history at Bir Zeit University, was an excellent teacher. His knowledge of the many complicated strands within the Palestinian political movement was comprehensive. He taught the history of the Palestinian people from a broadly sympathetic standpoint, but the Israeli state and Israeli people were not depicted as pantomime villains during his course. He was involved in campaigns to help free Palestinian prisoners from Israeli jails, and he had also built up some contacts amongst Israeli left-wing and peace activists over the years. Like almost every Palestinian man you meet in the occupied territories, he had spent time in an Israeli jail as a political prisoner, in his case as a very young man many years ago.

His historical method was based on source material and a search for facts. Despite this, in the class on pre-Nakba Palestinian life, Sa'd lost his critical edge somewhat. He used a projector to show us various black and white photographs of family, working and farming life in Palestine in the 1930s and 1940s. As he slowly flicked through the depictions of life before the creation of Israel, he sadly said to the class, 'Doesn't everyone seem happy? … There is a type of perfection to it, don't you think?'

Three years later, I interviewed Sa'd in his office in downtown Ramallah in May 2008. It was a wide-ranging discussion on the contemporary political situation in the territories. He expressed cynicism about Israeli government interests in a comprehensive peace deal.

'I think it is clear that they do not want to solve the conflict. They are just looking for ways to manage it. While they talk of peace, they continue to build settlements, and the checkpoints continue,' he said quickly while fill-ing his pipe with tobacco.

He made the case for an academic boycott and a wider campaign in the West against Israel, arguing that this was as much to help the Israelis as anyone else.

'Over the last couple of years, I really have come to be-lieve that a boycott like there was against South Africa is the best tactic. Something like this can force change within Israeli society, because no change is coming at the moment. Even recently, when there was talk about an international academic boycott of Israeli universities, there were many articles and discussion in the Israeli media. It forced universities to think about their policy towards the occupation,' he said sipping his coffee.

'The point is, anger on the Palestinian street is growing, and it is in Israel's own interest to come to a comprehen-sive agreement with the Palestinians and to end the occupation. But they need to be pressured into that by the international community, because they are not going to move by themselves.'

After focussing on the growing difficulties within the West Bank and the Gaza Strip, I raised the 'refugee issue' and my own trip to Lebanon the previous year. Sa'd quickly said that 'the refugee issue is the most dif-ficult because the right of return of those refugees to their homes is a collective and individual one.' He men-tioned work that had been carried out between Pales-tinian and Israeli academics some years previous on the issue, but even in this case there had been no unanimous conclusion on how to 'solve' the problem.

'The Israeli 'Law of Return', allowing every Jewish person in the world to come to Israel makes it all the more difficult for the refugees. For instance, since the 1990s they have had to watch thousands of Russian Jews arriving in Israel, coming to the land the Palestinian refugees had to flee and cannot return to.'

I asked him about the role of the Nakba and the way some Palestinians seem to regard pre-1948 Palestine as a dream world. I mentioned his comments and the projector display of pre-Nakba Palestine during my course in Bir Zeit three years ago.

He went quiet for a second.

'Well you know, if you ask a Palestinian refugee in the camps about their old town or village, they will go into great detail. Even if they themselves had not been born in the village in the Galilee or wherever it was, they would have heard the stories from their parents. They will be able to say exactly where in the village their home stood and what was in the garden. They can tell you who lived beside them, and all the names of the families who lived near them. They can say where the trees stood, where the mosque and the church was exactly. It is there in their minds, it exists for them as a real place, even if the village was later destroyed by the Israelis, he said quietly. But also, in looking at Palestine before 1948, I do believe there was great potential. The Palestinians have been regarded as the most educated of the Arabs for decades. They would have been able to use that potential. Also you have to remember that Bir Zeit, which is a small university town now, was bigger than Amman in 1948. There was development here, and the Arab Palestinian society was progressing, but that ended in 1948.

But yes, I suppose Palestinians do dream of what life was like in the past, but it is understandable that when you live on top of a sewer in a refugee camp you do not want to think about your real life,' he concluded.

All nationalisms have mythology inherent within them, some more than others. Of course Palestine before 1948 was not paradise on earth. There was some sectarian strife, a British occupation, poverty and significant economic gaps between rich and poor, iniquitous land distribution among Arabs and people certainly did not smile all the time. The crushing destruction of Palestinian Arab society in 1948 and the resulting decades of oppression, expulsion and occupation have led to an understandable exaltation of the past. Israel has taken the Palestinians' land and homes, but their memories of what life was like before the Nakba can remain beautiful and pristine, a mental refuge from the present.

*

The keys to Palestine violently exchanged hands during the Great War. Britain and its allies were eventually victorious. The Ottoman Empire, snidely referred to as the 'sick man of Europe' by Western diplomats, had backed the wrong warhorse. Having sided with Germany, the Ottoman Empire's lands beyond Turkey were lost. British forces, under the command of General Edmund Allenby, marched through Jaffa Gate and into the historic old city of Jerusalem in December 1917.

Back in 1916, prior to the Allies' victory, under candlelight in smoky rooms in London, large maps were taken from glass cases and the Middle East was carved up between Britain and France. While the war was still raging in 1916, British civil servant Sir Mark Sykes and French diplomat

Georges Picot met secretly to plan the futures of people living thousands of miles away. Their tools for nation-building were numerous, but a ruler was certainly one of them. A straight line thousands of miles long was drawn across the Middle East creating the northern border of Jordan, the southern border of Syria and many other demarcation lines. Once the ruler was put back in the drawer, the God-like strokes had decided the political, economic and national fate of many hundreds of thousands of Arabs, none of whom were ever consulted.

At the end of the bloody conflict, the spoils of war were shared out. France got Lebanon and Syria. Britain got Jordan (then called Transjordan) and Palestine. This was eventually referred to as the British Mandate following approval by the precursor to the United Nations, the League of Nations. The Skyes-Picot Agreement was not the first or last time that British officials were involved in partitioning land. Less than five years later, officials and politicians in London would pore over maps of Ireland and play a significant role in the future partitioned fate of another small piece of troubled land.

Throughout the Great War, leading Zionists, chief among them the brilliant and well-connected Chaim Weizmann, had petitioned the British government to support the establishment of a Jewish homeland in Palestine. Following constant lobbying by Weizmann, the British Cabinet eventually agreed, and a declaration signed in November 1917 by Foreign Minister Arthur James Balfour, proclaimed that Britain wanted to see a 'national homeland' for the Jewish people established in the Holy Land.

British cabinet members agreed to the Zionist goal for a variety of reasons. For some, it was religious. Prime Minister

Lloyd George was a Welsh nonconformist who had biblical sympathy for the idea of the Jews returning to Zion. Other British civil servants, policy makers and politicians simply feared the Jews, believing the anti-Semitic line that the Jews controlled the world. Many saw Jewish connections in everything from the 1917 October Revolution in Russia to the economic levers of American power in Wall Street. By giving the Zionists what they wanted, it was believed by some politicians that Britain had appeased a powerful people. Britain was still at war with Germany and wanted any support it could get. There were rumours that German officials were also considering making a pro-Zionist statement in an attempt to help its faltering war effort. Whatever the justification, the Zionists rightly viewed the Balfour Declaration as a significant diplomatic victory. Gaining the support of what was then the world's most powerful nation for such a mission was an important boost to the Zionist political project.

With the Balfour Declaration, the British had promised a land they did not yet own to a people the majority of whom did not want to live there, having had no consultation with the people who currently did live there. Few other historical documents sum up so neatly the monumental anti-democratic God complex that shaped the minds of the elite who ran the world's largest empire from London. The British Mandate controlled Palestine from 1920 to 1948. Imperial tactics utilised by the British across the world were also used in Palestine. The British authorities played the Jewish and Arab sectors, off one another: divide and attempt to rule.

In the 1920s and 1930s, the Zionists openly constructed the *Yishuv*, promoting more and more Jewish immigration with ever-larger waves of *aliyah*. The Zionist leadership in Palestine often clashed with the British Mandate authorities over restrictions on the number of Jewish immigrants allowed to enter. The Zionist movement believed it to be too small. Most Palestinian Arabs were understandably fearful of the Zionist push for a 'homeland'. They also often clashed with the British over the number of Jewish immigrants allowed in, but because they believed it to be too large.

The Zionists built kibbutz, labour unions, businesses, schools and universities, slowly and methodically increasing the amount of land in Jewish hands, either by purchasing the land of rich Arabs or by seizing disputed land. Yet until the very eve of the 1948 war and the foundation of the Israeli state, only six per cent of land was in the hands of Jewish landowners. It was not until the violence of 1948 and the exodus of over 750,000 Arabs that the majority of land and property belonged to the Jewish population.

Many of the leading Zionists described themselves as socialists, though most did not see 'class unity' stretching as far as their Arab neighbour. Encouraging Jewish landowners and businessmen to employ only 'Hebrew labour' was part of this socialism, one that was envisioned as being essentially for Jews only. Thus, in truth, it was not socialism at all. The Zionist movement, while having its own, sometimes violent, internal political schisms, was united by the certain goal of a Jewish state in Palestine. This unity of purpose, despite squabbles between different shades of Zionist opinion, was of central importance to the eventual successful establishment of the State of Israel.

In contrast, the Arabs did not have a centralised political leadership or a singularity of purpose. While the British offered the Zionists the Balfour declaration, the victors in the Great War had also promised the Arabs a homeland if they took up arms against the Ottoman Empire. They dutifully did so, with the Arab Revolt of 1916-18 inflicting a devastating blow to the Turkish side of the war. The promise from the British to the Arabs was not fulfilled.

The Arab nationalist consciousness grew during the period of the British Mandate that followed the end of the Great War. It was, however, never organised to the same extent as the Zionist fervour. Political leadership among the Arabs tended to group around rival historical families or the Grand Mufti of Jerusalem rather than around an ideologically motivated political party or movement. Palestinian politics had not developed highly organised parties or movements, and still looked to clans and well-regarded families to provide leadership. Palestinian Arab society often reacted with confusion to Zionist gains, as social conditions for the Arabs were much poorer than those of the new Jewish immigrants. Education, health and employment levels were dismal. The resulting 'Arab Rebellion' in 1936 was badly led and, in the end, turned out to be an unsuccessful attempt to assert Arab nationalism against the Zionists.

There was no credible left-wing movement in Palestine at the time arguing for unity among Jewish and Arabic workers, and this contributed in part to the victory of sectarian politics. Rightfully frightened and angered by the political implications of Zionism and the growing strength of the Yishuv, most ordinary working Arabs desperately gave their support to the leading rich families and some fiercely reactionary Arab politicians. Some of their leaders were to express support for the Nazis during the Second World War.

The British Mandate authority was sometimes rhetorically pro-Zionist in its statements, and other times, more pro-Arab. It published the findings of a number of commissions it had established during its reign, commissions which attempted to find future workable political solutions for the Holy Land. Most were researched and written from London and concluded that some variation of a partition of the land between Arabs and Jews would be preferable for the British. The Second World War (1939-1945) increased the pace towards the creation of the State of Israel. The hellish experience of life in the concentration camps, as articulated by survivors, convinced a rapidly-growing number of Jews, particularly those from the West, that their survival could only be guaranteed in their own state, protected by Jewish arms.

Dusk was quickly descending upon the Empire on which the sun had once never set. The new world order following the Second World War ensured that Great Britain was no longer all that great. Colonies, most significantly India, gained independence or moved in that direction, and with the rise of the United States and the Soviet Union, Britain was no longer considered to be a real superpower. The strategic and economic benefits of controlling the Holy Land had always been questioned by many in Britain, and by the mid-1940s it became clear that Britain wanted out of Palestine as soon as possible.

In February 1947, the British referred the Palestine Mandate to the United Nations (UN) for discussion. On

29 November, the United Nations General Assembly passed a partition plan for Palestine which would see the creation of both a Jewish and an Arab state.

The plan divided Mandate Palestine into three: almost 56 per cent for the Jewish state, 42 per cent for an Arab state and the area around Jerusalem to be put under international control. A majority of the UN General Assembly accepted the plan, including the United States and the Soviet Union. The Zionist leadership also accepted the arrangement, which was no surprise as it was extremely generous to them. Jews only made up one third of the population and currently only held six per cent of the land, yet they were to get 56 per cent of Palestine for their state. However, the Zionist acceptance was only tactical. Inside the boundaries of this proposed Jewish state there would be half a million Jews and 440,000 Arabs. This was such a narrow Jewish majority that the Zionist leadership could never accept it on any medium- to long-term basis. Either a large number of Arabs would have to be moved, or the borders of the Jewish state would have to be expanded. Both would happen in the chaos and violence that ripped apart the Holy Land in 1947–8. By late 1949 the new Jewish state had expanded its borders to over 78 per cent of the land.

The Palestinian Arab leadership and the neighbouring Arab states rejected the UN plan. This is often referred to by modern Israeli politicians as a colossal 'historical mistake'. It was supposedly the first example of the Arabs' ability 'never to miss an opportunity to miss an opportunity'. But this is dubious historical analysis. From the standpoint of the Arab leadership in 1947, acceptance of the UN plan would have been ridiculous. Arabs would lose huge percentages of the land, and over 400,000 of them would be living as a minority in a Jewish state. Of course, with the benefit of hindsight and knowledge of the subsequent history of Arab defeat, Israeli conquest and the dispersal and occupation of the Palestinians, perhaps a tactical acceptance of the plan at the time would have been better in the long run. Perhaps any deal, no matter how unfair, would have been better than nothing in 1947.

Violence between Zionists forces and Arab fighters increased across Mandate Palestine in late 1947 and as the date of Britain's departure in May 1948 loomed it descended into full-blown civil war. Attacks on civilians took place on both sides, and violence swept Palestine in the winter months of 1947 and on into early 1948. Decades of sectarianism fuelled the violence as the Zionists and Arab fighters tried desperately to gain ground while holding what they had.

The Zionist extremist paramilitary group, the Irgun, conducted many terrorist attacks on Arab civilian centres. Following a series of bomb attacks on Arab civilians, in Haifa in December 1947, local Arabs attacked Jewish oil refinery workers, killing 39 people. In retaliation, the Irgun planted bombs in crowded Arab centres like Jaffa, while Arab irregular forces conducted ambushes on Jews travelling along the roads. Zionist forces were better armed, more numerous, centrally organised and better disciplined than the irregular, more locally-based, badly-led Palestinian fighters. The Zionists would easily gain the upper hand as the weeks and months passed by.

On 9 April 1948, the most infamous massacre of the period took place in the Arab village of Deir Yassin near

Jerusalem. Zionist fighters entered the village and killed civilians including women and children. The rape of some local women and the killing of a large number of infants were reported. Approximately 100 people were killed. Survivors had their belongings stolen, and they were paraded through the streets of Jewish West Jerusalem where they were ridiculed by the public. News of the massacre created blind panic among Palestinians in neighbouring towns and villages. Thousands fled on hearing lurid tales from survivors and read those reprinted in the Arab media.

The British were also itching to leave. While there were voices from within the British establishment that cursed the day the Balfour Declaration was issued, in practice, the British Mandate helped facilitate the Zionist enterprise. By allowing the Yishuv to grow, a Jewish state-in-waiting, the British authorities were fundamentally pro-Zionist, despite some disputes along the way. Even if some of the Jewish militant groups turned their guns on the British after the Second World War, by May 1948, the British Mandate placed the Zionists in a position of strength from which they could declare the Jewish state. In contrast, the Arabs had not built up the structure of a state, nor would they have been allowed to do so. The British, who were meant to maintain law and order in the Holy Land up until May 1948 did not intervene to protect Palestinian villages and cities attacked by Zionist forces, nor did they do anything to prevent the Palestinian exodus.

The British Army had remained for three decades, eventually marching out again through Jerusalem's historical gates. They left some legacies particular to the British Empire, such as red post boxes, a comprehensive civil service, a deeply divided people, talk of partition and problems that made eventual descent into ethnic cleansing, bloody war and chaos inevitable. On the Mediterranean coast in central Tel Aviv, David Ben-Gurion rose to read aloud the Israeli Declaration of Independence just hours before the British left. The neighbouring Arab countries immediately attacked the new state. After 1948, the future fortunes of two people took starkly different paths.

*

Few experiences can be as tranquil as eating the catch of the day at the famous Byblos Fishing Club on a warm, sunny afternoon in northern Lebanon. Staring out on the jet blue waters of the picturesque harbour with local Lebanese fishermen going about their work at a lazy pace, there is little noise but the gentle sound of waves breaking against the bobbing boats. The walls along the empty restaurant are laden with pictures of 1950s Hollywood superstars, French singers and political personalities who visited the seafront location before the devastating civil wars of the 1970s and 1980s. These were the days when Beirut was called the 'Paris of the East'. The Byblos Fishing Club was then an important stop-off point on the international playboy circuit. The original owner, 'Pepe the Pirate', smiles out from faded photos, standing beside a string of local and international stars, particularly glamorous women.

But Byblos in the summer of 2007 is far from being a hub of VIP activity and social extravagance. In fact, it is almost utterly deprived of tourists, be they famous names or just ordinary backpackers. The stunningly preserved medieval town, the lavish Roman archaeological sites and the largely intact crusader castle are easily negotiated, as no one else is there to see them. Cafes are shut, and the town's souk, with its well-stocked selection of tourist trinkets, food and clothing is deathly quiet. The string of car bombings in the capital Beirut in the preceding months and the increasing political instability had kept foreign arrivals to a minimum.

While waiting to receive the bill from the bored, under-worked waiter, the distinctive swoosh of a helicopter's propellers could be heard. A military chopper flew low over the previously silent restaurants and tourist shops of Byblos. It was heading 40 kilometres north, to join a military operation in the clear skies above the Palestinian refugee camp of Nahr al-Bared, where the Lebanese army had been pulverising the homes of the 30,000-plus Palestinians who lived there for the previous couple of weeks.

In every Internet café, every bar, every small store and sitting room you could see into, the Lebanese watched the decrepit skyline of the Nahr al-Bared camp on TV. Thick plumes of dark, swirling smoke rose steadily from the camp's desperate interior. The consistent coverage on Lebanese television and the more intermittent up-dates on the international Arab stations kept a worried public glued to their screens. Pictures of Palestinian refugees gathering their belongings and fleeing the camp were splashed on the local *Daily Star*. On the move again, hundreds of miles from their original home, Palestinian refugees were once again in flight following their original exodus.

The camp had been established in 1949, the year follow-ing the Nakba. Palestinian families were living in the open, shivering in the cold and dealing with the elements in the uncompromising Beqaa Valley in east Lebanon. They were moved by the Red Cross from their tents to a camp in Nahr al-Bared. Most of the refugees had originally lived in the northern Galilee before fleeing the Israeli military, and so the various streets and squares in the modern Nahr al-Bared camp are named after towns and villages in what is now the Galilee area of Israel.

Almost sixty years later, and the Palestinians were once again back in the political centre-stage with an unwelcome bang. Lebanese army forces were shelling and bombing the camp in a supposed bid to destroy an extreme terrorist organisation called Fatah al-Islam which was said to have an Al-Qaeda-type political programme. All the major Palestinian organisations had condemned the group, and its support was minuscule among the refugees, making Palestinians a minority of the Fatah al-Islam militants, the majority of whom were Saudis and Syrians. Yet the massive bombing and shelling campaign waged by the Lebanese military affected all Palestinians living in the camp.

As innocent Palestinian refugees fled the camp the majority of the Lebanese political parties, excluding Hezbollah, supported the army's actions. Lebanese nationalism was at its height, with flags flying everywhere and patriotic videos and TV programmes beamed into millions of homes. The Lebanese army was using a massive military hammer to crush a small extremist nut. The Palestinians on the receiving end were not getting a huge amount of sympathy from most Lebanese.

One evening, we spoke to a nice young waiter at the Zaatar-w-Zeit restaurant along Beirut's bohemian student thoroughfare, Rue Bliss. He talked of his future plans to study abroad.

'I love Lebanon with all my heart,' he said touching his chest. 'But with things like this going on, you know the future could be war,' he nodded his head slowly. 'You know what is going on at the moment ... we are fighting those ... Palestinian ... terrorists.'

The mild-mannered waiter spat out the words 'Palestinian' and 'terrorists'. It is clear who he blamed for much of the trouble in his country.

It is not only in neighbouring Arab countries where there is friction between refugees and the inhabitants of the local towns. Although much less fierce, a number of Bir Zeit residents on the West Bank told me quietly that there was some lingering resentment against the refugees who lived in the local Jalazoun camp. Locals asked why they had not stood and fought for their own homes and villages in 1948. Why had they fled in the face of Israeli arms? The people of Bir Zeit had not fled following the Israeli occupation of the West Bank in 1967, so why could they not have displayed the same fortitude? This simmering tension between Palestinians with different histories is understandable; defeat and expulsion will divide any people, leading to accusations, infighting and bickering.

The refugees who live in the camps in the West Bank and the Gaza Strip have a unique story to tell, because they were occupied by Israel *twice*: first in 1948, when they fled their towns to the then Jordanian-controlled West Bank and the Egyptian-controlled Gaza Strip, and later in 1967, when the Israelis invaded and occupied both of these areas.

Bethlehem is one such town. The birthplace of the infant Christ does not look or feel like the sparse, rustic town of many Nativity plays, and the religious sites are no longer magnets for Christian pilgrims, as violence in the area has kept most away in recent years. The Israeli Wall runs within and alongside the town, right up tight against the local refugee camp. If the three wise men had to return to modern Bethlehem to worship at the baby Christ's feet, they would have serious problems negotiating the Wall and checkpoint system around the town. As for the shepherds, their land would most probably have been annexed by the Wall.

Young Palestinian children run giddily through the narrow laneways of the Bethlehem refugee camp. Reluctant to be photographed, they have inherited a wariness of new faces that many years of war have created. The camp is home to some 'wanted militants' as Israeli security forces call them. At the entrance to the camp near the Wall, a mural depicts the tents that the original refugees in 1948 lived in. Beside that stands a one-storey, shoddy, square, small building. This is one of the remaining structures the refugees were eventually transferred into when they moved from their tents. Now, the modern camp is architecturally similar to most others in the territories. Three- and four-storey white breeze-block constructions, are crowded into small areas with extremely narrow laneways between them, and services are far from adequate for the thousands of refugees who live there.

The small but impressive library in the camp was partially funded by Irish tax payers' money. In recognition of this, an Irish tricolour hangs in the corner of the main room, and it is hard as an Irish person not to feel some pride when you enter the building. In the community centre, a local camp leader gave a presentation on

the situation in the area to a large group of foreign students. It quickly developed into a discussion about
whether two states or a singular bi-national state was the
best 'solution' to the conflict. A young French man who
worked in the camp and was wearing a Fidel Castro T-
shirt argued that the only 'solution' to the conflict is one
state, where both Jews and Arabs would live as equal citizens. He said that two states would not be created, and
even if they were, they would prove to be very unstable
in the future. On the other side, a middle-aged Palestinian man, a community worker in the camp, said that two
states would be the only viable option. He said that one
state for both Palestinians and Israelis would never happen – the Israelis especially would never allow it. But as
you walk around the camp's alleyways, it feels that such
political talk of a one- or two-state 'solution' is far from
the grinding, depressing reality on the ground.

*

The Palestinian refugees ended up in Lebanon, the West
Bank and elsewhere as a result of the events of 1947–
8. After Ben-Gurion's declaration of independence, the
neighbouring Arab countries invaded Israel, but were
repulsed by the armed forces of the new state. The new
Israeli army was better trained, supplied and motivated
than the armies of Jordan, Egypt and Syria. But the Jewish state was to lose 6,000 in the war, about one out of
every hundred Jews living in the area at the time. This,
the first 'Arab-Israeli War', is regarded with huge pride
by Israelis. Israel, a new state in the opening days of its
life, was able to hold its own against all the Arab armies.
It shed much blood along the way, but the Arab armies
were prevented from destroying the new state.

While this war between the Israeli army and the Arab armies has proved rather uncontroversial in Israeli historiography, it is the 'civil war' between the Jews and Palestinian Arabs in Palestine during 1947–8, and the exodus of over 750,000 Palestinians during this period, that have proved to be hugely controversial.

Hundreds of thousands of Palestinians fled their family homes out of fear or because they were expelled by Jewish forces. Over 500 abandoned Palestinian Arab villages and thousands of homes were deliberately blown up or destroyed by Israeli forces.

Arab homes and farm land that were left standing were occupied and farmed by Jews, who became the new owners as recognised by the Israeli state. Israel in its early years introduced a wide sweep of legislation to give legalistic credence to this ethnic cleansing and massive expropriation, with acts such as the Absentees Property Act (1950) and the Land Acquisition Law (1953). The former owners of the property, seething with bitter anger and now living in tented refugee camps across the Arab world and prevented from returning to their homes had a more simple term for it – theft.

*

While hundreds of thousands of Jews from across the globe were welcomed into the new state under the Israeli Law of Return (1950), the same law prevented the previous Palestinian residents from returning, simply because they were not Jewish.

In December 1948, the United Nations General Assembly passed Resolution 194. Article 11 of the resolution reads:

> Refugees wishing to return to their homes and
> live in peace with their neighbours should be
> permitted to do so at the earliest practicable
> date and compensation should be paid for the
> property of those choosing not to return and
> for the loss of or damage to property which
> under principles of international law or in eq-
> uity, should be made good by the Governments
> or authorities responsible.

This resolution has never been implemented and has
been ignored by successive Israeli governments who
argue that their state was not responsible for the Palestinian exodus. The United Nations now defines refugees
as including the offspring of those who left their homes
in Palestine. The Israelis disagree. According to the
UNRWA, the UN body established to care for the
refugees, there are just over 1.9 million Palestinian
refugees and ten refugee camps in Jordan; 400,000 and
12 camps in Lebanon and 450,000 with ten camps in
Syria. There are an additional 16 camps in the West
Bank and 745,000 refugees, and 23 camps in the Gaza
Strip with just over one million refugees. In total, as of
2008, UNWRA recognises 4,562,820 registered Palestinian refugees with 1.4 million of them still living in 58
official camps. The actual figure of unregistered
refugees and their descendants makes the total figure
much higher.

The facts of the Palestinian exodus that are now accepted
by most international historians played little or no role in
shaping the official Israeli narrative regarding the struggle
to establish its state. Most Israelis are still taught variations
of the central Zionist narrative, one which states that the
land in 1948 was sparsely populated, and that the Zionist

forces always wanted peace but were forced into war by Arab armies. It further explains that most Palestinians who did leave did so of their own free will or because they were instructed to by their own leaders, leaders who promised the Palestinians they would return when the Arab armies were victorious. The Zionist myth also emphasises the war with the Arab armies in 1948 over the Palestinian civilians who fled. For example, the history of the birth of the state published on the Israeli Ministry of Foreign Affairs website ignores the Palestinian refugee issue entirely. The website chronicles the foundation of the state, followed by the immediate invasion by Arab armies from the neighbouring countries. The Palestinian civilians who were forced out in their hundreds of thousands are not mentioned anywhere.

Arab and international historians always questioned the mythology outlined above, and Palestinian refugees knew from their own experience that the Zionist narrative was untrue. Palestinian families in the refugee camps in Syria, Lebanon and Jordan hung the keys to their old homes, outside the tents and later the small buildings they inhabited as makeshift dwellings. Despite the evidence, it was not until recent years that there has been a fundamental re-evaluation of the official historiography within Israel concerning the foundation of the state.

The so-called Israeli 'New Historian' group in the early 1990s began to study new material from the period of the 1948 War made available in the Israeli state archives. They began to completely undermine previously sacred concepts fundamental to Zionism. A number of controversial books were published in Israel of historical accounts that showed that the creation of the state was a direct result of the forced removal of thousands of

Palestinians, acts of terror against the indigenous Arab population and the deliberate whipping up of fear among Palestinians. The Arab leadership had not made widespread calls on Palestinians to flee their land, and even if they had, it would have no bearing on the Palestinians' legal right to return to their homes. Some of the Israeli New Historians have labelled what happened in 1948 as ethnic cleansing.

The response to the new historical material tells a story. Traditional Israeli historians reacted with fury, alleging that the New Historians have political motivations. While the writings of the New Historians have been discussed in great detail in Israel, the traditional Zionist historiography of how the state was born is still cherished by the majority of Israelis. The New Historians themselves have come to terms in different ways with the material they have unearthed. Trail-blazing Benny Morris has become increasingly right-wing and bellicose, arguing that the forced removal of Palestinians did happen, but it was necessary for the creation of a Jewish state. In contrast, Haifa-based Ilan Pappé has been led down a very different political path by his work, becoming a 'post-Zionist' and arguing against the Jewish state as a fundamentally negative concept. He now campaigns for a bi-national singular state where both Jews and Palestinians would have full equality and religious liberty. He maintains that unless the Right of Return of the 1948 refugees is addressed by the Israeli state, then true peace cannot reign.

While the focus on the why and how of the Palestinian exodus is important, it must be remembered that it is what happened after 1948 which was most crucial. Israel prevented the Palestinians from returning to their homes, and no matter why you leave your home, it is still your home. The Palestinians could not return because of Israeli brute force and legislative larceny. The facts and consequences of 1948 remain at the very heart of the problem in the Holy Land.

*

Old Jaffa in May 2008 was awash in blue and white. The old port city, situated just south of Tel Aviv, was the most important urban centre for Palestinian Arabs prior to 1948. Six decades later, the local authorities had smothered the former Palestinian Arab city in a fluttering mass of Israeli national flags.

Blue bunting hung across the central intersection at Clock Tower Square in the old city. Israeli Independence Day was marked ostentatiously in Jaffa. There were more flags and patriotic paraphernalia there than you would find in downtown Tel Aviv and parts of Jewish West Jerusalem.

The roadside along the beach promenade was blocked daily with large numbers of coach tours carrying their passengers to visit the ancient port. Older tourists sipped coffee outside in the sun, or walked slowly up the hill to get a spectacular view of the harbour or the Tel Aviv skyline to the north. Young American teenagers crowded into the tourist stores along Beit Esheq street, purchasing cheap containers of Dead Sea mud used as balm for the face and feet, Arabic water pipes, *argileh*, T-shirts emblazoned with the Star of David and Israeli Defence Force caps. There was a youthful, busy buzz in Old Jaffa as Israel celebrated its 60th birthday.

The energy on the streets was fuelled principally by the visiting Americans who came as part of the 'Birthright' tours. They were easy to spot. A large group of 20 or so, all under the age of 26 and wearing the same 'Birthright' T-shirts, they followed one guide through the laneways and markets stalls of Old Jaffa.

The foreign contingent was marshalled by at least two fully armed chaperones, with one leading the way and the other drifting towards the back keeping an eye on the slower walkers. The armed guards are ostensibly there to protect the young Americans, although it is incredibly difficult to imagine an Arab shop keeper or local resident attacking such a group on a peaceful afternoon in Jaffa.

The 'Birthright Tours' were established in 2000 by an Israeli organisation with the backing of wealthy benefactors. It provides a ten-day, all-expenses-paid trip to Israel for any Jewish person under the age of 26 from anywhere in the world, although the United States is the focus of the group's work. According to the organisers themselves, their intention is to

> Send thousands of young Jewish adults from all over the world to Israel as a gift ... to strengthen the sense of solidarity among world Jewry, and to strengthen participants' personal Jewish identity and connection to the Jewish people.

In effect, the tours are a way of trying to promote the idea of aliyah to Israel among young Jews living in the diaspora, particularly Americans. It is the active encouragement of Jewish immigration to the Holy Land, and the tightly-scheduled itinerary makes sure to put the best spin possible on life in the Jewish State. The tour never enters the West Bank.

On the Monday following the official celebrations of Israeli Independence Day, I was wandering through the darkened laneways of the Old City in Jaffa. I came to a small ornate square, with a piece of artwork hanging in the middle of it. It was a massive plastic orange hanging three or four feet above the cobblestones, suspended from the surrounding buildings by four thick elastic ropes.

'This is a popular sight here. It represents the importance of the orange crop for this community historically, and how it will continue into the future,' said an Israeli guide in perfect English.

The guide had just arrived into the narrow square leading a large following of young American Birthright Tour visitors. They all gathered around the orange exhibit. Laughing and giggling, this was a good-humoured bunch, and they seemed to be only half-listening to the guide when he addressed them. Most were attracted to the bouncy orange and pushed and pulled the elastic ropes.

'This part of Jaffa is one of my favourite places,' said the guide.
'We will start walking through the narrow alleyways of the Old City and make our descent to the port. Along the way you will see many art galleries. If you have any questions please ask me.'

There were no questions, and one of the armed chaperones started to move forward through the adjacent stone arch to lead the way.

'Why is there a number one written up there on the wall?' enquired one of the young Americans. He pointed up towards a blue sign attached to the side of an old three-storey building with a number one written on it.

'Well, you would think that it is because it is house number one, obviously,' replied the guide. Some of his trans-Atlantic audience laughed quietly at the apparent stupidity of the earlier question.

'Eh...But it is also the street number,' said the guide. Here in Jaffa, many of the streets are numbered rather than named. There are some reasons for this, but one of the major ones is, well, it is back from the past ... the guide stumbled a little as if he was trying to pitch his address perfectly.

'Well, back in 1948, when the Arab residents fled ... or left ... or whatever happened ... the people in charge after the Arabs left went— well, they decided to number the streets here rather than keep the old names. They did that because of the refugees who left Jaffa – it would be harder for them to say they wanted their homes back and say that it was on whatever street if the streets no longer had names. So they numbered them – because of the refugees.'

A silence followed. Maybe most of the young Americans knew the history of the area and the exodus, and maybe they did not. But surely there had to be an urge from someone to ask, 'Where are the refugees now? Why were they not allowed to return to their homes? Is it not wrong to take someone else's home? By numbering the streets and getting rid of their former names, are we not denying history?'

But there were no questions.

These young, boisterous American Jews were being encouraged to immigrate to a country in which they were not born. They were being enticed by this tour to leave their home and travel to Israel where they would attain full citizenship rights because they are Jewish. They will then receive financial and other benefits from the Israeli government who will do all it can to help make their assimilation into Israeli life as trouble-free as possible. But looking at buildings along the numbered streets of Old Jaffa, they did not ask questions about the former inhabitants. 'Whatever happened' in 1948 was not going to be discussed. Some of them had started taking photographs of each other while straddling the elastic orange and laughing – these were their memories of Jaffa.

'OK, well some of the streets now have names after the different signs of the zodiac as well, so things change. OK. Any questions? No? OK, let's go towards the harbour.'

7

A Cold House for Arabs

Many people who have visited Old Jaffa and Tel Aviv on Israel's Mediterranean coastline have made this wonderful journey by foot. You leave Amiad Street and wander through the bustling flea market, which sells everything from postcards, to argileh, to second-hand mobile phones. Reaching Old Jaffa's central artery, Yeffet Street, you then make a right turn past Said Abou Elafia and Sons eatery, easily the busiest and most popular street bakery in the old port city, where orders are made and filled in speedy Arabic and Hebrew. Men and women savour the hot, fresh bread standing at the street corner as the distinctive aromas of the seemingly unlimited varieties of pitta bread, cheese pastries, toast and spicy *za'atar* pleasantly engulf your senses.

Despite the wonderful smells begging you to stop, you march ahead on your journey, finally reaching the century-old Jaffa Clock Tower, built during the Ottoman period as a symbol of progress to rise high above all the older neighbouring buildings. After admiring the tower for a few moments, take a left. You leave Old Jaffa, with its ancient minarets, tight market streets, Arab cafes, carpet sellers, Jewish restaurants, the shouts from the street traders and the general dirt and grime of the city.

Walk through the bustling intersection between Yeffet Street and the coast road and descend the slope. To your right is the Abu Nabout's Great Mosque and around the corner the old Kishle Prison. You stride past the middle-aged men roaring, laughing and exchanging money as they play backgammon. The sizzling chickpeas, browning nicely in the hot grease at the falafel stand, make you hungry. It is impossible not to stop to watch the vendor spread the homemade hummus thickly on the warm envelope of open pitta bread before stuffing the small balls of falafel in with a rich variety of salad and sauces following quickly in their delicious slipstream.

Suppressing your growing hunger pains, you wander down towards the beach and turn to face one of the most ancient port cities on the planet. Over the centuries, Jaffa harbour has seen figures from history as diverse as Jonah, King Solomon, Richard the Lionheart and Napoleon Bonaparte come and go. Jaffa oranges have made the port known the world over, as the fruit has been exported widely for generations.

At last reaching the coastline and standing on a height slightly over looking the promenade, you survey the panorama across the beautiful Mediterranean. In the near distance, you can clearly see the glistening skyscrapers along the beachfront of Tel Aviv. Descending the steps from the edge of Old Jaffa, start walking north the few kilometres towards Tel Aviv along the wide promenade. Away from Jaffa's fishermen and noisy markets, you start to meet joggers and sunbathers enjoying one of the most spectacular stretches of urban beachfront anywhere along the Mediterranean.

You can hear the Muslim call to prayer behind you, but the sound is drowned out by an Israeli military helicopter flying south, low over the coastline. Families picnic in the wide green spaces and along the low empty hills alongside the promenade. This area was once the bustling neighbourhood of the former Arab Manshiyyeh quarter, long since destroyed.

Ten minutes into your pleasant journey, you come across beach bars with brooding armed security guards brandishing metal detectors. Israeli pop music blares out from inside. A few tanned patrons sip bottles of the local Goldstar beer at tables in the sand, laughing as they watch their friends play frisbee on the beach. The soft sea breeze provides some slight relief from the scorching summer temperatures. Across the busy traffic intersection to your right stands the Hassan Bek Mosque, historically the northernmost point in Jaffa, but now surrounded by bright, modern high-rise constructions. The mosque looks uncomfortably ancient and isolated as the David Intercontinental Hotel towers above its minaret.

A group of young soldiers on leave walk past languidly in their olive green uniforms, swinging the weapons strapped over their shoulders. After a little while you stop, taking your camera from your bag. You peer through the lens out towards the striking blue sea, looking past the young bikini-clad Israelis playing beach volleyball. In the hazy distance you squint through the glare and see a gunship. You swing left and begin surveying the scene with the digital camera. Focusing on Jaffa's port jutting out into the sea, it looks like a picture from a history book with its old sandstone walls all rustic orange. After capturing that, you swing to your right.

The uneven high-rises of the hyper-modern Tel Aviv stand defiantly before the sea's edge. The 'white city', less than a century old, looks brash, young and confident. The Opera Tower brightly reflects the powerful Middle Eastern rays. When you pictorially capture these two neighbouring coastal cities you review your digital pictures. There is a clear architectural message to be understood between these two neighbouring urban centres, a message that is about much more than just building design. This skyline is a physical metaphor for the deep problems of this historic, dangerous and disputed holy place. Much of what is to be learned about this troubled land can be seen along that short stretch of coastal walkway. You are looking at this region's central modern story: this is the triumph of Israel and the defeat of Palestine.

*

The city of Jaffa, located a short distance south of modern Tel Aviv, was the most important commercial trading city in Palestine prior to 1948. The international port was the economic gateway for foreign businesspeople and migration to and from Palestine, and Jaffa was the hectic home of newspapers, factories, tradesmen and merchants from across the globe. There was money to be made here, and in the early part of the 20th century the city grew massively. Israel's modern cities like Haifa and Jerusalem have prominent Jaffa Streets and Jaffa Roads indicating how central it was as a nexus of commerce.

Principally home to Arabs, Jaffa was also home to a minority of Jews. The Jewish immigration in the late 19th and early 20th centuries meant that suburbs developed, and many Jews settled to the north of Jaffa. With the growing power of the Jewish Zionist movement in the 1920s and 1930s, Jaffa's centrality began to wane under the control of the British. There were outbreaks of sectarian violence between Jews and Arabs during this period, such as the significant riots of 1921. Some Jewish families, fearful for their safety, felt they had to move to the north. Yet the eventual economic, political and demographic eclipsing of Jaffa by Tel Aviv was not the result of organic migration. Rather, like much of the Israeli state, it also resulted from a conscious force of will.

Tel Aviv, which began as a tiny Jewish suburb to the north of Jaffa, quickly became the city of choice for Jewish immigrants from Europe. The city itself was only officially founded in 1909, and its name meant 'Hill of Spring' in Hebrew. Although the name conjured up images of green and lush hillsides full of blooming flowers, trees and fresh flowing streams, Tel Aviv in 1909 was little more than sand dunes and arid land. But its 'spring' connotes rebirth and renewal, concepts that the Zionists believed that they were in tune with in creating their new 'Jewish Homeland' in Palestine. Though Jerusalem remains the political focus and controversial religious centre, Tel Aviv has always been, and still is, the quintessential Zionist and Israeli city. No longer just bare sand dunes, less than a century on, it is a bustling, modern, Western-style metropolis.

Under the imperial eye of the British Mandate, Tel Aviv grew in stature while Jaffa was slowly dismantled as the pre-eminent historical locus it had once been. For the secular Zionists who did not fancy the intense religious lifestyle in Jerusalem, an earthy existence on the kibbutzim or the Arab atmosphere in Jaffa, Tel Aviv became a most agreeable home. A little bit of European life was rapidly created in the Middle East. Tel Aviv became the urban magnet for the cosmopolitan Jews of European descent, the Ashkenazi, who eventually became the ethnic elite in the Israeli state.

In 1920 Tel Aviv had 2,000 residents, and by 1925 it had 34,000. It was to further expand at a breathtaking pace during the 1930s. Soon, David Ben-Gurion made his home there. Development was quick, with Bauhaus architecture leaving its mark all over modern central Tel Aviv. A European-style café lifestyle bloomed along Tel Aviv's boulevards as Ashkenazi secular Jews seeking some Western sophistication, established it as their new home. Wide, tree-lined streets like Rothschild Boulevard were constructed, as was a grid system of paths and roadways. In its very design, Tel Aviv was to be fundamentally different to the labyrinth of narrow alleyways that twisted their way through Old Jaffa.

Tel Aviv for the Zionists represented progress and a modern Jewish future, while Jaffa to the south was seen as backward and part of the Arab past. Ben-Gurion spoke for many Zionists in 1924 when he cast his mind to the role Jaffa would play in a future Jewish state: 'the destruction of Jaffa, the city and the port, will happen and it will be for the best.' It was clear that the old Arab Palestine represented by Jaffa would be replaced by Tel Aviv, which personified Zionist modernity. This replacement would take place by force if needed. The implication of the Zionist project, even if it was not often explicitly stated, was to be the destruction of Palestinian Arab society.

In late April 1948, Irgun launched a devastating mortar attack on central Jaffa. Some wealthy Arabs had fled months before after a number of terrorist attacks which had already taken place in the city, and out of fear of an inevitable war. The bombardment of Jaffa, ordered by the Irgun leader and future Israeli Prime Minster, Menachem Begin, would instead spark off a terrifying exodus by the Arab population.

There was some defence from Arab fighters but they were to be overwhelmed by the larger, more organised and technically advanced Zionist forces. Begin and the Irgun had purposely intended to demolish the centre of Jaffa and create a mass flight of its Arab inhabitants. They saw Jaffa as a hostile Arab entity bordering Jewish Tel Aviv. Begin believed that Jaffa simply could not remain an Arab city if the Jewish state was to be secure. He later wrote that 'the strategic aim was to subjugate Jaffa and free Tel Aviv once and for all from the loaded pistol pointed at its heart'.

Most of the Arab inhabitants of Jaffa escaped through the harbour. Packed boats overflowing with terrified refugees sailed south to Gaza and some all the way north, past Tel Aviv, to Beirut in Lebanon. Whole families and generations of Jaffa residents carried with them their house keys. Most believed they would be returning home soon after the fighting ceased. They were to be tragically mistaken. While hundreds of thousands of Palestinians were to leave their homes and villages across the Holy Land in 1947–8, it is the memory of the flight from Jaffa by sea that has become one of the most potent in the collective Palestinian consciousness. Over 100,000 were forced out and prevented from returning to what had been the single most significant city in Palestinian Arab life for centuries.

Jaffa was later occupied by another Jewish armed group, the Haganah, the military forerunner to today's IDF. Haganah units took up positions in the depopulated streets of Jaffa in May 14. Only about 4,000 Arabs remained in Jaffa after the desert dust settled following the war and ethnic cleansing of 1947-48.

After 1948, the area was called the 'Big Wasteland' as new Jewish immigrants lived side-by-side with what was left of the impoverished and fearful Arab community. In the decades that followed, poorer Jewish immigrants from Eastern Europe, particularly Bulgaria, were encouraged to move in. Some Jews from Middle Eastern and North African countries, the Mizrahim, also made Jaffa their new home, as they were moved into the empty Arab homes. Many newly-arrived Jewish immigrants left Jaffa as quickly as they could, as the rubble from the 1948 war was still piled high and the area was in a mess both economically and socially. New Jewish immigrants spoke of seeing Arab ghosts late at night in the buildings they now lived in.

*

I have stayed in Old Jaffa on five separate occasions, and it remains a city that can seduce the visitor with its pleasant bohemian charm. It is mixed, with both a Jewish and Arab population, and if you so wish, you can see its community as a 'model of co-existence' as the guide books and Israeli authorities often claim. Approximately

45,000 people now live in Jaffa, two thirds of whom are Jewish, the remainder Arab. However, even a superficial awareness of the history of the ethnic cleansing, destruction and straightforward robbery that took place in Jaffa after 1948 makes a visit to this beautiful port city a profoundly troubling and complex one.

The old city of Jaffa has not been wiped off the map, unlike the 500 other Palestinian towns and villages destroyed by the Israeli authorities in the early decades of the state. The magnificent architectural qualities of the historic old city of Jaffa and its potential attraction for tourists meant that following a long debate, the Israeli planners decided not to bulldoze it. Rather, they choose to create an artistic colony.

The contemporary Old City is still a maze of confusing alleyways, now home to a myriad of different art galleries and studios. The former Palestinian homes are now attractive workshops for Jewish Israeli sculptors, painters and photographers. Abstract paintings and modern photography hang from the outside walls of buildings where once generations of Palestinian Arab families lived. Weird and wonderful sculpture is displayed in small squares, where the public can view it under the warm blanket of the Mediterranean sun.

Art lovers from Tel Aviv drive south at the weekend to browse and to drop into the various high-quality restaurants and cafes that provide refreshment after a long day traipsing around the cobblestoned streets. There are wine bars for a relaxing drink in the evening. The atmosphere is of easy-going bohemia, alternative and liberal. It is natural to lose yourself in the pleasant present, forgetting about the uncomfortable past.

But despite this past, contemporary Jaffa is peaceful for the most part. The depleted Arab population that remains continues to engage with the local business and social community.

On occasion, animosity breaks out. One afternoon, I was overlooking Tel Aviv and its working-class southern suburbs from the rooftop of the Old Jaffa Hostel. Engrossed in the detailed coverage of the Israeli election in the *Jerusalem Post* and *Haaretz*, I was researching one of my final pre-election articles for *Daily Ireland*.

The large roof garden on the Ottoman building allowed you to survey the narrow alleyways that spread out like a web from Yeffet Street in Old Jaffa. You could also see east to the poor but bohemian Florentin district, then across the city towards central Tel Aviv and inland to the working-class suburbs. The constant bustle of Middle Eastern market life provided a sonic backdrop to the spectacular view.

But my work was suddenly disturbed by shouting from the direction of the Clock Tower Square. The roaring and yelling got louder. I went to the edge of the roof and leaned out to look towards Yeffet. I dropped my paper and ran down to the market to see what the commotion was about.

Activists from the far-right-wing Jewish Herut party had arrived in the Clock Tower Square – and they hadn't come to taste the excellent local hummus. They were looking to provoke the local Arabs, but they were to be a little disappointed. The Arab shopkeepers and market stall owners remonstrated loudly against the Herut stalwarts, but no riot ensued. Some fruit and vegetables were thrown, but in a region where blood is spilt every day, this was obviously a minor incident.

Herut members moved up and down the streets handing out fake money to local Arabs. They called on them to accept thousands of shekels and 'transfer' themselves out of Israel and relocate into one of the neighbouring Arab states. The fake money was at times knocked out of the activists' hands by angry Arabs and Jews alike. Piles of it were left strewn around Jaffa for many hours, gently blowing in the late evening sea breeze.

Herut, meaning freedom in Hebrew, had based its election campaign on stoking fear among Israeli Jews about the so called 'demographic threat' posed by Arabs in Israel. Also sometimes called the 'demographic time bomb', the political implications for the Jewish state arising from the growing population size of its Arab community is an issue that focusses the minds of many Israelis. Because of the higher birth rate among Arabs than Jews, some Israeli politicians, including cabinet ministers have called for the removal of the Arab population who live in Israel. Some argue this should be done by force, euphemistically referring to it as a 'transfer'. Others argue that this should be done by economic inducement, or simply by unilaterally re-drawing the borders of Israel to leave large Arab towns outside the state, very euphemistically called 'soft transfer'.

Herut had now come to Jaffa, a city with a significant Arab population and a rich Arab history, to spread their particular unsavoury philosophy. One of the leading Herut election candidates was the striking-looking, Russian-born Yana Chudriker. The former Israeli beauty queen featured in many of the party's posters and advertisements that seemed to adorn every second public bus in Tel Aviv, Jerusalem and Jaffa. In the poster, Ms Chudriker donned a burka with the not-too-subtle catch line 'The Demographics will poison us' strapped underneath in Hebrew. In the party's TV election broadcast, Ms Chudriker was again wearing a dark burka. After some words to camera, she eventually pulled off the burka and swung her flowing long blonde hair free. The message was insidiously simple: The Arabs are taking over. We need to get rid of them if our Jewish state is ever to be at peace and truly free.

While not infrequent, attempts by some Israeli political activists to inflame this anti-Arab strain within Israeli Jewish society are particularly evident at election time. Herut was to poll poorly in the 2006 election, but other parties who shared its idea of 'transfer' did win seats in the Knesset.

The impression of Jaffa as essentially Arab, backward, traitorous, dangerous and not quite being part of Israel is one that persists in the present day. Waiting for a taxi along the modern Yerushalayim Boulevard can be a disenchanting experience, as many empty taxis seem to fly past along the main motorway linking Jaffa to Tel Aviv. I asked one taxi driver who eventually picked me up why the empty taxis passed by.

'I always keep my doors locked when driving through Jaffa. There is so much crime here. There are many Arabs here and I do not want to drive them, I would not pick up here usually. I normally open the window and talk to someone first, I can tell by the accent.'

Taxi drivers who decide who they pick up on the basis of race are, sadly, an international phenomenon.

Nonetheless, his attitude and the attitude of many others I spoke to in Tel Aviv and Jaffa showed that even when there is no open conflict, there remains ethnic and political friction between the two neighbouring cities.

While many Jews from Tel Aviv like to travel to Old Jaffa on the weekend to eat hummus and visit the art galleries, division remains. Some Tel Aviv residents, particularly those from the Zionist right wing, gaze south towards Old Jaffa from their homes with a mixture of fear and loathing. Jaffa is home to the 'other within' – the Arab citizen of Israel.

In October 2000, an assembly organised in Yeffet Street by the Committee for Jaffa Arabs became a violent demonstration in which stones were thrown and tyres burned. The protest was held following the outbreak of the second intifada within the occupied territories. Young Arabs from Jaffa, inspired by a sense of solidarity with their Palestinian cousins in the occupied territories and angered by the discrimination against their own community within the Jewish state took to the streets. Decades of simmering angst and suppressed sectarian tension momentarily exploded. Riots continued for days between Jews, Arabs and armed security forces within Jaffa. The Hassan Bek mosque was attacked by a Jewish mob, while Jaffa Arabs stoned Jewish-owned businesses and the police.

Jaffa's mixed community had been shaken by events in the occupied territories. For just a few short days, the intifada had spread from Ramallah, Nablus and Gaza and onto the streets in Jaffa, the violence reaching into the very centre of Israel itself. This short outbreak of violence had a profound impact on relations between Tel Aviv and Jaffa and between local Jews and Arabs.

Tel Avian Jews stopped travelling south to shop in Jaffa, and an unofficial Jewish boycott of local Arab businesses began. Local Arabs were consequently angered as the Jaffa community was economically affected.

Even when it's not Israeli Independence Day, many of the buildings in Jaffa have Israeli flags flying high and proud from their roofs and windows. These are not official buildings; the flags have been raised by private Jewish residents in a clear expression of patriotism. You are less likely to see such flags fluttering over homes in central Tel Aviv. While the ethnic and national identification of Tel Aviv residents is undoubtedly Israeli and Jewish, the orientation of Jaffa still seems to be problematical for local Israeli Jews. They feel that they must make an extra effort to fly their nation's flag over the buildings to emphasise that Jaffa is in fact Israel.

The old port city's beautiful winding streets are now a labyrinth of coffee shops, furniture stores and art galleries. Local Arab resident groups argue that a deliberate policy of gentrification is taking place in Old Jaffa which is seeing the gradual removal of the Arab community and its replacement with expensive restaurants and tourist shops mainly frequented and owned by Jews. The coast of Old Jaffa has certainly been developed as a tourist location; classy seafront restaurants with breathtaking views of the Mediterranean and a visitor centre that narrates the history of Jaffa from a Zionist perspective attract many. The rolling hills, ornate bridges and small streams provide the perfect backdrop for wedding photos.

The area is often described in tour guides as one place in Israel where Arabs and Jews mingle and live together.

The active flea market just east of the old city port is indeed populated by both Jewish and Arab sellers and buyers. There is an encouraging mix of Arabic and Hebrew in the air as the haggling reaches a fever pitch. But significant sections of the wider community exist in poverty and live with a major drug problem. Residents complain that the city is treated poorly by the governing authorities compared to its pampered northern neighbour. Locals claim that sewerage waste from Tel Aviv is sent through Jaffa, a vile indication of the relationship between the cities.

Many foreign visitors and Israelis only drop into the old port city long enough to pick up delicious falafel or some of Jaffa's famous freshly cooked bread. They rarely visit the sprawling working-class communities around Old Jaffa that are home to poor Arabs and some working-class Jews, many of Russian origin. Poverty breeds crime in the area, and gang wars between different families has led to a rising death toll and injuries as a result of drive-by shootings. Much of the cannabis smoked by the Jewish students, sunbathers and soldiers in Tel Aviv is channelled through Jaffa, a lucrative trade with criminal turf wars the predictable consequence. It is not only the national conflict that kills in the Holy Land.

*

The old Manshiyyeh Quarter north of Old Jaffa was destroyed during the fighting in 1948 and later bulldozed. It is now home to high-rise hotels, a busy motorway and the seaside promenade that stretches up north towards Tel Aviv. One of the few Arab buildings still standing from that historic quarter is the attractive square sandstone structure on the seafront. It has large dark panels of glass on each side with an Israeli flag fluttering above. From the stone wall to the east of the building is a magnificent view of Old Jaffa plunging out towards the Mediterranean. The former Arab building is now home to the official museum of the Irgun, the very Zionist force that pulverised the Old City with mortar fire in April 1948, leading to the flight of the vast majority of the Arab population.

It is a dark irony indeed that a museum commemorating and hailing the actions of the Zionist paramilitary force who led the destruction of Arab Jaffa is now located a short distance from the old city. With its ominous presence it is as if the building is keeping a watchful eye over the port city, a constant reminder to the remaining Arab population of their defeat, the expulsion of their families and friends and their subordinate position within the Jewish state.

The curator of the Irgun museum has created a living love letter to the right-wing military organisation that was incorporated into the IDF after 1948. The video installations, photographs and text on the wall tell tales of attacks on British forces and the 'liberation and conquest' of various Arab neighbourhoods in 1948, including those in Jaffa. No mention is made of any of the numerous attacks on Arab civilians and atrocities undertaken by the Irgun.

The central topic for the museum is the so-called 'Campaign for the Liberation of Jaffa'. The visitor to the museum is promised maps, photographs and videos that will 'enable the visitor to experience one of the finest battles of the War of Independence'. The exhibition is honestly proud of the Irgun's role in the destruction of Arab

Jaffa and in the wider Nakba. The triumphant text along the wall describes the scene, the Irgun 'mortars relentlessly bombarding the centre of the town causing the mass exodus of its inhabitants'. Across the road from the museum, the Hassan Bek Mosque still stands. Once the most northerly point in Arab Jaffa, it has now been subsumed into Jewish Tel Aviv. The museum text refers to the mosque as having 'cast a shadow of fear over Tel Aviv'.

When I dropped into the museum, there was already a tour group of middle-aged and older Americans inside. They were sitting in the museum's lecture room listening to an elderly Irgun veteran tell tales from his adventures before 1948.

He looked physically fit and was obviously enjoying himself as the audience hung on his every word. He spoke from the top of the room, in quick but low English which made him difficult to hear. Above his head hung paintings of the spiritual founder of right-wing Zionism Vladimir Jabotinsky, the leader of the Irgun, Menachem Begin, and the leader of the even more extreme Lehi, Yitzach Shamir. Shamir had chosen 'Mick' as his underground codename in honour of Michael Collins, Republican leader of the Irish War of Independence against the British. Shamir, like Begin, would later become an Israeli Prime Minister.

Most of the tour group members were older women, and they seemed transfixed by the Irgun veteran's tales of derring-do. The elderly veteran emphasised that the Irgun had fought the British army – he did not mention the attacks on Arab civilians.

He told them about a bold midnight raid on a British army base in northern Palestine, where he and his fellow Irgun fighters made off with ammunition. Some of the American women actually started to 'ooh' and 'ahh' loudly as he described his days as a plucky militant. He described his capture by the British, his time in Acre jail in northern Palestine and his eventual escape to freedom. The story was an audacious tale of a courageous national liberation fighter who joined the Jewish underground to fight the British and gain Israeli independence. He was just like any other fearless freedom fighter the world over, ready to take on the brutal occupier to liberate his nation.

But the Zionist struggle for freedom was not a simple tale of national liberation. The former Zionist fighter did not mention the bombardment of Jaffa, the expulsion of Arabs from other towns or any of the attacks on civilians. His focus was on the supposed fight against the British Empire, rather than on the war against the Palestinian civilians. He spoke about the attacks on British soldiers, not emptying villages of their Arab inhabitants. Despite these important historical blind spots his audience was pleased with what they had heard and patiently queued to have their pictures taken with him afterwards. It was the story they wanted to hear.

*

Nazareth has long since superseded Jaffa as the largest and most important Arab city in Israel. Located near the Sea of Galilee in the north, it is familiar to many international pilgrims who have travelled to the place that the Christian Holy Family called home and the town where the infant Jesus Christ grew up.

Nazareth now has over 70,000 inhabitants, over 60 per cent of whom are Muslim and the remainder Christian. The Muslim call to prayer gently mingles in the air with sounds of the bells ringing from the various Christian churches. It is a sonic reflection of the religious plurality at the heart of Palestinian Arab identity, a plurality often ignored by the Western media in their constant focus on Hamas and their rather shallow reading of the role played by Islam in Palestinian life.

When I visited in early 2006, tourist figures were slightly up compared to the previous two lean years. Tourism, a vital component in Nazareth's economic life, had been on the slide since the outbreak of the second intifada.

While I sat sipping coffee, I watched a steady stream of chartered buses park along Paulus Street and unload their pilgrims to visit the Church of the Annunciation and other religious sites. The familiar aromas of Arab street life, pungent strong coffee and the lingering scent of cooked falafel and meaty shawarma filled the heavy hot air. Looking over the old city in the evening from the roof of my hostel, I could hear the patriotic Palestinian songs of Ahmad Ka'bour blaring out from some local's stereo system. It drifted defiantly through the dark, star-filled sky over Nazareth. The momentary calm was shattered by ear-crunching sonic booms from Israeli fighter jets on their way south to conduct missions over the West Bank.

With such a large population centre, and with just days to go before the general election, one might have thought that Nazareth would be the focus of some intensive electioneering by the Israeli political parties. But Nazareth, like most predominately Arab towns in Israel, exists in a political universe parallel to that of official

Israeli society. There were few large election posters from the three major parties – Likud, Kadima or Labour – and the posters at every street corner and displayed in shop windows were only for the Arab parties.

While a very visible Wall was being constructed inside and around the West Bank, there was also another long-standing, albeit invisible, wall inside Israel's borders. This wall is the division between the Jewish and Arab communities who live within Israel.

Almost all the Arabs living within Israel are descendants of some 160,000 Palestinians who remained in Israel after 1948. Like the Palestinians who fled to the neighbouring Arab states, many of those who remained within the borders of what became Israel also lost their homes. If they had fled their home and stayed somewhere else within Israel, they were defined as 'present absentees' by the Israeli government, with the effect that they could become citizens of Israel, but their property could be expropriated by the state.

Nazareth was relatively lucky during the fighting in 1948. Zionist leaders were concerned that the flight of tens of thousands of mainly Christian Arabs from Nazareth would have provoked an outcry from international Christian leaders, and as a result, no massive expulsion took place.

While finding some shade, I got talking to a middle-aged Arab man in a café close to the main market. It was clear that Nazareth was sleep-walking towards the March 2006 general election.

'I did not vote last time, I will not vote this time,' he said in poor English.

Inquiring as to my reason for being in Nazareth, he

found my reply amusing.

'Coming here to write about these elections? Don't you have enough trouble in Ireland?'

The two major Arab parties wrestling for that sector's vote in Nazareth and elsewhere were Hadash, a holdover from the old Israeli Communist Party, and the more nationalistic Balad party. The red flags and posters of Hadash were very prominent in Nazareth. One elegantly painted Hadash poster portrayed an elderly man dressed in traditional Arab garb sitting by a tree on a hilltop. He was surveying a town in the valley that looked both prosperous and peaceful. A young boy plays at his feet wearing a keffiyeh. It is a political party that boasts both Arab and a smaller number of Jewish members. Then Hadash leader Ahmed Tibi took part in a pre-election debate on the future of Arabs within the Israeli state. He was quoted in *Haaretz*:

> We are a collective that is a national minority, like Quebec in Canada. Our situation today is that of citizens without true citizenship. Because we are considered Arabs more than citizens, we are constantly told we are tenants, conditional citizens, a fifth column.

Despite enjoying nominal equal protection under the law, the leaders of the Arab community have long complained of systemic discrimination against their community in terms of jobs, education, health services and political representation within Israel. These claims have been supported by numerous independent reports and economic analyses of the Arab Palestinian community within Israel, conducted by both Israeli and international groups.

At present, 1.3 million Arabs live in Israel, just under one fifth of the total population of the country. The majority of Arabs live in the Galilee area in northern Israel, others in the so-called Triangle of small Arab towns in the country's centre and the remaining in the Negev desert in the south. The Israeli authorities count over 200,000 Arabs living in occupied East Jerusalem as 'permanent residents' of Israel. The bulk of Arabs in Israel are Sunni Muslims, with a significant minority of Christian and Druze. The Druze community is exceptional; many do not consider themselves Palestinian, and they serve in the Israeli army.

The historical identity held by the Palestinian Arabs within Israel is profoundly shaped by long-standing discrimination, but also by a number of brutal iconic events. In 1956, Israeli military border police shot and killed 48 men, women and children in the northern village of Kafr Kassem. This is an important incident still remembered in the community. Just over ten years later, in 1967, the Israeli state officially ended military rule over the Arab minority in the state, a rule that had been in existence since 1948. Despite the lifting of military rule, persecution and prejudice persisted.

In 1976, Arabs called a general strike in response to the construction of more Jewish settlements and towns within the Galilee. Arab leaders were concerned that the Israeli state was attempting to purposely tilt the ethnic balance in the area. In March of that year, six Palestinians were killed during clashes with Israeli forces that took place within Israel itself. While repression was rife, the shooting dead of Arabs at demonstrations held within Israel was not common. These events are commemorated every year, on an important political anniversary that is unique to the Palestinian community living within Israel, Land Day on 30th March.

Until the late 1960s, the Arab minority within Israel lived under direct military rule by the Israeli army. The deepening alienation of the Arab community from official Jewish political society can be seen in the recent collapse in voter turnout. In 1999, three-quarters of Arabs voted in the Prime Ministerial election, the vast majority for the Labour party candidate, Ehud Barak. The decorated former army general stood on a clear platform of launching serious peace negotiations with the Palestinians in the occupied territories. This was a significant policy shift from the right-wing, hawkish incumbent Benjamin Netanyahu of Likud, whom the Arab community deeply disliked. Political leaders in the Arab community coordinated a sweeping campaign to galvanise solid support for Barak.

Two years later, following the controversial collapse of the Camp David peace talks, the eruption of the second intifada and the subsequent killings of Arabs in Israel's northern towns by Israeli security forces, the Arab community felt deeply let down by Barak. The community boycotted the 2001 election in protest at Barak's bitterly disappointing premiership. Just less than one fifth of Arabs voted in 2001. In 2003 there was no boycott, and Arab voter turnout was 62 per cent, while in the most recent general elections in March 2006 it had fallen further to 56 per cent. The statistics for the past decade show a general fall in the number of Arabs who bother to vote in Israeli elections

Palestinian Arabs in Israel are officially exempt from service in the IDF. While the vast majority would refuse to wear an Israeli uniform anyway, failure to serve has a lasting impact on future employment possibilities. Some employers use the absence of a military record as an excuse not to employ Arabs. Arabs are also in practice excluded from employment sectors involved in military and defence matters, which constitute a massive part of the Israeli economy. Thus, Arabs find the door closed to them in many areas of employment, areas that have been a significant factor in the country's economic boom in recent years. In 2006, only five per cent of jobs in government offices were filled by Arabs.

Housing has also long been a problem for Arabs. Arabs with expanding families find it extremely difficult to get planning permission for the expansion of their homes or development. The resulting lack of architectural growth in Arab towns (despite the increasing population) is reflected in the low land ownership in the community. Only 3.5 per cent of the land in Israel is owned by the Arab sector. Thousands of Arabs live in villages and towns that are 'unrecognised' by the Israeli state, which means that they are not provided with basic services such as water, roads and education.

But it is in the realm of immigration that the contrasting experiences of Arabs and Jews in Israel are most stark. Under the Israeli Law of Return, any Jewish person on the planet, regardless of whether they have any connection at all with the Holy Land, can 'return' at any time to Israel and become a citizen with full rights. But if a Palestinian currently living in Nazareth has family who fled in fear in 1948 to the camps in Lebanon, his or her family is not allowed to return. This is despite the fact that the house or land they left behind might still exist. They are not allowed to return to a place where they or their family actually lived

and called home. They are not allowed to return in defiance
of international law, a law that defends the right of refugees
who have had to move during times of war to return to
their homes. They are not allowed to return home despite
United Nations' resolutions that have endorsed the Palestinian 'Right of Return'. The clear truth is they are not
allowed to return home simply because they are not Jewish.

*

Haifa is an industrial port city in northern Israel. With
the beautiful Bahá'í gardens and imposing Mount
Carmel, it is unlike other such cities in being pleasing
on the eye. When visiting it before the Israeli 2006 general election, I wanted to get a sense of where the Arab
parties stood. Arab Israeli citizens make up a substantial
minority of the Haifa population. Indeed, despite some
suicide attacks, Haifa has been held up by many as another example of peaceful coexistence in Israel between
Arabs and Jews.

There are Arab-owned restaurants in the popular German
Colony in the city. Jewish and Arab family and friends
enjoy their meals along the fashionable Ben-Gurion
Avenue on a balmy evening as the spectacular Bahá'í gardens light up above them. Mixed groups of noisy Arab
and Jewish school children are led by teachers onto the
Carmelite subway as they take a trip towards the summit
of Mount Carmel. In the public park adjacent to the zoo
in Carmel Central, Muslim families sit down on the
grass to enjoy picnics while Jewish children play football
beside them. There are also some extensive cross-community projects in the mixed city and co-existence is
more a reality here than in the vast majority of other
Israeli urban centres. But this reality of co-existence is
not perfection – it is more nuanced than that.

When undergoing a security check at the city's train station I was questioned by the female security guard as part of the procedure:

'Where are you from?'
   'Ireland.'
   'What religion are you?'
   'Well ... none really,' I said a little baffled by the brazen nature of her second question.
   'What do you mean, "none"?'
   'Well, I mean, I was christened a Roman Catholic,' I said, not wanting to get into a theological debate with an armed young security guard who did not come across as being all that friendly.
   'Then you are Christian,' she said definitively. 'Are you carrying a gun?'
   I laughed instinctively.
   'Are you carrying a gun?' she repeated louder this time, not so amused.
   'No, I am not carrying a gun.'
   'OK, go ahead.'

Religion and ethnicity still play pivotal roles, even in mixed Haifa. The reaction of many Arabs residing in Haifa and elsewhere in Israel to their subordinate position is not to get involved in politics. They want to stay within the safety of their own family and community and try to make do as well as they can. 'Keeping your head down', not discussing politics in mixed situations, trying your best not to cause 'trouble' are all techniques that some within the Arab population seem to deploy.

The local university is citied as a bastion of excellent co-existence between Jews and Arabs. And indeed, Haifa

University has higher levels of Arab enrolment than other Israeli third-level institutions. Talking to Haifa students, there is apparently some good interaction between young Arabs and Jews. However, such interaction seems to require a de-politicised context for it to work smoothly. Toby, a German friend who studied at Haifa, knew both Arab and Jewish students. He told me he found it 'almost impossible' to talk to Arabs in the university about the occupation or wider political issues. He said that the female Arab students in particular wanted to focus on 'parties and university trips'.

'Whenever you'd try to address the conflict, they would just say something like "You know, I prefer not to talk about these things too much since it makes life too difficult",' he said. 'I think the best way to describe Israeli Arabs is that they do care and talk among themselves, but in public they are extremely careful and try to make the best out of their own lives. It is better to keep your mouth closed as there is no use. If you complain it will only give Israelis further reasons to ask why the Arabs should have equal rights, if they do not feel Israeli,' concluded Toby, who had extensive experience with young Jews and Arabs living on both sides of the Green Line.

Other Arabs in Israel are of course politically engaged, and many of the leading figures in the Arab parties are some of the community's most articulate and high profile champions. In Haifa in March 2006, I attended a lively election rally in the Wadi Nisnas area, jointly organised by erstwhile rivals for the Arab vote, Balad and Hadash. The local Arab population clearly saw Haifa as very much *their* city and were confident enough to express their political beliefs loudly on the streets.

The icons, symbols, flags, anthems and official holidays of the State of Israel are all Jewish. Some historians and activists talk of a deliberate 'memoircide' conducted by the Israeli state in attempting to remove historical traces of a Palestinian Arab past. After the Palestinian exodus in 1948, those abandoned Arab towns which were not bulldozed were given new Hebrew names.

A modern movement of leftist Israelis and Palestinians have attempted to revive the Arab names of abandoned villages. The Zochrot (Remembering) group often erect signposts in both Arabic and Hebrew pointing towards Palestinian neighbourhoods and towns that were razed during the creation of the Israeli state. These signposts are normally quickly removed by the Israeli authorities. Despite official claims that Israel is both a Jewish state and a state for all its citizens, the reality for the Arab sector is that they are profoundly discriminated against and excluded from Israeli society.

A complex identity is held by the Arab community that did not leave in 1948. They now make up 20 per cent of the Israeli population and 10 per cent of the Palestinian people as a whole. The sometimes tortured debate over what terminology to use when describing this community reflects some of the problems. For official Israeli society the community are simply defined as 'Israeli Arabs', or the 'Arab sector'.

Furthermore the Jewish state tends to divide this sector into official sub-groups such as Christian, Druze, Bedouin, Sunni, etc. This strategy goes beyond mere semantics and contains important political distinctions from the Jewish side. Firstly, the term 'Israeli Arab' emphasises the Israeli citizenship of the community.

The absence of the adjective 'Palestinian' is important. The attempt to prevent any overt cultural and political bonds forming between the Arab community within Israel and in the occupied territories or refugee camps abroad has always been a central component of Israeli governing policy. It is vital that these three groups not be joined under the one term 'Palestinian'. Secondly, by sub-dividing the Arab community in Israel by religion, it at least officially makes that sector appear to be divided and less like a unified and potentially troublesome mass of people.

In contrast, the Arab community uses different terms for self-identification such as 'Palestinian Arab citizens of Israel', 'Arab citizens of Israel', 'Palestinian community in Israel' or just 'Palestinian'. Of course, some within the community would not use these terms, but the majority, particularly of the young, would use the word 'Palestinian' as part of their self-identification.

The Palestinian people in the occupied territories and in Israel itself are physically divided with little opportunity now for many of them to meet family and friends living on the other side. When I was living in the West Bank in 2005, I often asked locals about their attitude towards the Arabs who are citizens of Israel. All answered with the line of national solidarity as if it were a reflex: 'We are all brothers and sisters!'

But when the issue is teased out further, things became a lot more complicated.

*

It was an Arab footballer, a citizen of Israel, the captain of an Arab club team and a player wearing the national jersey of the Jewish state who broke Irish soccer fans' hearts in Tel Aviv in March 2005.

On an organised day trip to Hebron later that summer, I was speaking to our Palestinian guide about Abas Suan, Israel's new soccer star. Our guide was from Bethlehem, a Christian with perfect English. We soon got to the Israel versus Ireland World Cup qualifying match that had been played in Tel Aviv the previous March. A last-minute goal by substitute Abas Suan meant that it ended in a 1-1 draw. This soccer story was more than a little unique. The Israeli hero and midfielder, Abas Suan, was an Arab. The result made him a sporting sensation in Israel.

'Of course I supported Ireland. You don't think I would be supporting Israel, now? I did not want to see them in the World Cup,' said my guide laughing.

'But what about Abas Suan scoring the goal?'

'Oh yes, a Palestinian. Yes, it was a great goal,' he said smiling and waving his hands in the air as if celebrating the super strike.

'But really, would you be proud of him as a player or would you see him as a traitor?'

'As a traitor? No, of course not. He is a Palestinian, they are all our brothers. We are just divided. I do not know all that much about him myself; do you know anything about him?'

'He has a deadly long-shot,' I said ruefully.

In truth, I had kept half an eye on Suan's life following his late 20-yard drive past Irish goalkeeper Shay Given. At the time, feeling deflated and cursing Ireland's inability to hold onto the lead, I had turned away in disgust and began dissecting the game with friends in a Dublin pub following the final whistle. The somewhat surprising news that it was an Arab player who had scored the equalizer only hit later, as I poured over the coverage in the Sunday papers.

Immediately after the match, Suan became a pin-up boy for Israeli supporters across the world. Some pro-Israel bloggers online and writers in the print media celebrated the fact that an Arab citizen of Israel had become a pivotal part of the team. Because of his goal, he became an instant national hero. Arab citizens of Israel could be treated as equal citizens – just look at the adoration of Suan, it was said. There was some truth to this. An Israeli friend of mine went to the Irish game with her father. Following the match they sung Suan's name along with the other tens of thousands of fans in the stadium. Suan himself was poignantly quoted in the Hebrew media in his moment of ecstasy just after he had left the pitch: 'I dedicate this goal to the whole country. I hope that the people who didn't respect me respect me now,' he told pitch-side journalists breathlessly.

The captain of the Arab club team Bnei Sakhnin FC, located in northern Israel, was now an Israeli star. He quickly won major advertising contracts. But as the weeks passed by, it became clear that despite his hopes, not all Israelis would respect him.

When Bnei Sakhnin later played against their bitter rivals, the more successful, right-wing Beitar Jerusalem FC in a league game, the atmosphere was hostile. Some of the Jewish fans sang loudly that they hoped that the then 29-year-old Suan would develop cancer. They unfurled a banner proclaiming that the midfielder did not 'represent us'. There is a nasty political and sporting rivalry between both these clubs, which can explain some of the hatred directed towards the Arab international, but clearly, not all Jewish Israelis looked on Suan as 'one of them'.

Even within the sectors of Israeli society where Suan was briefly held aloft as an example of potential Jewish and Arab solidarity there were strains. To become accepted as a 'true' Israeli, Suan had only to score a last-gasp screamer against one of the best shot-stoppers in the modern game in a hugely important World Cup qualifier. Most Arabs living in Israel would never have such an opportunity or possess the ability to so impress Jewish Israeli society and to become 'accepted'

*

The Israeli authorities argue that while the economic and political situation for the Arabs within its borders may compare unfavourably with that of its Jewish citizens, it contrasts well with conditions for Arabs living in other Arab states in the region. It points to Arabs' protection under law and the right to vote as signs that Israel is clearly a democratic country for all its citizens. Discrimination and inequality unfortunately exists in all modern Western-style democracies like Israel, say government spokespeople from their offices in West Jerusalem.

However, it is rare for Western democracies to have complex webs of laws and restrictions based on ethnicity, which is the case in Israel. The circumstances that the Arab population live under are somewhat analogous to those of Northern Irish Catholic nationalists under Stormont rule from 1921 until the early 1970s.

Following the partition of Ireland in 1921, Northern nationalists made up a significant minority in Northern Ireland. Like Arabs in Israel, they had the right to vote, although at the local level it was restricted and based on property ownership. As a clear minority, they could never expect to see their own legislation passed at a 'national' level. They also suffered discrimination in education, health services, housing and employment. The ruling government in the North was run by the Protestant Unionist majority and Catholics had little political voice at the centre of power. The cultural and national expressions of the minority community, such as the Irish tricolour flag, use of the Irish language and Irish sporting institutions were either officially banned or ignored by the Unionist elite. The official symbols, anthems and icons of Northern Ireland inspired no allegiance from the nationalist minority.

Despite decades of sectarian and political discrimination there were no significant street protests or campaigns by the Catholic minority until the Civil Rights Movement in the late 1960s. The community had always kept its head down, but inspired by rights-based demonstrations among blacks in the United States, Catholics, particularly the young and working-class, took to the streets of Belfast and Derry demanding equality.

The civil rights struggle was met with force and opposition by the Unionist majority. British troops were sent to the North. On the streets of Derry on January 30, 1972 the Northern nationalist community had its own 'Land Day'. British paratroopers opened fire on a peaceful civil rights march killing 13 unarmed civilians. What became known as 'Bloody Sunday' and other violent encounters with the British occupation forces led an increasing number within the nationalist community to conclude that peaceful protest would not change the discriminatory system. Nationalist military forces won recruits from among the young Catholic working class. What followed was a bitter war between the IRA, the British state and armed Unionist gangs (often with covert British military support). It lasted for almost 30 blood-filled years, costing the lives of more than 3,000 people and leaving a renewed legacy of sectarian hatred in the tiny geographical area of Northern Ireland.

Many of the leaders of this Civil Rights Movement were from the first generation of young Catholics to receive a university education in the North. Some Arabs within Israel, like Northern nationalists before the Civil Rights Movement, attend third-level education. While the supporters of the British government in Northern Ireland pointed to the Republic of Ireland, and said that Northern nationalists should be happy because their economy, education and health services were better north of the border, Israel does the same with the Arabs, highlighting the failure of other Arab states to provide as well for its people. Like the nationalist minority in Northern Ireland, the Arab minority feels no allegiance to the iconography of the state they live in. Thus, the Arabs in Israel do not fly the Israeli flag or sing the Israeli national anthem 'Hatikvah'.

I had only been home a few months after my stay in the West Bank, when I thought again of the Arabs in Israel. I was playing host to a couple of friends I had made in the Holy Land. I invited Atalia, a young Israeli whom I had met in Tel Aviv the previous summer, and Toby, my former flatmate, to the Dublin Theatre Festival production of *Bloody Sunday: Scenes from the Saville Inquiry*.

The real-life Saville Inquiry was established by the British government in 2000 to investigate the shootings on the streets of Derry on Bloody Sunday in 1972. It was instituted as part of the peace process. Families of the 13 victims had long campaigned for a new inquiry, since the inquiry held immediately after the incident, the Widgery Inquiry, which exonerated the British para-troopers of any wrong-doing, was considered to be a whitewash and an attempt by the British establishment to cover up the paratroopers' actions.

The Abbey Theatre's reconstruction of the Saville Inquiry was engaging, as was the dramatisation of evidence from numerous people who had attended the march and who spoke of its peaceful nature and how they reacted when the firing began. During the play's interval Atalia turned to me.

'You have heard of the Orr Commission, right? It is amazing how much like the Orr Inquiry this is. It is un-believable,' she said.

In October 2000, in a series of incidents that shocked Israeli society to its core, 13 unarmed civilians lost their lives on the streets of several northern Arab towns when Israeli security forces attacked protestors with live ammunition. In the occupied territories, similar tragic situations were a regular occurrence, but on the Israeli side of the Green Line it caused a sensation. The demonstrations had been originally sparked by the out-break of the second intifada and the violence that erupted in the occupied territories. When Arabs in Israel took to the streets in a number of Israeli towns, they were met by force.

The Orr Commission of Inquiry was established following the killing of the 13 Arabs, who were Israeli citizens. The Orr hearings were marathon sessions that continued for two and a half years and were presided over by Jewish Israeli Chief Justice Mr Theodor Orr. By the time they ended in August 2002, a total of 92 public hearings had been held with over 430 individual testimonies recorded.

The publication of the Orr Commission report in 2003 was heralded by some as an important moment for the Arabs in Israel and an eye-opener for Jewish Israelis. Among other things, the commission found that there had been years of neglect and discrimination against the Arab community in Israel. Obviously, Arabs were aware of this, but it was significant that such findings were made by a member of the Israeli Jewish legal establishment.

According to Justice Orr's fiindings:

> The state and generations of its government failed in a lack of comprehensive and deep handling of a large Arab minority inside the Jewish state. Government handling of the Arab sector has been primarily neglectful and discriminatory. The establishment did not show sufficient sensitivity to the needs of the Arab population and did not take enough action in order to allocate state resources in an equal manner. The state did not do enough or try hard enough to create equality for its Arab citizens or to uproot discriminatory or unjust phenomenon.

The report called for police reform. The Israeli police were not regarded as 'guardians of justice' by the Arab population, but rather as a hostile force sent to discriminate against them on behalf of a hostile government and state. Since October 2000, over 20 Arab citizens of Israel have been shot and killed by Israeli forces. Arab advocacy groups say that relations between Arab citizens and the Israeli police are still very poor.

The Orr report chastised some Arab politicians who it claimed had inflamed tensions during the period. But Justice Orr was also sharply critical of the former Israeli Prime Minister Ehud Barak. The report found that Mr Barak simply did not care about the Arab sector and the problems it suffered despite the rhetoric of peace and negotiation that he used to gain the Arab vote and win the 1999 election. This apathy would help to fuel the anger that would eventually explode onto Israeli streets in October 2000.

> The commission found it was proven that Mr Barak was not aware of or sufficiently attentive, being prime minister of Israel, to the processes occurring in Israel's Arab society, which created during his tenure a real fear of the outbreak of widespread rioting.

'A cold house for Catholics' was how the former Northern Ireland Unionist Party leader David Trimble described Northern Ireland in its early decades. He used the phrase during his 1998 Nobel Peace Prize acceptance speech. To equate years of systematic sectarian discrimination against thousands of Catholics to a cool draught or breeze was seen by some Irish nationalists and civil rights advocates as an understatement to say the least. Others welcomed it as an important statement of honesty by a leading unionist.

While similarities can be drawn between the two situations, it is evident that Israel is far more than a 'cold house' for its Arab citizens. While dealing with discrimination, Arabs must also live within a state where some of the political leaders and much of the Jewish populace would rather see them thrown out. In the March 2006 election, a party led by a former Israeli Cabinet Minister made the removal of Arabs from Israel a central tenant of its election platform. Avigdor Lieberman's Yisrael Beiteinu party said it wanted to separate Arabs and Jews. It wanted Arabs in towns in central Israel unilaterally thrown out of the country. In May 2004, Mr Lieberman was widely reported as saying of the Arabs, 'They have no place here. They can take their bundles and get lost.'

The irony of the Moldovan-born Lieberman promoting what has been called 'soft transfer' of Arabs from their land was not lost on Hadash politician Ahmed Tibi in *Haaretz*.

> It is inhumane that my aunt who used to live in Taibeh and was expelled to Kuwait, and whose house is still standing, could not even come here for a visit. She died two years ago but this is a true story and there is no Arab family that does not have such a story. This is while any Lieberman can come from abroad and settle outside Israel, in Nokdim [in the West Bank] and he wants to deport me to another country ...

While the majority of Israeli politicians would not use Lieberman's extreme language, it could be reasonably argued that there is an endemic anti-Arab bias at the heart of the Israeli political system. Prime Minister Ehud Olmert, leader of the Kadima party, speaking prior to the March 2006 election ruled out any coalition with parties that are not 'Zionist and Jewish'. This essentially meant that as a matter of principle, the Arab parties would not be considered to be suitable partners in government. If the Arabs are truly equal citizens, it must be asked why Olmert would rule them out entirely as political allies.

The creaking logic of Israel as a self-styled Jewish and democratic country, a state for the Jewish people, built on the enforced exile of hundreds of thousands of Palestinian former inhabitants, a state that now contains a growing Arab minority within and a brutal occupation without, has the continuing potential to unravel in the most extremely violent and horrible ways. The plight of the Palestinian population within Israel is one often ignored by international media and human rights organisations. In part this is understandable. The military occupation of the West Bank and Gaza and the horrors it creates are always likely to garner more international media attention. But the problems faced by the Arab community within Israel are a key factor in the region and has the potential to be explosive.

*

In October 2006 a politically weakened Prime Minister Olmert invited Avigdor Lieberman, leader of Yisrael Beiteinu, into his coalition. Only one Labour party member of the government resigned in protest. Mr Lieberman was appointed Minister for Strategic Threats and a Deputy Prime Minister; this was a man who had previously called for the execution of Arab members of the Knesset who had met representatives of Hamas for political discussions. In an interview with Israel's Army Radio in November 2006, Lieberman reaffirmed his belief that Arabs should be removed from Israel. He declared that Israel must 'hold a surgical removal once and for all. He later added, 'If we want to safeguard Israel's character as a Jewish and Zionist state, there is no other solution.'

Arab politicians and community leaders immediately called Lieberman a racist and demanded his dismissal. The calls were ignored by the Israeli political establishment of which Mr Lieberman and his followers were now central components. The public proposal for the ethnic cleansing of the Palestinian population of Israel had been voiced openly at the epicentre of political power. Until January 2008, Lieberman was the second most important and powerful politician in Israel. He resigned from government because of concerns he had over negotiations with the Palestinians. In future elections, it is likely that Lieberman could again become Deputy Prime Minister, and not impossible that he may even be Prime Minister. The Palestinian Arab community in Israel looks on with increasing fear, insecurity and pessimism at its collective future.

8

Jew Don't Evict Jew

One hot, sticky morning in July 2005, I set off to attend a somewhat unique summer festival. This eagerly anticipated gathering of thousands had all the necessary ingredients of an enjoyable day: music, food, dancing and plenty of colour, all combined under the pleasant blanket of a perfectly blue sky. It was glorious T-shirt-wearing weather.

There were weeks of excitement in the build-up to the festivities. Newspapers published weighty supplements previewing what would take place. Local TV and radio devoted whole programmes to it. Extensive policing and security measures were planned months in advance. Unlike summer festivals back home in Europe, where the liquid aspect is fundamental to the festival experience, this one was alcohol free. Though nobody was inebriated, there was an undoubtedly intoxicating mix of youthful radicalism and mature, intense belief to be enjoyed in the fields surrounding Kfar Maimon, and the attendees seemed happy and content enough without wine or beer. Most of the tens of thousands of Jews who arrived in Kfar Maimon in southern Israel were religiously inclined, and so would shy away from excessive alcohol intake.

Kfar Maimon, a tiny rural Jewish village situated less than 16 kilometres from the Gaza Strip and 8 kilometres outside the Israeli city of Netivot, was in July 2005 the colourful last stand of the 'orange movement'. This was the mass movement that had since the beginning of the year sprung forth and blazed a vibrant and noisy path across the Israeli body politic. Orange was the official colour of the local governing authority over Gaza's Jewish settlements. This movement organised demonstrations big and small all over Israel, supporters blocked motorways during rush hour traffic and special prayers were said at the Western Wall in Jerusalem.

Thousands gathered in southern rural Israel carrying their orange flags and wearing their orange ribbons, hats and t-shirts. They were there to protest against Israeli government plans to remove Jewish settlers from the occupied Gaza Strip, and orange was their colour of choice. They were angry about the controversial and bitterly divisive Gaza disengagement plan. What was organised in Kfar Maimon was a massive festival, celebration and protest initiated and attended by members of the religious sector of Jewish Israeli society.

In the week prior to the major demonstration, small numbers of protestors had already arrived from all corners of Israel. An orange tent village had emerged and had attracted Israeli TV and print media to this isolated southern spot. In the end, some 20,000 police and soldiers would prevent approximately 30,000 protestors from marching from Kfar Maimon all the way into the Gush Katif Jewish settlement in Gaza. Although this was the stated intention of the organisers, in reality, everyone knew that the protestors would not be allowed to march brazenly into war-torn Palestinian Gaza. Thus, this was principally a symbolic gathering to show the Israeli general public the depth of opposition to the Gaza plan. It was a festival of resistance to any plan to concede one inch of Jewish land.

On the Sunday prior to the protest, the Israeli security authorities, backed by the government, denied the organisers a permit for the event. This deemed everything that took place in Kfar Maimon that week illegal. The state warned private bus operators across Israel not to transport people to the protest. Despite this, the organisers decided to plough ahead, and on Tuesday 19 July thousands marched from Netivot to the orange base in Kfar Maimon.

Once the rotund favourite of the religious settler movement, then Prime Minister Ariel Sharon had stunned his loyal followers when he announced the 'Gaza disengagement plan' earlier that year. He declared his intention to remove the 7,500 plus Jewish settlers who had lived in the Gaza Strip for decades and to dismantle their settlements. The settlers would be offered compensation and new homes, but if they refused to move, they would literally be pulled from their homes by the Israeli army.

With just weeks to go before the Israeli army began the forced removal of settlers, the destruction of their homes, the exhumation and relocation of their familial burial plots and the abandonment of their synagogues, the orange opposition had intensified its protest movement to new heights.

*

Three European friends and I went 'undercover' to Kfar Maimon. The departure point alone of our journey would have shocked our orange travelling companions had they discovered it. We had begun our day in the occupied Palestinian West Bank and would end that evening in the company of radical, religious Jews.

We woke up early that morning on the floor of a Ramallah apartment. We all struggled with lingering hangovers following a party the night before attended by international and Palestinian students. German friends Stephan and Toby, English Ben and I tried to ignore our aches and pains and decided to travel into Israel to attend the orange demonstration. I wanted to talk to the protestors and get a sense of the tactics and strategies of the anti-disengagement movement for a forthcoming article for *The Sunday Business Post*.

I can almost be 100 per cent certain we were the only four people to make the interesting trip from Ramallah to Kfar Maimon that day. Travelling from the headquarters of the PA in the occupied West Bank to southern Israel and the largest gathering of religious Zionists in many decades was undoubtedly a unique journey. The geographical distance was relatively small, less than 200 kilometres, but we were covering significant ground on the political landscape.

After negotiating the usual number of Israeli checkpoints we finally left the West Bank. When we reached

West Jerusalem we saw the protestors wearing distinctive orange ribbons and hats, waiting for private chartered buses to bring them south. Toby, who had some good conversational Hebrew, spoke to one of the organisers and told them we were Christian Zionists from Europe interested in showing our solidarity. His Hebraic sweet-talking worked, and we donned the mandatory orange ribbons and patiently waited for the next bus to bring us southwards.

The reality that it was none other than Ariel Sharon who had started this disengagement was extremely unpalatable for the protestors we spoke to. Obviously distressed, they grappled for reasons why their former hero could be doing such a thing. For Yitzack, a friendly religious Jew in his thirties waiting outside Jerusalem Central Bus Station for his ride to Kfar Maimon, it was all conspiratorial.

'Sharon is doing this because of his troubles with the law. It is just so hard to understand, but he has these legal and money problems. By doing this, by taking Jews from their homes, he is keeping people from looking into his financial problems. It is a diversion,' Yitzack said in a sad tone.

He then started to ask us about where we were from and why we were going to the protest. Eventually he directed some probing questions towards me about the strength of the Christian Zionist movement in Ireland.

'Weak,' I answered a little guiltily.

Yitzack agreed with the authors of a bestselling Israeli political book, who claimed the inspiration for Sharon's Gaza plan had sprung from an attempt to deflect attention from the 'Greek Island' financial scandal in which Sharon and his son had been implicated. Yitzack looked genuinely personally hurt when he started to talk about Sharon.

'All this because of money. All of this, watching Jewish people throwing other Jewish people out of their homes. And their homes are built on Jewish land. All of this just because of money,' he said despondently.

For other protestors bound for Kfar Maimon, it seemed just another miserable confirmation that no politician, no matter who they were, could be trusted. Prior to the 2003 general election, Sharon had actually opposed a similar Gaza plan supported by the Labour party. After securing the support of tens of thousands of religious voters and settlers, he had essentially carried out a brazen volte-face on the issue after he had won the election. He decided to implement the very plan that he had previously opposed. Opponents said he lacked any democratic mandate to undertake such a significant venture – it was a fair point. When asked about Sharon's motivations for removing the Gaza settlers most protestors waiting for the bus simply said, 'Sharon is just a traitor and cannot be trusted.'

Israel, like Ireland, is a place where patiently queuing for the bus, like peace, is a nice idea, but in reality, it is war. Even among the religious types who were waiting to display their fidelity to both God and country in Kfar Maimon, it was every person for themselves as they pushed onto the old decrepit bus when it finally opened its doors. The bus was a model which had been fitted with very high, small windows with extra-thick plastic installed for security reasons. It was the type of bus used by Jewish settlers throughout the occupied territories.

During our journey south there was a brief communal prayer when one of the passengers walked up to the top of the bus and recited into the microphone – but that was the only occasion for collective religious expression. The pilgrimages I had made as a child with my grandmother to Knock in County Mayo were far more religious. Every 30 miles, or so it seemed, the bus would come alive with another decade of the rosary from the ageing pilgrims as we spirited towards the western location for the Blessed Virgin's claimed appearance in 1879. I had expected significantly more in the way of vocal religious devotion as we drove along the wide, open motorways cutting through the southern Negev desert. In fact, the atmosphere inside the bus was mostly hushed, but with a palpable sense of purpose. This was serious business for these orange protestors.

There were many privately-owned cars and other buses driving south along the motorway, all flying the orange ribbons from their windows and radio aerials. Thousands had obviously decided to ignore the government ban on the march and make their way to Kfar Maimon all the same.

Stephan fell asleep on the journey down. To get some shade, he had covered up his face with the hat he had bought from a nearby stall when we had waited for the bus. It was inscribed in Hebrew with the unforgettable motto of the orange movement: *Jew Don't Evict Jew*. For a people whose collective memory is very much formed by eviction, exodus and homelessness, such an evocative slogan stirred much emotion in Israel.

I had nothing to read, having been warned by the perceptive Toby that taking the liberal and pro-disengagement

Haaretz out of my bag might blow our cover as international fellow ideologues. After a few hours we were stopped at an Israeli checkpoint as we approached the southern city of Netivot. This was something that I had grown very familiar with in the West Bank, but never in Israel itself. OK, so the armed police officer did not get on the bus, check all of our ID cards, throw some of us off the bus and stare at the rest of us menacingly as he would have during even the most routine of checkpoint situations on the West Bank. The police officer spoke for a few seconds to the bus driver and had a quick look down the length of the bus. It was nothing serious, but to be stopped at all at such a checkpoint within Israel was still unique.

There were some grumbles from protesters about the Israeli police checkpoints along the southern motorways en route to Kfar Maimon, grumbles that would surely have brought more than a wry smile to Palestinians in the occupied territories, where Israeli government restriction on travel is as fundamental a part of life as breathing.

The private bus was finally halted by Israeli police on the motorway a few kilometres outside of Netivot. The orange gathering had been declared illegal so access was to be somewhat restricted. But the authorities did not entirely restrict access to Kfar Maimon, because to have done so would have risked serious and possibly violent protests by the orange movement. There was some confusion among the passengers as to whether the protest had been officially banned by the authorities. We were still well over eight kilometres from our destination. We had no choice but to wearily disembark from the bus with our fellow passengers. We then set off to walk for more than an hour and a half in the afternoon sun before reaching the festival.

Religious Jewish parents with their children, young teenagers in groups and older individuals marching on their own were all making their way along the empty rural road to Kfar Maimon. The festival-goers were plodding slowly forward in silent determination. In the fields on either side of the road, thousands of soldiers and security personnel were stationed and preparing themselves. Israeli army helicopters flew low and noisily overhead. Military jeeps sped past us towards the village. One stopped to hand out much needed water bottles to the protestors melting in the heat. At this stage I wished that I had also bought a *Jew Don't Evict Jew* hat to protect me from the unforgiving sun.

Qassam rockets fired by Palestinians from the Gaza Strip had landed in the vicinity of Kfar Maimon before. I searched the perfectly clear sky for any sign of one. This massive gathering of right-wing Israelis would surely be regarded as an attractive target for some of the Palestinian militant factions.

I spotted a middle-aged woman with an orange ribbon in her hair catching my eye after I had been looking into the sky. She smiled and nodded slowly. Maybe she was also looking for potential lethal rockets. Or possibly she believed that I like many of the religiously devout who attended that day was scouring the heavens for signs of a last-minute intervention by God himself to thwart Sharon's scheme. This was not academic: the most religious among the settlers and their supporters did believe that God would, or at least could, intervene to save the day and prevent the disengagement.

In the weeks prior to the disengagement, books and articles were published describing numerous 'miracles' that had taken place in the largest Gaza settlement, Gush Katif. Tales of how Gush Katif residents had survived relentless barrages from Palestinian rockets were wrapped up in urban legend and sold as miracles by some of the religious settlers. These were precious signs for some that the Almighty would not allow the abomination of Jews ripping other Jews away from the historic biblical land of Greater Israel. Some who marched in the sun that day in Kfar Maimon had little hope that earthy politicians would come to their rescue. Only God Himself could save them at this late hour.

We trod forward in the blistering heat. After walking for more than 90 minutes, the earlier trickle of orange supporters who had been wandering along the road had by then developed into a large swell of nationalist Jews. The protestors who approached Kfar Maimon filled the road completely from one side to the other.

Eventually we saw satellite dishes shimmering in the distance. Then we could clearly see the rows of mini buses from the various Israeli and international TV networks parked in a long convoy along the roadside. We now knew that we had finally arrived at this orange festival, and there was a noticeable extra spring in the step of the weary walkers.

*

The construction of Jewish settlements, or 'colonies' as Palestinians often call them, in the West Bank and the Gaza Strip began soon after the end of the 1967 War. Following Israel's spectacular victory over its Arab neighbours, it won the West Bank, including East

Jerusalem, from Jordan and Gaza from Egypt. Swept along by the euphoria following the stunning victories, Israeli politics was then seized by a debate about what to do with the newly-occupied territories and the hundreds of thousands of Palestinians who lived in them.

For those on the Zionist political right, the occupation of these lands could allow the partial fulfilment of a long-held desire to construct a 'Greater Israel', as promised to the Jews by God. This bigger and better Israel would begin in the west at the Mediterranean and expand in the east to the River Jordan, and perhaps even further to that biblical river's east bank. Others, including many on the Zionist left, felt that the occupied lands could provide security for Israel from its Arab neighbours. Pre-1967 Israel was so small, they argued, that both the West Bank and Gaza would provide a buffer zone against any future invasions. So began the initial construction of a small number of Jewish settlements on land that was internationally described as occupied.

Later, in 1967, a political lobby group of settlers and their supporters, the Land of Israel movement, started to campaign for and then began to establish larger settlements in the occupied territories. They won support from both the Zionist right and the left and among both religious and secular Jews. In the following decades, the more overtly religiously-based Gush Emunim (Bloc of the Faithful) campaigned energetically for settlement construction in the occupied territories.

During the years 1967–77 over 30 settlements were built for about 5,000 settlers in the West Bank, not including East Jerusalem. On the election of the first right-wing Likud government in 1977, the pace of settlement construction increased rapidly. In the 1980s and 1990s under both Labour- and Likud-led governments, settlement construction grew faster still. Ironically, the most intensive construction occurred after the signing of the Oslo Accords in the early 1990s under a Labour government. Not including East Jerusalem, some 260,000 Jewish settlers now live in 121 settlements throughout the West Bank.

The Zionist right have always been depicted in the foreign media, and thus in the minds of international observers, as the driving force behind illegal settlement construction. While the left wing had the communal, peaceful kibbutz, the right wing had illegal war-mongering settlements. This was always a colossal oversimplification. In fact, the Labour party has through its actions (and sometimes through its inaction) arguably done more to fuel the construction of illegal settlements on occupied Palestinian land than the right wing has.

Jews who moved to the West Bank and the Gaza Strip had various reasons for doing so. In this they were much like the early Zionists, who arrived in Israel during the aliyahs in the early 20th century. Some settlers were motivated by strongly religious impulses, believing that they were settling in the Land of Greater Israel as promised to the Jews by God. They understood themselves to be living in a messianic age and by settling on the land, they would quicken the coming of the Messiah.

Other settlers, probably a majority, had less celestial and more commercial reasons to move to the occupied territories. Government aid and tax incentives attracted Israelis who flocked from the country's crowded cities to live in sometimes large suburbanite villas with excellent facilities and infrastructure in the West Bank settlements. High-quality roadways were built through the West Bank for Jews only to allow the settlers commute into Jerusalem and Tel Aviv quickly, avoiding the Arab Palestinian towns along the way. Massive settlements like Ariel, Bet El, and most significantly Ma'aleh Adumim became pleasant suburban cities with a high quality of life. Ma'aleh Adumim stretched out from the occupied Arab part of Jerusalem and cuts large swathes through the centre of the Palestinian West Bank.

A drive of any short distance through the occupied territories quickly reveals the topographical power relations between Jewish settlements and Palestinian towns and refugee camps. The West Bank is made up of sloping hills, and on the top of these hills Jewish settlements have been built. They are all fairly aesthetically uniform residential developments with red slate roofs and white walls. Their location on the hills is of course strategic. Israeli planners argue it provides security as a hilltop is a perfect place to spot potential threats from all around. Local Palestinians will point up at them and say 'they are looking down on us'. For Palestinians, the positioning of the settlements above them is a direct metaphor for their own political position, as occupied and oppressed by the Israelis.

The high locations are also favourable in terms of controlling the crucial water sources in the West Bank. Israel controls the water supply in the West Bank. The Palestinians have their water quota fixed by Israel. There are no such constraints set on Israeli use of water and Israel is free to pump according to its needs. Settlements are said to use five times the amount of water per capita as the Palestinian population in the occupied territories. Some settlements deep in the West Bank are small, isolated villages with long, wide roads up to their entrances. This is to allow armed residents and Israeli security to spot if a non-Israeli-registered car is making an approach. Palestinians often cite attacks by armed settlers as an ignored aspect of the Israeli occupation. Jewish settlers counter-claim that they have to remain armed because of security threats posed by Arabs.

The smallest and most isolated settlements are the ones inhabited by religious zealots. In Hebron for example, Jewish settlers have taken over the upper floors of three-storey Palestinian homes in the city. Wire mesh is in place above the narrow market streets of central Hebron to prevent settlers from throwing missiles down upon Palestinians.

Hebron's settlers are known to be particularly vicious towards local Palestinians, and yet the Israeli state has no plans to remove them. The city centre is a war zone, with Israeli troops patrolling the market with their guns propped up and aimed at Arabs. Israeli troops are stationed on each corner you pass on your way towards the historic Abraham Mosque. Iron mesh security cages and military watchtowers with gun turrets are built right in the centre of Hebron's streets.

On one visit to Hebron I witnessed four intimidating Israeli soldiers shouting very loudly at a foreign member of the Temporary International Presence in Hebron (TIPH). This independent organisation was established to oversee the division of security matters in the city between Israeli and Palestinian forces. The foreigner kept his cool, though his back was literally against the wall. He kept pleading with the soldiers, 'Do not touch my camera'. We walked by quickly.

Skinned camels hang from hooks outside street butchers while vegetable and fruit stall owners roar and shout in deafening Arabic. The city is home to religious sites that are important to both Jews and Arabs and boasts an ancient history of coexistence, as well as moments of bloody violence. Since the late 1990s, the PA has taken limited control over certain neighbourhoods in Hebron, but Israeli forces are still there in large numbers, nominally to provide protection for the religious settlers. There is nothing even approaching a cordial relationship between the extreme settlers and the Palestinian locals: in February 1994, a local Jewish settler shot dead 29 praying Palestinians in the Abraham Mosque.

Criticism of the settler enterprise from the international community – including criticism, at least in rhetoric, from the United States – has been ignored by successive Israeli governments. Both right-wing Likud and left-wing Labour-led administrations rushed to build these settlements on Palestinian territory. Palestinians believe that the construction of the patchwork of settlements, roadways, checkpoints and army bases across the West Bank is a tactic to prevent the foundation of a viable Palestinian state. But to the supporters of the settlements, like those who gathered in Kfar Maimon, international law and world opinion is insignificant when God himself has promised you the land.

*

To Irish eyes, the scene at Kfar Maimon was a strange hybrid between the Drumcree protests by the Protestant Orange Order in Northern Ireland in the late 1990s and a pleasant summer musical festival. The comparison to Drumcree went beyond the colour scheme of the day and the steely determination in the air: both the Jews in

Kfar Maimon and the Orangemen in Drumcree believed that they were defending their historic rights. In the case of Drumcree it was the so-called 'ancient right' for the Orangemen to walk along the 'Queen's highway'.

The Orange Order has historically been regarded by many Irish nationalists as a sectarian organisation that has been instrumental in discrimination against Catholics. Sections of the intended Drumcree march route went straight through a nationalist, Catholic estate. The local residents did not want people whom they considered sectarian marching in a parade past their front lawns. For a number of years in the late 1990s, standoffs between police, Orangemen and nationalist residents led to outbreaks of vicious violence. Riots became annual occurrences.

According to the Kfar Maimon organisers, theirs was also a protest based on a defence of an ancient right. In this case, it was the 'right' of the land of Israel to stretch from the Mediterranean to the River Jordan, at the very least, as bequeathed by God to Abraham. Sharon's plan to pull the settlers out, some literally kicking and screaming from their Gaza Strip homes, was a violation of this Biblical real estate deal, according to the angry protesters.

Like any summer musical festival, this event was attended by large numbers of young people. Teenagers travelled to Kfar Maimon from across Israel. The most ardent and extreme among them came directly from the West Bank settlements. Such people worried that if the State of Israel could remove settlers from Gaza that they and their families in the West Bank could be next.

Loud religious music drifted through the dry air over Kfar Maimon, only stopping for the reciting of prayers. Then Orthodox Jewish men began the physically strenuous Hasidic dancing; arms tightly around each other's shoulders, dancing in wildly excitable circles, the groups of men were clearly enjoying themselves, noticeably perspiring as they spun around at a hectic, dizzying pace. Female orange protestors stood a few feet away minding the children who were laughing and supportively clapping their men

Families sat together in deep conversation under the welcoming shade of fig trees. Other Jewish men wearing tallitot were swaying back and forth praying and reading aloud from the Torah. There was a wonderful atmosphere of purpose that one only feels at a highly-charged political occasion. We heard rumours that during the night there had been some scuffles between protestors in the tent village and Israeli security forces and mounted police had been briefly deployed among the demonstrators. But that tension seemed to have long since dissipated, and the atmosphere when we arrived was peaceful and ebullient.

'Your cameras cannot capture everything here. It just cannot capture it all. It cannot capture the heart of these people. There is so much heart here,' said a smiling young protester wearing a bright orange T-shirt upon learning that we were foreigners.

'There are 100,000 people here, brought together by this disaster. Sharon does not know what he has done. He has brought all this on himself,' said the protestor who was merry and enjoying himself, surrounded by like-minded friends.

But the heat had obviously melted his head, because while the crowd was large, it was clearly not 100,000. I did not have the heart to quibble with him over the numbers.

By the time I attended the festivities in Kfar Maimon I had grown accustomed to a certain type of interaction between Israeli soldiers and the public, having resided in the occupied territories for the summer. In the West Bank, the relationship between soldiers and Palestinian civilians is, at best, layered with intense friction, hatred bubbling underneath. At worst, well, it's much worse and leads to the ever-growing body count.

However, in southern Israel that day, despite the presence of thousands of well-armed soldiers, the atmosphere was far from tense. Orange protestors handed flowers to smiling members of the IDF and attempted to give them ribbons. Some uniformed troops laughed and joked with orange activists. Many soldiers would have sympathised with the orange protest's aims, coming from nationalist families themselves.

While there was no violence at Kfar Maimon, some Jewish religious leaders in the orange movement had decreed that physical resistance to the disengagement was permissible. Protest leaders and some right-wing rabbis had essentially urged Israeli troops to mutiny: they directed IDF soldiers to refuse to accept orders from their generals to remove the Gaza settlers. From the far fringes of the movement there was talk of even more extreme action against Sharon's plan – and maybe even against the Prime Minister himself.

*

Claims of similarities between Nazi and Israeli state policies emanated from an unexpected quarter in 2005. In the early period of the anti-disengagement movement, some of the movement's members called on opponents of the disengagement to wear an orange Star of David. The star was purposely reminiscent of those used by the Nazis to identify Jews during the Third Reich. At protests some highly-strung orange protestors screamed 'Eichmann had orders, too!' at Israeli soldiers, hoping to pressurise them into disobeying their orders to remove the Gaza settlers.

Adolf Eichmann was a leading Nazi who oversaw the deportation of Jews to the concentration camps. He was central to the command structure that organised and carried out the Holocaust. Eichmann survived the war and eventually fled to Argentina, but in 1960, the Israeli secret service, Mossad, captured him in Buenos Aires. They secretly brought him back to Israel where he was put on trial and later hung after being found guilty of crimes against humanity. The Eichmann trial and the evidence delivered against him by Holocaust survivors created a worldwide sensation, but it was within Israel that its impact was felt most powerfully. Historians see the public trial as one of the crucial moments in the history of the young Jewish state.

In the early years of the state, the Holocaust and its survivors were not part of the central Zionist narrative. Israeli Jews were taught to see themselves as strong warriors. In contrast, survivors who lived in Israel were sometimes regarded as oddities and the events surrounding the Holocaust were unclear and remote for a generation of young Israelis. The Israeli leadership had not wanted to focus on the victimhood of the Holocaust, but rather on the military victories and successes of the young Jewish state. But the evidence in the Eichmann trial brought the horrors of the Holocaust alive for many Israelis once again, including the many hundreds of thousands of newly-arrived Jewish immigrants from the Middle Eastern countries, the Mizrahi, who largely did not suffer during the Holocaust.

By evoking the name of such a hated Nazi, specifically Eichmann, some within the orange movement made a major error. To compare the IDF to the Nazis appalled most Israelis and cost the protest movement much potential support from wider Jewish society.

The extreme discourse and the stark division within Israeli society sparked by the disengagement reminded some of a decade previous and the intense political rupture caused by the signing of the Oslo Accords. That tension reached its zenith with the 1995 assassination of Israeli Prime Minister Yitzhak Rabin by a young, right-wing Jewish extremist. Yigal Amir gunned Rabin down following a massive Tel Aviv peace rally. For some Israelis, the anger and hatred during the summer of 2005 caused by the Gaza plan had eerily reignited memories of the difficult year of Rabin's murder.

In the most surreal, macabre story of them all, teenage surfers from the largest Gaza settlement Gush Katif threatened to commit mass suicide. The young settlers promised to take their boards out to sea on evacuation day and drown themselves. In the end the kamikaze surfers did not take to the Mediterranean waves when the IDF came knocking on disengagement day, 15 August.

However, despite the divisive and potential violent backdrop, the Israeli army's modus operandi was 'softly

softly' in Kfar Maimon and towards the orange movement in general. In certain parts of the village, young
protestors and soldiers sat in circles singing and playing
guitar together. This contrasted with the violent reaction
of the IDF I witnessed during other 'illegal' but
avowedly peaceful protests in Bil'in and elsewhere in the
occupied territories.

There were various strands of religious Judaism represented at Kfar Maimon, including the somewhat excitable
followers of Rabbi Menachem Mendel Schneerson. We
walked past a group of his chanting devotees. They began
talking to us and we revealed that we were Gentiles. They
were very pleased. One of the men took out a leaflet
produced specifically for us – Gentiles that is.

'This leaflet gives you all the information for the seven
commandments that you need to follow to help make a
new world free of misery and poverty,' he said in an American accent, as he cheerfully handed us one leaflet each.

I gazed at his classic Hasidic attire in sympathy, the dark
suit, tie and wide black hat. The formal ensemble more
suited for a cold Eastern European village than to the
burning Middle East. How hot could he be in that get-
up? He must lose two stone in sweat every day during
the sweltering summer in Israel.

'It will not take you long to read,' he assured me.

I was fairly interested. Already there were three
commandments fewer than the usual ten, so surely that
would make them easier to follow.

'Seven you say?'

'Yes only seven. You only have to follow seven, while
Jews have over 600 to follow. '

'Tough deal,' I said.

According to the literature, Rabbi Schneerson, whose face smiles from posters erected by his followers along all major Israeli highways, happiness can be brought to the world if these commandments are followed.

The majority of the thousands at Kfar Maimon were both religious and Zionist. They were less focused on the Gentile's morality and more on Israel's political direction. They saw Sharon's plan as an affront to both the biblical land of Israel and modern Israel as a Jewish state. The removal of the Gaza settlers would be both treacherous and dangerous in equal measure.

But beyond the smiles, chanting, food stands and dancing, many other Israelis saw a political movement reach its peak at Kfar Maimon that for them threatened to cause a fundamental rupture within Jewish Israeli society itself.

*

As the August date for disengagement loomed, Israel became increasingly tense. Media coverage was at saturation level. A deep period of collective soul-searching was played out at all levels of Jewish society. Israeli political commentator Ari Shavit wrote that in the summer of 2005, his country experienced an 'unprecedented trauma of identity'.

According to the opinion polls, the plan was supported by a majority of Israelis though a significant minority opposed it – a minority that grew in size as the date for disengagement approached. The country split, as with much else, along broadly religious and secular lines over the issue. Most secular left-wing Zionists were in favour and most religious right-wing Zionists were against. The debates in the media and on the streets were sharp, cutting, brutal and at times hysterical.

The orange movement crystallised for many secular Israelis their fear of the powerful influence that religious political groupings and their supporters had accumulated in Israel. The growing political power of the religious Jewish community is something that has long concerned the secularists. Because of Israel's political system, larger, mainly secular parties have always had to rely on the votes of religious parties to form coalition governments. Thus the religious parties have wielded influence far disproportionate to the size of their community's population.

The foot soldiers of the orange movement were supplied by the nationalist religious sector. More specifically, it was the young members who were the most prominent, angry and active. These teenagers were to be seen everywhere in West Jerusalem in the summer of 2005, both male and female. They stood on the corner of Jaffa Road and Ben Yehuda Street, handing out orange ribbons and headbands to passers-by.

The teenage boys hung the ribbons to their school bags, and the girls tied them in their hair. The boys wore oversized orange t-shirts while the girls donned long denim dresses with orange ribbons around their waists. They looked much like disaffected teenage youth in most western countries. Like the skaters, Goths and Emos, who spend their weekends sitting around the Central Bank in Dublin city centre, this youthful orange generation were moody, dressed alike and felt like they were rebelling against authority. But that is where the comparisons end.

While the rebellion expressed by the Dublin teenage youth is fleeting, generational and often apolitical, the young religious Israelis were moved by a deep sense of nationalism and religious belief. This explosive synergy had created a potent phalanx of committed reactionary idealistic youth, who were dislocated from 'official' secular Israeli society. Israel had now become one of the few places in the world where the 'hippies', or those who look bohemian, are actually the conservatives and the right-wingers.

When I returned to Israel seven months later, the events at Kfar Maimon had taken on an almost legendary significance within the religious-nationalist sector. Much like Woodstock in the 1960s, or the General Post Office during the 1916 Rising in Dublin, people who had not attended lied and said they had. It was regarded as a considerable boost to your commitment to the Jewish settler cause to say that you had been among the tens of thousands of orange supporters in Kfar Maimon. A key litmus test of your fidelity to Zionism was whether you braved the spectacular heat, ignored the outlawing of the event and drove down south on that July day.

By March 2006 most of Israeli society had moved on from the events in Gaza the previous summer, but the orange activists remained obsessed by it. For supporters of Sharon's plan, the disengagement had gone well. There had been no cataclysmic civil disruption on the streets, mutiny in the IDF gunshots from the settlers aimed towards Israeli troops.

One night, walking through Jerusalem I saw a gathering. In Zion Square, the heart of Jewish West Jerusalem young orange supporters had erected a large screen. On the screen, they played an all action home-produced documentary packed full of riots, clashes between orange protestors and mounted police. The scenes were taken from some of the events organised by the orange movement during the Gaza disengagement. A few hundred people huddled together to watch the documentary, many still wearing the orange ribbons from the previous year's battle. The style of the documentary, using video clips from street protests interspersed with loud music, was reminiscent of films I had seen emanating from the global anti-capitalist movement on the riots at G8 summits in Genoa and elsewhere in recent years.

A new, clearly identifiable sub-group of young religious Zionist Israelis had been established during the build-up to, and aftermath of, the Gaza disengagement. This group had been described by Sharon at one stage as a 'fellowship of gangs'. They are now, it seems, completely sidelined from the official Israeli state. The orange people, particularly the young, have concluded that the Israeli state is controlled by secular leftists who do not share their faith in Zionism and Judaism. They are active and politically engaged in contrast to their young secular brethren who have become disillusioned with politics.

*

The original Jewish settlers in the Gaza Strip tended to be of the less religious and more economically-driven kind. Of the 21 settlements in Gaza most were established in the late 1970s and early 1980s. Unlike the West Bank, Gaza is lacking in important Jewish religious sites, but many of the Gaza settlers were seduced by generous government financial incentives – not by religious fervour.

While scraping a living in a poor southern Jewish town in the Negev Desert, making a move to a settlement like Gush Katif promised settlers a larger home, more money and a sense of a renewed purpose in life. The settlers and their supporters who I interviewed at a number of orange protests in 2005 described how they felt that their lives in Gaza had given them a mission. No longer were they just another 'normal' working class Jewish citizen trying to make do in a banal periphery town; they were 'somebody' when they lived in the Gaza settlements at the cutting edge of the Zionist project.

These settlers regarded themselves as ideological and political Zionist pioneers in the same mould as the early Jewish immigrants to Palestine. They positively and consciously compared themselves to those who created the Israeli state. If the land in the Gaza Strip is considered occupied and not Jewish, why is the rest of the land on which Israel now exists considered to be unoccupied and Jewish, many settlers honestly enquired?

The Gaza Strip is only 12 kilometres across at its widest point and just 45 kilometres long. In 2005 it was home to over 1.3 million Palestinians, most living in poverty with endemic unemployment levels. The Gaza Strip was home to some of the most overcrowded places on earth – in the Palestinian end, that is. In the area where the Jewish settlements were built, there was actually plenty of room. The 21 Jewish settlements in Gaza were home to just over 7,500 settlers. The Jewish settlements took up 165 square kilometres. The 1.3 million Palestinians were squashed into the remaining 210 square kilometres that was left of Gaza.

The majority of protestors I met at Kfar Maimon in 2005 knew that the settlers would be removed, despite the march and the wider campaign. But there was an un-spoken and more achievable goal for the anti-disengage-ment movement: it wanted to make the removal process so horrific and difficult that it would be nigh-on impos-sible to do it again. By highlighting the images of women and children pulled from their homes, and by implanting lasting memories of tens of thousands marching against the plan, it would lessen the chances of any future removal of settlers from the West Bank.

This, in a way, was always part of Ariel Sharon's ingen-ious strategic plan.

In August 2005, the world's media cast Ariel Sharon as a man amazingly converted to the idea of peace and compromise. International reporters descended on Gaza just days before the disengagement began. As was to be expected, they quickly articulated an easily digestible story line to the effect that the formerly hard-line general and war-mongering politician had changed into a man of peace. He was taking this courageous plan and implementing it, despite strong opposition from the religious and right-wing fanatics in his country.

This was also how the international community, long since ground down by years of bad news from the region, looked at it as well. Sharon was feted as a man of peace by some and on his first visit to the United Nations head-quarters following the disengagement he was roundly congratulated by world leaders. But the motivations behind Sharon's plan were far more complicated than the simple storyline served up by the international media. There was more going on than just some sim-ple-headed desire for peace.

Just casually leafing through Ariel Sharon's military and political CV is enough to make a Palestinian wince with fear, and a right-wing Zionist's heart soar with pride. Sharon's career was one built on a hard-line militaristic attitude to the Arabs, constant practical support for the settlement enterprise and absolute opposition to numerous peace initiatives. When Sharon was Defence Minister in the early 1980s he was found guilty by the Israeli Kahan Commission of bearing 'personal responsibility' for the Sabra and Shatila massacres during which hundreds of Palestinian refugees died during the Israeli invasion of Lebanon. 'Ariel, King of Israel' as his followers endearingly crowned him, had a long history in right-wing Zionist politics and a bloody one in military matters. In more than one Israeli Cabinet he was instrumental in the construction, development and expansion of Jewish settlements.

His October 2000 visit to the Temple Mount complex in Jerusalem, site of the al-Aqsa Mosque, was rejected by many Israelis and Palestinians as a calculated attempt to cause a reaction among Arabs. It worked and is generally regarded as the 'spark' that lit the second intifada. Later, on becoming PM, Sharon ordered a brutal intensification of the occupation. Ostensibly in reaction to a shocking suicide attack on an Israeli hotel, 'Operation Defensive Shield' saw Israeli forces in 2002 re-enter Palestinian city centres in massive numbers. Many Palestinians lost their lives, while civic society and the Palestinian's feeble government structures were destroyed in aggressive attacks on infrastructure. Just mentioning his name to a Palestinian on the West Bank was enough to garner an angry response. More so than any other Israeli politician, he was quite simply utterly detested by all the Palestinians I spoke to.

So why, then, did Sharon decide to create despair for his supporters, bafflement among Palestinians and joy in the international community when he announced he was going to dismantle the Gaza settlements? From the beginning, many on all sides in Israel were very dubious about the veteran politician's motives. One question consumed Israeli Jewish society for the first half of 2005. Why was Sharon doing this?

The voices and desires of the Palestinians who lived in the occupied territories were entirely absent from the great internal debate that had gripped Israeli society.

*

For the Palestinians on the other side of the Green Line in the occupied territories, the disengagement was equally bewildering. The Israeli government carried it out unilaterally, with absolutely no discussions and interaction with the Palestinian leadership, so the PA could do little or nothing to prepare for it.

I met the Chief of Staff to PA Chairman, Mahmoud Abbas, in a group question and answers session just weeks prior to the Gaza disengagement. Rafiq Husseini hosted us in a large boardroom in the Muqata, the building in Ramallah where the late Palestinian President Yasser Arafat spent his last few years. During 2002, the Israeli military surrounded the compound and Arafat was holed up in the building, sometimes in complete darkness. Since Arafat's death in November 2004, the Muqata has become a centre of pilgrimage for Palestinians, as Arafat is buried within the grounds. It was, however, his wish that this would not be his final burial place. Rather, his body is to be moved and buried in Jerusalem if and when that beautiful, bitterly contested city becomes the capital of a future Palestinian state.

The Muqata is now the governmental centre for the PA leader Mahmoud Abbas and the ruling Palestinian bureaucracy. The front of the building is deeply uninspiring, and hardly what one would expect from the headquarters of a proto-governmental power. A shabby white building, that looks like it was designed in a hurry and constructed under fire.

Sections of the building still bear the scars from the Israeli siege of 2002. Bullet holes are visible all along the outer walls and some of the rubble created by the Israeli tanks and bulldozers had still not been removed. Inside was much better, with lush carpets, large boardrooms, an excellent air conditioning system and many photographs of the late Arafat. It was hardly the standard of facilities you find in the West Wing, but it at least smelt and felt like a potential governmental hub.

Mr Husseini was a busy man, but he greeted us warmly and generously and gave us over an hour of his time in a large cabinet room. A Palestinian in his fifties who has spent much of his life in England, Mr Husseini trained as a virologist at the City University in Birmingham. He spoke like all diplomats, in a precise and almost detached manner. This detachment continued even when he was conversing about such a passionate issue as the Israeli occupation. He clearly outlined the PA's problems with the Israeli government, but he was also critical of Palestinian corruption and mistakes that his own leadership had made in the past.

Mr Husseini is part of what some hope is a new breed of honest bureaucrats in the corridors of Palestinian power. Intelligent, affable, English-speaking and Western-educated – all attributes that would help Mr Husseini in discussions with United States and European Union officials. He has also appeared regularly in Western media with the sometimes-unenviable task of arguing the Palestinian case. He was a good-humoured man despite the difficult nature of his job. Holed up deep inside the Muqata, he has had to go on difficult journeys to the Gaza Strip and across the Palestinian territories to represent the PA and Mahmoud Abbas.

When he met us he talked about the recent history of the conflict, highlighting events that he thinks were pivotal, such as the assassination of Rabin in 1995. The topics he focused on and the issues he did not mention reflect the priorities of the PA. He maintained that direct negotiations were needed between Israeli, Palestinian and international officials. Settlement construction must be halted by the Israelis to show their goodwill. The Palestinian refugee issue was absent from his wide-ranging opening remarks.

When the anti-Wall protests in Bil'in were mentioned, he praised those who took part, but bluntly concluded that they will achieve nothing. His perspective is that of the PA leadership, and of Mahmoud Abbas in particular. They believed that talks with the Israelis were the only way to create a Palestinian state. Armed struggle or even a campaign of civil disobedience was no longer considered as a tactical option for the PA.

But there was one issue that very much occupied Mr Husseini's mind: the upcoming disengagement and what happened the 'day after' for the Palestinians in the Gaza Strip. He angrily criticised the lack of coordination and planning from Ariel Sharon's government, which, he said, made the task for the Palestinian authorities in Gaza a hugely difficult one.

'They have not spoken to us, so we cannot organise anything. It makes it much harder for us to make sure things improve on the ground from the day after the disengagement. They are doing this unilaterally with no coordination with us, which makes everything so much harder. The point for us the day after the disengagement takes place is to make sure that the people in Gaza feel like they have some hope,' Mr Husseini added.

When it came to talking about Sharon's motives for pulling the settlers out of Gaza, Mr Husseini, like all Palestinians, was cynical.

'If there is no hope the day after the settlers leave, then there could be chaos. I think we have to be honest in saying that. And I think that is what the Israeli side wants. They want chaos in Gaza so they can say that the Palestinians cannot run their own state. We have to make sure there is not a Somali-type situation after the settlers leave, with factions fighting on the streets. We have to try to make it more like Singapore than Somalia, so we can show the world a good news story from Gaza. It is going to be difficult because the Israelis are doing this unilaterally, with no coordination with us. But we must try.'

The allusion to Singapore seemed hopelessly optimistic at the time and sadly the vision of Somali-type street battles has subsequently been proved frighteningly apt.

While settlers were removed, Gaza remained effectively occupied by the Israeli army. Israel controls the borders, the air space and the coast. Palestinians are prevented by the Israelis from opening their international airport in Gaza, and they are also banned from building a new international sea port. The Israeli army has made numerous invasions of the Gaza Strip by land, and there have been extensive bombing raids by the Israeli Air Force that have killed hundreds of Palestinians and blown up the electricity generator for the whole of Gaza. Added to this nightmare, the international economic sanctions that followed the January 2006 election victory of Hamas has led to an intensification of social and economic deprivation for Gaza's Palestinian inhabitants.

They are living in a tiny prison with over one million Palestinian inmates. The Israeli prison guards may have stepped outside the prison walls, but they still control its perimeter and it is they who decide who can enter and who can exit, but they can also violently re-enter the prison whenever they so choose.

Violence between Hamas and Fatah gunmen in the Gaza Strip has also increased and turned into open street warfare since the disengagement. Despite the 2005 removal of the Jewish settlements, the Gaza Strip remains the most impoverished, choked, unstable and desperate part of the Palestinian occupied territories.

*

So why did Ariel Sharon pull the Gaza settlers out? Some in Israel argued that the public anti-war letter signed by a number of leading Israeli fighter pilots published in 2002 shocked him. These were not the usual peacenik activists, but very experienced military men who said that they would refuse to take part in what they believed to be illegal bombing raids over Gaza.

The publication of the 'Saudi Peace Plan' at the 2002 Arab League summit and the Geneva Accords in October 2003 also put pressure on Sharon. Each called for at least a partial ending of the occupation of Palestinian territories and the establishment of a Palestinian state. The Saudi plan adopted by the Arab League was very significant. It promised Israel official recognition from all Arab states if Israel retreated to its pre-1967 borders and returned the Golan Heights to Syria.

Sharon did not want to be forced by international pressure into negotiating and signing a deal with the Palestinian leadership. Having built a career on opposing and undermining previous peace initiatives, Sharon decided to make a sweeping unilateral move, one which he knew would be supported internationally. And within Israel, even the peace camp that once despised him would have to support his Gaza plan. However, for others on the left in Israel and among Palestinians in the occupied territories, Sharon's reasons were more sinister and politically brilliant.

By initiating the disengagement Sharon won universal international backing. It diverted world attention away from the construction of the Wall in the West Bank. Palestinian support groups argued that the disengagement plan was purposely announced early in 2004 at the height of international criticism of Sharon's Wall. Gaza took the world's gaze away from the Wall.

The Sharon government also helped to hype the orange protests. Israel in the summer of 2005 was supposedly 'one step away from civil war', as one of Sharon's ministers, Tzachi Hanegbi' said. Sharon was cleverly instigating a long-term plan. If Israel comes to the precipice of internal disintegration because of the removal of just 7,500 settlers from Gaza, how could Israel ever be expected to remove the massive settlements from the West Bank? How could any future Israeli Prime Minister risk suffering domestic disaster by removing tens of thousands of West Bank settlers from their homes, following any future negotiations with the Palestinians?

Pushing through this Gaza plan may have been politically risky for Sharon in the short term, but in the long term, many of his supporters believed it bolstered the future of the settlements on the West Bank. In the week prior to the Gaza move, Sharon said that the major Jewish West Bank settlement of Ariel 'would remain part of Israel for ever'.

Most crucially, by instigating the Gaza disengagement, Sharon received an historic letter from the American president George W. Bush in April 2004. This letter, signed in the Oval Office and delivered to Sharon's headquarters in Jerusalem, could prove to be as important, momentous and disastrous as the Balfour Declaration of 1917.

The United States had since 1967 taken the stance shared by the rest of the international community, namely, that the lands seized by Israel in the 1967 War were illegally 'occupied'. It could be argued this was just rhetorical posturing, because the US has given almost unlimited political support to Israel for decades. However, under the administration of George W. Bush, even this veneer of opposition to existing settlements on occupied lands was further diluted.

This sharp diplomatic turn by the Washington administration towards the Zionist right was first reflected linguistically. Members of the most pro-Israeli Washington administration in history, such as former Secretary of Defence Donald Rumsfeld, talked about 'contested' rather than 'occupied' territories. Then, under the cover of world support for Sharon's proposed Gaza Plan, President

Bush penned a public letter to the Israeli PM that fundamentally altered US policy towards the Palestinian territories. In his letter praising the removal of Gaza settlers as 'real progress' towards peace, he also comments on the major settlements in the West Bank. The US President wrote:

> In light of new realities on the ground, including already existing major Israeli population centres, it is unrealistic to expect that the outcome of final status negotiations will be a full and complete return to the armistice lines of 1949.

Thus by removing just 7,500 settlers from Gaza, Sharon had transformed US policy towards the massive West Bank settlements. The homes of tens of thousands of Jewish settlers would remain on occupied Palestinian land in any final peace agreement according to the US President, who had also paradoxically, proclaimed himself in favour of a Palestinian state. All this despite the pleadings of Palestinian leaders who said the settlements and their security installations cut the West Bank into pieces, making it nearly impossible to establish a viable state.

When the dust had settled following the removal of the settlers it seemed that the wily old Sharon had got what he wanted. What was occurring in the summer of 2005 was not the beginning of the end of the Israeli occupation of Palestine, but rather the magnificent skilful reorganisation thereof.

*

Disengagement itself turned out to be a military 'success' for the IDF. No shots were fired by settlers at the military forces and the resistance from the settlers turned out to be predominantly non-violent. While no shots were exchanged between Jewish settlers and the IDF during the Gaza disengagement, there were some fatalities. As usual, it was Palestinians who made up most of the casualties.

Just days before the disengagement, Eden Natan Zada, a 19-year-old Jewish extremist and army deserter from a West Bank settlement, opened fire on a public bus in a northern Israeli Arab town called Shfaram. He killed four Arab citizens of Israel before being lynched by by-standers. Zada had deserted from the Israeli army because of his refusal to take part in the Gaza disengagement.

He had been inspired by the calls made by some among the orange movement for soldiers to disobey orders. He was hoping, presumably, through his actions to cause civil strife in the northern Israeli towns thus halting the Gaza plan. He failed.

On disengagement day, most settlers left quietly. Others had to be carried from their houses by soldiers, weeping for the loss of what had been their homes. All of this was carried live, 24 hours a day on Israeli TV for the week it took to complete. The settlers who were re-moved received compensation packages from the government and were put up in temporary accommodation.

The whole process was undoubtedly a deeply shocking and traumatic one for the settlers and their families. Initially hailed by the Israeli state in the 1970s and 1980s as brave pioneers of the Zionist enterprise, the same state pulled them from their homes and literally destroyed their communities as they watched in disbelief. A year after the disengagement, many settler families still lived in temporary accommodation in the south and many complain that the government have not done enough to help them.

The Zionist left who supported the Gaza move were happy that the plan was carried out despite religious opposition. However, the bitterness and division created during the hot orange Israeli summer of 2005 continues to linger. Deep fault lines exposed over the disengagement in internal Israeli society will be difficult to ignore. The settler movement feels that they have been callously betrayed by their state and they and their supporters remain hurt, angry – and organised.

9

Divided Within

The young Jewish boys, with long hair hanging over their ears and dressed in their dark religious attire judged us warily. Until our arrival they had played happily on the vacant street close to the taxi stop. But once we came onto their scene we became the centre of their close attention.

Dusk was descending lazily over Netivot as we waited for the last scheduled Sherut to arrive and take us the long road north to Jerusalem. The taxi stop was positioned awkwardly close to a roundabout, but this mattered little, as the streets were mostly empty of traffic. The stop was also located in a clearly religious neighbourhood in the heart of the southern Israeli city. Bearded Orthodox Jews wearing distinctive black hats, dark long jackets and white shirts quickly walked up and down the street with their sharp, darting, instant steps. They all seemed to have somewhere to go to in a hurry, in what on the surface felt like a slow, unexciting town. The women trod wearily past pushing their prams, wearing their head scarves, long sleeved tops and dark, ankle-length skirts. Over time the local children eventually bored with staring at us and once again began to run up and down the empty streets playing joyfully.

Our brief visit to Netivot had been uneventful. There were a couple of other people waiting for taxis to take them to the few neighbouring Jewish towns established in the barren Negev desert. A young woman wearing the ubiquitous long, demure skirt enquired from a passerby the departure time of the final bus to the Gaza Strip settlement Gush Katif. Her family home was to be demolished in less than a month, as part of the Gaza disengagement.

Netivot is a sleepy urban centre. It suffers one ill that is not much reported in the region, focused on in detail by the international media: Jewish Israeli poverty. It is nothing compared to the poverty in the Palestinian occupied territories, of course, but Netivot was relatively poor compared to other Israeli towns and cities.

Ugly apartment blocks are spotted around the city centre, adding an aesthetic element to the general downbeat feeling that hung in the air. The architecture overall was uninspiring and mundane. Netivot could not be described by even the most lyrical of Israel's supporters as a beautiful urban miracle that had taken root and flowered in the uncompromising harsh desert sand. It was more a land of dust and cement than a paradise of milk and honey. This was not a glistening, fresh city like Tel Aviv or a beautiful, ancient treasure like Jerusalem. There was no sense of excitement and vigour screaming from the walls. Rather, Netivot exuded a jaded, disappointed persona. It looked like the city was finding things hard in its inhospitable, arid, unfriendly surroundings.

Walking along Netivot's streets with three other internationals, our progress was carefully scrutinised by local adults as well as children. It would be rare for Israelis from the major cities, let alone internationals, to visit a city like Netivot, situated on the margins of Jewish society. There is little here to attract tourists seeking religious sites, beautiful scenery or adventure.

Netivot is one of the 'development towns' established by the Israeli state in the 1950s. These towns became the home of poor Jewish immigrants from Arab countries, the Mizrahim. Jewish communities had lived in Arab countries for centuries, and for most of that time, in peace. In countries like Egypt, Morocco and Iraq they had an enormous impact on society, culture and commerce. The Mizrahim spoke Arabic and were a Jewish part of wider Arab life. The creation of the State of Israel and the resulting Arab-Israeli hostilities made life increasingly difficult for Jewish communities living in Arab states. Hundreds of thousands of Mizrahim were to leave the Arab world in the 1950s to become citizens in the new State of Israel.

When they arrived they were put in temporary accommodation by an Israeli state that was dominated by Jews of European descent, the Ashkenazim. Many within the Ashkenazi community considered the Jews from Arab lands to be socially backward, and the Mizrahi suffered discrimination within the new Jewish state. The community had to abandon Arabic as their spoken tongue and much of their Arabic culture as part of the difficult transition into Hebraic Israeli society. The Mizrahim are generally of a darker skin colour than the Ashkenazim.

The new development towns constructed for the Mizrahim in the 1950s were purposely built on the fringes of Israeli life, in the southern Negev desert. Sderot, Netivot and Ofakim were established in an attempt to settle the Negev with a significant Jewish population. Importantly, all the towns were built close to the Palestinian Gaza Strip.

In recent years the development towns, particularly Sderot have been the target for Palestinian rockets attacks. These have killed civilians and struck buildings and town squares in and around Sderot. Since 2005, thousands of rockets fired from Gaza have hit targets in southern Israel.

Although the Qassam rockets fired by Palestinians can be deadly, they are small and inaccurate, in contrast to the larger-scale bombardments by Israeli forces. This is, of course, little comfort to the residents of Sderot and now Netivot. Such rocket attacks have become commonplace and feature high in domestic media coverage, normally above reports of much harsher Israeli bombardments in Gaza.

Despite this coverage, governmental reactions to the attacks on the southern Israeli cities have been criticised as inadequate by local mayors. Residents of the development towns like Netivot and Sderot are left to believe that because they are living on the Israeli periphery, they matter less than residents of Tel Aviv or Haifa. In reaction, local residents have at times shut down Sderot and held general strikes in attempts to force their plight onto the political centre stage. Despite visits by the Israeli President and the installation of an early warning system for rockets, people living in the development towns still feel ignored by the Israeli elite.

On their foundation in the 1950s the towns received generous tax breaks to encourage settlement and industrial development. As the years passed, in keeping with broader socio-economic trends across Israel, the Mizrahim lost further ground in the internal Jewish class war. Towns like Netivot and Sderot experienced growing problems of unemployment and poverty.

That situation was compounded from 1977 onwards, when successive Israeli governments started to provide tax incentives and economic sweeteners to settlers in the recently conquered West Bank and Gaza Strip. This led to a transfer of economic resources away from the southern development towns. Israeli society was consumed by the practicalities and enthralled by the debates surrounding the occupation and the settlements. It was a country giddy following its victory in the 1967 War.

As a result, the development towns in the south were increasingly neglected and sidelined. The settlers and their passionate supporters who believed that they were taking part in a great divine enterprise drowned out the more everyday and less inspiring difficulties faced by working-class Jews struggling to make a living in Netivot.

Netivot, when I visited in July 2005, was a desolate place on a balmy summer evening. According to the Israeli Central Statistics Bureau, over 24,000 people lived in Netivot in 2005, almost 100 per cent of them Jewish, as the development towns have no Arab populations. The population tends to be religious and politically right-wing. In general elections since the late 1970s, it was only the right wing, particularly Likud, who have bothered putting up posters or campaigning in places like Netivot or Sderot.

The right-wing Likud party under the charismatic leadership of Menachem Begin had won the allegiance of many poor Mizrahi Jews by promising social reforms in the late 1970s. Likud's historic election victory in 1977 was built on the support of Israeli Jews like those in the development towns. The Labour party, which had ruled Israel since 1948, had become wholly identified with the Ashkenazi, the rich and powerful in society.

The historic and bitter elections of 1977 and 1981 brought the internal Jewish Ashkenazi and Mizrahi divide to the forefront of electoral politics. It helped intensify already existing intra-Jewish tensions. Ashkenazi voters regarded the Mizrahi as uncultured and their Arabic past as something that could not be part of Israeli society, while the Mizrahim viewed the Ashkenazim as a pompous, spoiled elite. When *Guardian* journalist Eric Silver attended major Labour and Likud street rallies prior to the 1981 election, his observations on the contrast between the attendees was sharp:

> The Labour meeting was relaxed, middle class, self-satisfied, warming up with the old pioneer and 1948 war songs. The Likud supporters were young, lean, dark, and strident responding to the cadencies rather than the words of Mr Begin's repetitive oration, chanting the leader's name and beating their fists in the air.

In the busy campaigning weeks prior to the March 2006 general election, something dramatic happened. The issues surrounding the decades old Mizrahim and Ashkenazim divide returned to the centre of the political agenda. The ethnicity of the Labour party candidate for Prime Minister was to lead to weeks of pre-election Jewish navel gazing.

While I was covering the election campaign for *Daily Ireland*, a Moroccan immigrant and the product of the southern development town of Sderot became a significant player in the Israeli election. A clearly identifiable Mizrahim Jew was running for the post of Prime Minister for the first time. The face of the Labour Party leader Amir Peretz, with his paternal smile underneath his trademark bushy moustache, began to make appearances on posters on the street corners of Sderot and Netivot. Not only was a North African from a poor town running for the country's top political post, he was doing so as leader of the main left-wing Zionist party, the Labour Party.

Born in Morocco in 1952, Amir Peretz's family undertook aliyah when he was just four years old. Having arrived in Israel in 1956 they eventually made their permanent home in Sderot like thousands of other poor Jewish immigrants from North Africa. Peretz served his time in the Israeli army and was badly wounded during the 1973 War. Spending a long time in a wheelchair, Peretz's young life was difficult as he tried to make a living as a poor farmer.

Despite these setbacks, Peretz became a high-ranking trade union official and one of the original supporters of the Israeli Peace Now movement that called for the end of the occupation. He was later elected mayor of his home town of Sderot. These personal triumphs were achieved by working within a system that many from his own ethnic background believed to be fundamentally biased against Mizrahi Jews.

He also had a strong track record as a peace activist and supporter of a Palestinian state, standpoints not often taken by development town residents. There was a rush of pride in the southern urban centres when Peretz came to canvass in March 2006. Locals repeatedly told Israeli journalists 'he is one of us' as they greeted the Labour leader enthusiastically.

The interest in Peretz and his challenge for the top political position in Israel generated curiosity and some optimism beyond his home region. When Peretz became leader of the Labour party in late 2005, there were upbeat mutterings from the Syrian capital Damascus and also in Ramallah. Arab leaders, who had been driven to despondency by the belligerent stance taken by Ariel Sharon towards peace negotiations, saw Peretz as a possible alternative. The veteran Israeli peace activist Uri Avnery counted Peretz's political rise, along with other factors in 2005, as resulting in a positive 'political earthquake' in Israel:

> The election of Amir Peretz constitutes a major movement of the Labour party to the real left. This is true for the solution to the Israeli-Palestinian conflict as well as for the social problem.

In many interviews, Peretz himself made a link between peace with Palestinians and the need for a fairer Israel. He spoke of the poor Jews in Israel who had been left behind by Israel's high-tech boom over the last decade. The ripples of excitement caused by Peretz's candidacy for the top political job in Israel crept in increasing circles across the country.

In the north I attended one noisy election street rally in the Arab district Wadi Nis in Haifa just days before the March election. Hundreds of members of the mainly Arab parties Balad and Hadash were waving flags in the street, handing out leaflets, organising car cavalcades, beeping horns and roaring Arabic announcements from a loudspeaker tied precariously to the roof of a minibus.

Standing slightly apart from the main crowd, there were three Labour party activists handing out leaflets. One young Jewish woman held a massive poster of Peretz in front of her chest. I learned she was a student at the local Haifa University. I was impressed by the conviction of this small band of Labour activists, who seemed willing to take their message to the heart of what was essentially an Arab political rally. The vast majority of Arabs in Israel had long since stopped voting for the Labour party. When I asked her simply, 'Why vote for Peretz?', she smiled.

'He is different. He knows that there needs to be peace, and then we can start to work on all our problems here. Like poverty and the troubles faced by the old, and how Netanyahu has ruined our economy with economic liberalism,' she said enthusiastically.

'But has this not all been said before?' I asked unconvinced.

'No, I think he is different. He has to be different, because if he is not things are just going to get worse. Even worse then they have been before,' she said pushing a leaflet into my hand.

For his supporters, Peretz's campaign heralded something new and significant for an Israeli society plagued by huge gaps between rich and poor. These Jewish class divisions often corresponded to ethnic differences between the Mizrahim and the Ashkenazim, as well as the more recent Israeli arrivals Russians and Ethiopians.

Peretz's message was one that also promised substantial moves towards potential peace with the Palestinians and Israel's neighbouring Arab countries. Peretz's candidature boosted the morale of many within the Israeli peace movement, a movement that appeared to be in terminal decline following the second intifada. Some of these campaigners invested much hope in Amir Peretz in the early months of 2006 – and hope is a scarce commodity in the Holy Land.

*

I was fishing for quotes from a Palestinian perspective on the Israeli election on my return to Bir Zeit in March 2006. Sitting down eating my falafel in the packed university canteen, I spotted Ahmed, a twenty-something former student who I had got to know a little the previous summer. I waved at him and called him over.

Ahmed was obsessed by American rap music, like many of his contemporaries. He never told me his political affiliation, but I had a strong suspicion from listening to some of his comments that he supported Hamas, at least passively. After catching up, I quizzed him about general politics.

'Has the occupation changed much here in the West Bank since the Gaza Disengagement?'
'Look, it seems simple to me,' said Ahmed. 'They have moved the settlers out of Gaza and then moved

them over here to set up home in the West Bank. Simple as that, nothing changes, you see. No matter what they say, nothing changes.'

'But because the settlements have gone from Gaza does that not give you hope that they could be removed from here in the West Bank as well?'

'No, the Israeli settlements are going to stay here – and get bigger as well. They are not going to be removed by the Israelis. They are not going to go unless they are forced to go,' he said in a matter-of-fact way.

I decided to move onto questioning about the imminent Israeli election.

'Who would you like to see win the Israeli election?'

'What?'

'What would you think would be the best outcome for the Palestinians from the Israeli election? Do you think it would be better if Ehud Olmert won rather than Likud? Or do you have any hope in the new leader of the Labour Party, Amir Peretz?'

'Look David, I do not understand all the different parties in Israel. I know nothing about the different groups like Likud, Labour ... they are all the same. I hear them mentioned on the news but I see no differ-ence at all.'

'So you have no opinion at all?' I asked a little incredul-ously.

'No. Really – I do not care who wins it. It makes no difference to me. If Likud or Labour win, when I wake up in the morning the Israeli army is still on the streets and there are still checkpoints. And we still don't have our state back. It does not matter which Israeli party wins.'

Ahmed was politically savvy and had a deep understanding of Palestinian and international history as well as contemporary Middle Eastern politics. But this blind spot when it came to Israeli politics was not one that just afflicted Ahmed. Many Palestinians I spoke to expressed a similar ignorance about Israeli domestic debates.

In a town like Bir Zeit where education and knowledge were intellectual commodities to be proud of, a large number of local Palestinians I met were honest about their lack of understanding of political forces on the other side of the Wall. Even Palestinian academics, while keeping a watchful eye on goings-on in the Knesset told me that in the end, it essentially no longer mattered who occupied the Israeli Prime Ministerial office in Jerusalem.

During an interview with Muna Giacaman, I again raised the Israeli election. After talking about the recent Hamas electoral victory and wider Israeli-Palestinian politics, Muna was indifferent towards Israeli domestic politics.

'So do you have a preference on how it goes? Do you think Palestinians would like to see Ehud Olmert lose?' I asked her

She smiled.

'No. It does not matter to us at all. It does not matter because none of the parties will do anything different. It was announced on Israeli radio this morning that Israel will declare its own borders unilaterally in two years' time. That is with no consultation with us at all. And the so-called new plan that the Israelis talk about is the plan they have always had. They are going to keep hold of the large settlements that they know they can hold onto and leave us with nothing. This was Sharon's plan, this was Shamir's plan, this was always their plan.'

'You see no difference at all between Peretz or ...'

'No. No fundamental difference for Palestinians, anyway. No matter who wins, nothing major changes,' she said while waving her hand dismissively.

In the same month I was back in the West Bank conducting my interviews, so was Amir Peretz. In early March in an obvious attempt to look statesmanlike Peretz met PA President Mahmoud Abbas at the Allenby Bridge border crossing between Israel and Jordan. This followed previous meetings between Peretz and the leaders of Morocco and Egypt.

'We have no war with the Arab or Muslim world. We are against collective punishment', Peretz told reporters following the Abbas meeting. The hand of friendship was once again outstretched from an Israeli leftist politician to the Palestinians. The PA leadership, whose power had been severely curtailed by Israel for over a decade, looked to Peretz with a mixture of minor hope and desperation.

Palestinian civilian and civic society was utterly unimpressed by the words of this Israeli politician who looked like an Arab. Israeli Nobel Prize winners and men internationally regarded as peacemakers are not often seen in the same light by Palestinians who have grown increasingly wary of self-declared Israeli doves. It seems that in Palestine there is a twist to the old anarchist maxim, that it does not matter who you vote for, the government always wins. In Palestine it does not matter who Israel votes for, the occupier always wins.

*

Israeli commentators and academics, particularly leftist Zionists would find this dismissive Palestinian attitude almost laughable. And even friends of Palestine could reasonably question whether wilful ignorance of the political nuances of internal Israeli politics would be detrimental in terms of future 'final status' negotiations. Is it not important to 'know your enemy' as thoroughly as possible to garner as much leverage as you can in both war and negotiations?

Yet the refusal of many Palestinians to differentiate between the Zionist left and right is not borne of a lack of knowledge or the result of bone-headed stubbornness in refusing to see the political complexity of Israel. It is in fact a reasonable reaction to the role both the Zionist left and right have played in the bloody history of Palestine and the abuses heaped on the Palestinian people.

The leading Zionists at the time of the creation of the Israeli state were self-styled socialists and secular Jews. The existence of the kibbutzim in Israel gave the country an appeal to many on the left internationally. One of the greatest misconceptions about Israeli life still held by people in Ireland and elsewhere is that the famous communal farms are a significant factor in the Jewish state.

The kibbutzim have, over the generations, attracted Jews and non-Jews seeking communal living and 'real', existing socialism. In the pre-state period, the kibbutzim were indeed a pivotal phenomenon. The residents were in the avant garde of the Zionist movement. The labour Zionists in particular saw in the kibbutz a micro-metaphor for the larger state. They were celebrated as small plucky outposts of communal civilisation, building a new Jewish existence in the Holy Land.

In the rapid period of national invention undertaken by the Zionists in the decades prior to the creation of Israel, the symbol of the hardy, rural kibbutz worker was key. Naturally linked with the land, this powerful, confident Jew contrasted sharply with the traditional, stereotypical image of the Jew living in the diaspora; powerless, urban and downtrodden. The kibbutzim across Israel did supply both Israel's armed forces' top brass and its political elite with a high proportion of its membership. Internationally, the myth surrounding the kibbutz was a strong attraction for young socialists, some of them Gentiles, to these small utopias living and breathing in the Holy Land.

Many kibbutzim were founded in abandoned Arab villages, or on land previously owned by Palestinians. Thus, the communes were never regarded as utopian communities by the Palestinians, but as communes for colonialists.

Over the past 20 years the kibbutz has been relegated to in the margins of Israeli life. Young international Gentiles are no longer arriving in large numbers imbued by a strong sense of idealism. This distinctively Israeli icon is today not as seductive for the young liberal backpacker. In fact, such politically motivated young people, like the late American Rachel Corrie (1979–2003), are now more likely to join the ranks of the International Solidarity Movement (ISM) in the occupied territories than to spend the summer months on an Israeli farm. Corrie was killed by an Israeli armoured bulldozer in Gaza in March 2003 while heroically attempting to stop the Israeli destruction of homes in Gaza. The Palestinians regard her as a martyr, and her memory has inspired many artistic tributes, from a very successful play to a song composed by veteran British singer-songwriter Billy Bragg. Moved by a belief in human rights many young internationals have taken huge risks in recent years and stood in front of Israeli bulldozers as they smash their way through Palestinian homes.

But the kibbutzim are not merely unattractive to internationals. They are not as appealing to Israelis either. With an increasing number of young Israelis leaving the kibbutz movement and settling down in more conventional living quarters in the suburbs or within the major cities, the population of the communal farms has drastically decreased. Over the past two decades, many of the country's communal farm population have left, and there are now just 117,000 Israelis living on the kibbutzim. A significant percentage of these kibbutz dwellers actually work outside the farms in neighbouring cities and towns. Most of the farms have begun privatisation with people able to buy and sell shares in the once communistic co-operatives. The best days of this important symbol of left-wing Zionism are well behind it.

The real and consequential differences between the right- and left-wing Zionists are minuscule on the major issues such as the need to maintain the Jewish character of the state, the Palestinian Right of Return and the settlements. If you strip away the rhetoric that marks much of the political debate in the country, even among the smaller Zionist organisations there is broad consensus on the central concerns facing the Jewish state.

*

In March 2006 there were hopes that Amir Peretz could reignite the Labour Party and the peace movement and help to heal divisions between the Mirzahim and Ashkenazim community in Israel. But if anything, the Peretz campaign for Prime Minister exposed just how deep those divides within Jewish society still go.

Veteran Ashkenazi supporters of the Labour party found it hard to accept the Moroccan-born Peretz. Some within the Jewish Russian community were also said to be turned off Peretz because of his Arabic origins. Over one million Russian immigrants live in Israel following the 'Great Alyiah' which took place after the collapse of the Soviet Union in the early 1990s. The political role played by this increasingly important sector of Jewish Israel has been much debated over the past decade. The community has its own Russian-language newspapers, TV and radio stations. After contradictory early voting patterns, the community now seems set to vote solidly for the right-wing. The Russian community has already given Israel some of its most strident anti-Arab populist politicians, like Avigdor Lieberman. It was from the Israeli Russian media that the racial attacks on Peretz were strongest. One Russian language newspaper wrote of Peretz as an 'alley cat from Sderot'. An Israeli academic I shared dinner with in the run up to the election said, 'the Russians won't vote for him because he looks like Joe Stalin.'

Amir Peretz gamely attempted to ignore these developments in his early months in the job. However in the weeks prior to the general election he finally faced the racist and arrogant attitudes emanating from some Ashkenazi voters. In a revealing pre-election interview with *Haaretz* journalist Lily Galili, Peretz, still in election mode, refused to utter the word 'racism'. He chose his words carefully when he explained the fear and hatred his candidature had provoked among some Jews.

> There is no doubt that I'm treading on one of
> the most sensitive nerves in society, as sensitive
> as a spinal nerve. I am treading very cautiously.
> If, heaven forbid, I act carelessly, I may cause
> paralysis of the entire body ... I still want to
> prove that it is possible to transform the hidden
> ethnic struggle into a class struggle.

When asked to comment on the Russian community's dislike of him and his ethnicity, Peretz said sadly, 'I knew it existed, but I didn't know it was so strong.'

The division of Jewish Israeli society into differing ethnic groups is not much commented on outside Israel. It is an issue that does much to shape the contours of Israeli politics. The country has taken in Jewish immigrants from differing cultural and linguistic sources from across the globe. Some of the waves of immigration have left lasting problems, including, for example, the Yemenite Jews.

In 1949 'Operation Magic Carpet' saw the airlift of the Yemenite Jewish community to the new State of Israel following riots in Yemen. Leading members of the Yemenite Jewish population still believe their own culture and societal system was purposely destroyed by the Israeli authorities. Even more shocking are the allegations surrounding the theft of hundreds of Yemenite children stolen from their parents and sent to Ashkenazi couples. These abductions continue to leave a lasting wound within the Yemenite sector in Israel. A 2001 Israeli commission of inquiry into the disappearance of the Yemenite children 'unequivocally rejected claims of an all-inclusive establishment plot to take children away from Yemenite immigrants and hand them over to childless families for adoption', reported *Haaretz*. The commission findings were not accepted by many leaders of the Yemenite community. However, the commission did look into the cases of 1,033 missing children. The commission also blamed the authorities for a lack of proper contact with the families involved.

Because of Peretz's campaign, ethnic and socio-economic differences among the Israeli Jewish community became a significant topic in the 2006 general election. Yet its importance should not be overemphasised. Despite the discontent felt by many Jewish immigrants from African and Arab states about their treatment, they remain very loyal to Zionism. The same is true for the most recent *aliyahs*, with hundreds of thousands of Jews from the former Soviet Union and a much smaller number from Ethiopia. Amir Peretz himself never looked to win support in the Arab community within Israel, he was looking to unite only Jews of different ethnic backgrounds.

It is one of the central ironies of modern Israeli life, that although popular and official culture is dominated by an Ashkenazi, Western, and some would argue anti-Arab world view, 20 per cent of the population is Palestinian Arab and a significant section of the Jewish population actually heralds from Arab cultural backgrounds. Nevertheless any political linkages between what are essentially Arabic Jews and Palestinian Arabs along ethnic, cultural or political lines was and remains almost impossible.

Israeli society holds quite an extraordinarily diverse Jewish community together. The vast majority of Israeli Jews who have made *aliyah* to Israel from well over 100 countries, speaking a myriad of languages, and hailing from different ethnic groups and starkly contrasting cultural backgrounds find a common national identity. Shared experience during mandatory service in the Israeli Defence Force further helps to forge bonds within Israel.

The Mizrahi Jewish poor within Israel are still discriminated against. However, they are treated much better than the Arabs of Israel and those who live in the occupied territories. Their privileges are based on the Zionist nature of the state, as a state of the Jewish people. So regardless of how deep disenfranchisement within the poor Mizrahim working-class community may get, it is difficult to see any open break from the Zionist state by the community.

So while Jewish ethnic division is a source of concern, for many Israelis (and Amir Peretz's campaign certainly exposed fault lines within Jewish Israel) it is the iniquitous power relations between Jews and Arabs in Israel and the occupied territories that remain the central cause of violence and instability within the region.

*

The young settler supporter was standing on the Ben Yehuda side of Zion Square in West Jerusalem. It was a glorious morning. She was fixed behind a portable table, with orange ribbons hanging from each of its legs. Graphic photographs of Gaza settlers struggling with Israeli soldiers as they were pulled from their homes were taped to the front of the table.

Behind the table sat a large stereo system pumping out what sounded like traditional Hebrew music accompanied by a furious dance beat. It was blaring out across the quiet empty streets of commercial West Jerusalem. The shopping day was yet to get fully underway. Four or five young men wearing orange ribbons around their wrists were walking around Zion Square handing out leaflets.

I went up to speak to the young female activist. She said she was only 16, born in Jerusalem. She did not know much about Ireland, in fact I had my doubts whether she had ever heard of it.

'Do you mean Scotland?'

'No, Ireland. It's beside England,' I said helpfully.

'Like Scotland, that's beside England as well,' she said smiling.

She had not attended the Kfar Maimon protest the previous summer, because her parents thought her too young to go:

'It was Jewish land and other Jews took Jews off it,' she said angrily when recalling the Gaza disengagement the previous summer.

I asked her about the Palestinians who lived there.

'You know when the Arabs took over the hothouses and greenhouses at Gush Katif the plants died. Gush Katif was famous for the vegetables and herbs it grew, people loved them across Israel. It is not the Arabs' fault that the plants and vegetables did not grow. I do not blame them. They could not grow the same crops and vegetables. They could not do it, because the land was for the Jews, and only the Jews could make things grow there.'

She asked me where I had been on my trip. I thought it conversationally safer to focus on my itinerary west of the Green Line, rather than my time in the occupied territories.

'Did you like Tel Aviv?' she asked when I mentioned I had been there.

'Well, I was only there a few days,' I answered diplomatically.

'It is so different than here. It is almost like a different country.'

The differences between Tel Aviv and Jerusalem expose the growing gulf in experience between the secular and religious in Israel. If you walk along the streets of Tel Aviv or in the beautiful, middle-class, residential areas built along the side of Mount Carmel in Haifa you see no overt signs of religion at all. The neighbourhoods are much like modern areas in Western cities. In contrast, when you step into the Meah Shearim neighbourhood in Jerusalem you are practically stepping into another century. The Haredi population live in a close-knit community around Meah Shearim Street, in what looks much like a nineteenth-century Jewish neighbourhood in Eastern Europe, a shtetl. Traditional dress is the norm, with slight variations for each of the different ultra-orthodox sub-groups. Large signs erected on walls plead with women to 'dress modestly' when walking through the neighbourhood.

Many religious Jews were not supporters of the Israeli state when it was founded in 1948. They believed the creation of the state should have waited until the coming of the Messiah, at some as yet unspecified future date. Israel itself was founded primarily by thoroughly secular Zionists, who wanted to create a predominantly religious-free state. Following the 1967 War, the majority of religious Jews began to support the Israeli state, with a minority still opposed for theological reasons. The rapid success in the War against so many enemies was celebrated as an act of God. With such apparent heavenly intervention on the side of the Israeli state, leading religious Jews began to rethink their opposition.

Despite growing support among religious Jews, large swathes of modern Israel are relatively non-religious places. Trips to major cities like Tel Aviv and Haifa can certainly be undertaken without ever coming into contact with overt symbols or practitioners of the Jewish faith. Secular and religious education is kept separate, and popular Israeli culture is secular, Western and heavily influenced by America. However, the state is Jewish. It is the self-declared state of the world's entire Jewish population.

At the state's foundation the secular Zionists struck a deal with Orthodox Judaism in order to garner some support. The so-called 'status quo agreement' was signed. This meant that the state would respect the Jewish Sabbath and religious festivals. Personal status law, dealing with marriage, divorce and religious conversions are governed by orthodox rabbinical courts. This is a source of huge anger among many divorced secular Jews who sometimes have to leave Israel and travel to neighbouring Cyprus to get remarried. The laws also discriminate against other strands of religious Judaism, such as Reform or Conservative Jews who do not follow the teachings of the orthodox rabbis.

The tension between the secular and religious in Israel is constant and is often reflected in politics. Religious Ashkenazi Jews often vote for religious parties such as the National Religious Party (NRP), while religious Mizrahi Jews vote for the Likud or Shas parties. On the secular side, those who were really disgruntled with the religious influence on politics voted for parties such as Shinui, which stood on a strongly anti-religious platform and won an amazing 15 seats in the 2003 elections. Many secular Jews were resentful of the amount of money poured into religious education and the exemption from military service for religious Jews.

This virtual *Kulturkampf* at the heart of Israeli society often enters public discourse and the media at a time of a religious festival or during the annual row surrounding the Jerusalem Gay Pride Parade. The differences between the secular and religious Jewish community is not only reflected in politics, but also geographically. The most extreme contrast is the one between the two largest cities, avowedly secular Tel Aviv and strongly religious West Jerusalem. Tel Aviv has an active gay scene, while in Jerusalem, gay pride marches are denounced and attacked by religious activists. On the Shabbat in Tel Aviv, most shops, bars and clubs are open, but on the streets of West Jerusalem not even a car drives past, in line with strict religious rulings. In the 2006 election, the Torah and Shabbat Judaism party received 19 per cent of the vote in Jerusalem, but less than 2 per cent in Tel Aviv.

*

Following a lacklustre election campaign, my assignment was over and I left Israel in late March 2006. As I waited in the departure lounge of Ben-Gurion airport, tired after a fortnight of extensive travel, I languidly read the English-language Israeli papers. They were already focussing on the post election fallout and had begun to dissect the bartering process. The intrigues, meetings and promises had started among all the parties. Acting Prime Minister Ehud Olmert, leader of the largest party, Kadima, was attempting to cobble together a new governing coalition.

Amir Peretz's Labour party won 19 seats in the election, hardly a 'revolution' but a credible showing. He had won the same number of seats that the party had managed in the 2003 elections. While pushing some older Ashkenazi voters away from the party, Peretz had obviously also won some new working-class Mizrahim support from voters who had traditionally gone with Likud.

Kadima and Labour were quickly emerging as the major players in a four-party coalition. Amir Peretz was given the option of taking the Finance Ministry. In Finance, he could have had an instant impact on the lives of the Jewish poor. However, he plumbed for the second most important job in Israel, Minister of Defence. Hopes were already fading for those who had placed them in Peretz.

Peretz was a man with no high-profile military career. It was predicted that he would come under severe pressure from much of Israeli society to quickly demonstrate he was 'tough on terrorism'. Concerns about his previous peace activism and support for a Palestinian state would mean that Peretz would have to prove that he could be trusted with Israel's security.

But wait. Maybe Peretz, with his long-cherished and publicly-stated hopes for peace and justice could reign in the more militaristic aspects of Israeli 'security policy'. Maybe he could buck the trend and argue from a prominent position in Israeli politics for a fundamental re-think on the occupation of Palestine. He told Abbas at Allenby Bridge that he was 'against collective punishment'. That was certainly a start. As my plane took off from Tel Aviv airport I thought that surely, as the young Labour canvasser in Haifa had told me, Peretz would be different simply because he had to be.

*

The first day of August 2006 was a dramatic one in the Knesset. A packed and expectant chamber was sitting in emergency session. The Israeli war with Hezbollah had raged for a month. The Israeli bombing and invasion of southern Lebanon, and the Hezbollah rocket attacks on northern Israeli towns had focused the world's attention once more on the Holy Land. What would become known as the Second Lebanon War was reaching a crucial phase. Israeli Defence Minister and Labour party leader Amir Peretz rose to defend attacks that the Israeli military had carried out on towns and cities across Lebanon. With his round, warm face and newly-trimmed moustache, Peretz had only begun to speak when he was loudly and angrily heckled. Arab members of the Knesset screamed 'baby-killer' at him. There was uproar. Arab politician Ibrahim Sarsur was ordered to leave the hall by the Knesset chair.

Mr Sarsur was verbalizing what much of the Arab world was thinking. As of Sunday, 30 July, Peretz was a 'baby-killer' in the eyes of the Lebanese and Palestinians.

The Israeli Air Force attacked the southern Lebanese village of Qana on 30 July, killing at least 28 civilians, half of them children. This was just one attack of many in which Lebanese civilians would lose their lives in

Israeli aerial bombardments. When the conflict with Hezbollah began in early July, Peretz's language had been embarrassingly bellicose. He warned the Hezbollah leader Sayyed Hassan Nasrallah that he would 'never forget the day he heard the name Amir Peretz'.

It was clear now that the civilians of Qana and southern Lebanon would never forget the name of the former peace activist from Sderot. The Lebanese war had been preceded by weeks of heavy air attacks on the Gaza Strip ordered by the Israeli government with many Palestinians losing their lives. The civilians in Gaza now knew Peretz's name as well.

Peretz defended the attacks in Lebanon and Gaza as responses to the kidnapping of a handful of Israeli soldiers and the firing of rockets by Palestinians and Hezbollah. However the majority of the world did not agree. Israel's military response was condemned as disproportionate in most international capitals, except, of course, in Washington and London.

The one-time peace activist was now ordering the brutal bombing of Lebanon and Gaza. Mr Peretz's recent political life shows how morally corrupting Israeli politics can be. Even many of the so-called left-wingers and peace camps in Israel end up carrying out horrific actions. The Zionist left in Israel, despite what it and international supporters might say to the contrary, is in fact wholly complicit in the Palestinian occupation and the troubles that result in the region.

Another leftist, dovish politician had briefly raised hopes only to prove them false.

I received an email from a Palestinian friend on the West Bank just after the war in southern Lebanon ended. I asked him about the role Peretz had played in the conflict. He wrote back, 'with Israeli doves like these, who needs hawks?'

10

Apocalypse Now?

I was standing and staring at the photograph of a chicken. I had stopped to flick through newspapers on a newsstand located on a pathway in Afula. As I looked at the English papers, I spotted a picture story in one of the many Hebrew tabloids. The dramatic and amusing splash seized my attention. The story looked unique in that it was not focused on the 'conflict'.

Bizarrely, there was a close-up of a chicken standing upright with a strange, stoical look about it. The newspaper sub-editor had inserted a huge circle around the seemingly proud bird's head. From this circle came a line that pointed towards a screaming headline in Hebrew. I could not understand it. But I gathered from the font size and design that it was some catchy, witty tabloid headline in a style familiar to readers of the British and Irish press.

A young man wearing a baseball cap, sports T-shirt and jeans was walking towards me along the pedestrian path in Afula, a Jewish city in northern Israel. The uninspiring inland town is not on the tourist trail in Israel. Nonetheless, to get from Nazareth to Jerusalem by bus I had to stop off there for a few hours.

'Hi, do you speak English?' I asked, motioning with my hand at the cap-wearing pedestrian.

'Yes.'

I pointed towards the chicken story.

'What does that say?'

He glanced at the page and sniggered.

'It is saying that this is the bird that has brought Bird Flu to Israel.'

The potential Bird Flu pandemic had made headlines across the world in late 2005 and the early part of 2006. Scare stories about a possible global outbreak had hit the headlines of the Irish press and consumed much air time on the radio talk shows before I had departed for Israel. Concerns were raised in Ireland over whether the state was prepared to deal with an outbreak. The devastation it could cause to the European farming sector concentrated the minds of many politicians and experts. Fear, speculation, misunderstanding and tension were the abiding aspects of much of the international media coverage. It had whipped itself up into a dangerously powerful storm that would later quickly blow itself out and dissipate as rapidly as it had begun.

I already knew that Bird Flu had reached the Holy Land, but this was the first time I had seen a local newspaper do a feature on it. The general reaction to the outbreak seemed much less intense in Israel then it had been elsewhere in the world.

'You're not worried about this?' I asked, smiling.

The man shrugged his shoulders and smiled back.

'No, no. There are many more things that can kill us here than a fucking chicken. The end of the world will begin here, OK, but man, I don't think any of the religions believe it is going to be from a fucking chicken. 'Chicken,' he laughed. 'Where are you from?'

'Ireland.'

'Ireland, great! I am going to Ireland next year. Plenty of bars yes? Please tell me there are plenty of bars and drink?'

I was able to answer him in the affirmative. He continued happily on his journey following my unequivocal promise of the almost unlimited alcohol that my island would provide for him. I spoke to more people about the end of the world on my visits to the Holy Land between 2005 and 2008 than I had in my whole life up until then.

The site that will apparently host the last battle on earth as prophesied by St John in the Book of Revelations is located in northern Israel. Megiddo is now a national park, but many doomsday watchers believe that it is there and in Jerusalem that the final acts during Armageddon will happen.

I spent the last few nights before the Israeli election in March 2006 in Jaffa and Tel Aviv. I had already carried out a series of set-piece political interviews during my first week of coverage. Now I was trying to talk to young Jewish people for my *Daily Ireland* reports. My journalistic technique was simple, and one that lay outside the mainstream Holy Land beat of press conferences, political interviews and discussions with local media. I went in to a pub or café, sat up at the bar and tried to talk to anyone who came in and sat anywhere near me. Few wanted to discuss the impending vote or the occupation. Other issues, like the division between the secular and religious were more prevalent. But one topic that exploded into most conversations was the looming global catastrophe now originating in Tehran that Israelis feared.

One liquid night in the bohemian Florentine district of Tel Aviv I got talking to a curly-haired Jewish guy in his late twenties and his girlfriend. He was out celebrating his friend's thirtieth birthday. Our amicable conversation was conducted while screaming over some God-awful, deafening Israeli dance music. Our discussion focussed less on politics and more on Israeli pop and rock trends. The state of the local music scene was generally good, he claimed. He was dreadfully disappointed when I replied in the negative to knowledge of a number of local acts he listed for me. He, like other Israelis I spoke to, was angered by the world's top bands and artists who did not include a show in Israel as part of their world tours. He chiefly blamed the Palestinians for the violence that kept these artists away. I asked him if he had any plans for his own thirtieth.

'I won't see that. It is a few years away and I don't think I will see it,' went his extremely gloomy reply. It was one that was out of context in his generally upbeat party mood.
    'What?'
    'I won't be here for that, I don't believe so, anyway,' he said again.
    'Why?'
    'I am very pessimistic, to tell you the truth, my Irish friend.'

'How so?'

'I think Iran will attack here. Or something even more likely, I think there will be a huge dirty bomb exploded in Tel Aviv, something chemical or nuclear. It is so easy to do now and there are people who want to do it. Just put the bomb in a suitcase. We have to be a prime target for that, and I think it is coming.'

'Really?'

'Yes, really! You look surprised. You're supposed to be a journalist! Do you not read the news?'

'You are talking about the Iranian President,' I said.

'Yes, I am talking about him. Would you like it if a leader of a country near to Ireland was saying he wanted to wipe you out? And in a totally unrelated issue, of course, he wanted to get a nuclear bomb! Come on, would you not be worried? Would you not think, "this could happen", would you not want to get drunk thinking about it?' he laughed and slapped me on the back good-naturedly.

'But say he did attack, although I think it very unlikely. He would kill many Palestinian Arabs as well. He is supposed to be on their side,' I said, trying to tease out a more detailed response.

'Yes, but these people do not care about Palestinian or Israeli Arabs. Look, it is my friend's birthday over there,' he said pointing to about ten young people huddled in the corner of the bar.

'That is our group of friends, the guy on the right is a great guy, he is a loyal Arab. We are all friends together. We need to forget about all this and enjoy the rest of the night. I thought you Irish loved to enjoy yourself. He lifted his glass and took a deep swig of beer.'

'Israel has nuclear weapons as well, and Iran has not said it wants to develop weapons,' I said.

'Look my friend. Yes, we have, but we will not use

them. We are civilised. The man in Tehran is a madman. Olmert is not the best, and I will not be voting in the election, but he is not a madman like the Iranian leader.'

I told him I was leaving the bar anyway and politely refused his offer to join his friends and the 'loyal Arab' for further drinks. Drinking and laughing mixed with visions of potential destruction and annihilation.

*

He looked very unthreatening, even though he was one of the most hated men in Israel. Mordechai Vanunu sat in the corner with his legs crossed. He gazed towards the ground as we entered the room. His handshake was limp, and when he spoke it was slow and deliberate. It was little wonder that a man who had spent 18 years in prison, 11 of which in solitary confinement, would have somewhat stunted social skills. In fact, Vanunu gave a sense of stoic, assured self-restraint. He was still confident in his own righteousness, despite being domestic enemy number one for the Israeli state.

Since his 2004 release, he was banned from talking to foreigners and journalists about his incarceration and continuing legal difficulties. He completely ignored this. Speaking to a small audience of both foreigners and journalists in his new Jerusalem refuge, he told us his well-known biography.

His father was a Moroccan rabbi and immigrated to Israel in 1963. Vanunu studied mathematics and physics and was later employed by the Israeli state as a nuclear technician. He worked at the Negev Nuclear Research Centre in Dimona in southern Israel. He grew increasingly troubled at the secret Israeli nuclear programme. In

1986, he became one of the world's most famous whistleblowers when he leaked the shocking news that Israel had nuclear weapons to *The Sunday Times*. The Israeli state was greatly angered and used a 'honey trap' to capture Vanunu who was then staying in Rome. A female Mossad agent seduced Vanunu, and he was drugged and smuggled back to Israel by the Israeli secret service. Back in Israel he faced charges of treason and espionage. In 1988, he was sentenced to 18 years in prison. He was not released until 2004.

Because of his leak, it became known that Israel was the only state with nuclear weapons in the Middle East. Despite UN resolutions, Israel does not allow international supervision at its nuclear facilities. It is now believed to have at least 100 nuclear weapons and was the sixth country in the world to develop nuclear weapons capability. Israel has not signed the Nuclear Non-Proliferation Treaty (NPT). The Vanunu disclosure made neighbouring Arab states aware that they were living under the shadow of a potential mushroom cloud.

On his release, Vanunu remained unapologetic about his revelations. He had converted to Christianity and he found refuge in the beautiful St George's Cathedral complex in Jerusalem. That is where we met Vanunu a little over a year after he was released. When we spoke to him, the international media was full of the 'growing Iranian nuclear threat'. Vanunu was a little amused. With his campaigning in favour of nuclear disarmament, Vanunu has become a hero for much of the international peace movement. When we asked about the Gaza Disengagement, and the talk of the future possibility of peace, Vanunu was cynical.

'I demonstrated against Sharon in 1983 and 1984 [during the Israeli occupation of Lebanon] and other times during that period ... Now he stands before the world as a man of peace ... Can you believe that Ariel Sharon is a man of peace?'

He delivered his lines slowly, like a man who was not in a hurry.

'When we were demonstrating all those years ago, we could not believe that one day Sharon would actually become Prime Minister,' he continued.

Many of Israel's supporters now argue that nuclear capability is essential to protect itself from neighbours such as Iran, an Iran that they maintain is intent on Israel's destruction. Not surprisingly, Vanunu disagreed:

'The way that the international community should deal with Iran is by dealing with Israel's nuclear weapons first and show that there are no double standards,' he said.

'The proliferation of nuclear weapons across the region makes the Middle East more unsafe. Nuclear weapons are used by countries to dictate to others, they are used for power. They do not provide security. They are weapons that create genocide and the state of the Jewish people should be a state that should be most against such weapons,' concluded Vanunu.

*

The perception that Israel is permanently on the verge of existential extinction is one that continues to profoundly shape the collective consciousness of Jewish Israelis and the country's supporters internationally. Israel, a small, plucky, Spartan state has been created by a people who have been victimised for centuries. It is now surrounded by nations of millions bent on its destruction. An oasis of Western-style democracy in the desert of corruption and despots, the Arabs have tried and failed to destroy Israel because of the country's brave defence forces. Yet Israel must live day to day with the knowledge that its neighbours want to destroy it. An Arab desire to 'drive Jews into the sea' fuelled by hatred and a seething anti-Semitism.

Such a perception, although powerful, stands up to little objective scrutiny. Israel is a tremendous military power that can easily defeat its neighbours in full scale conflict. It is also a state that has the complete military and economic backing of the most powerful nation the world has ever seen. Some of its Arab neighbours have signed peace treaties with Israel, while others have made offers that have been rejected by Israel. Finally and most significantly, Israel is not the nation that in the present conflict with the Palestinians is fearful and oppressed. Rather, it is Israel that holds the position of power and aggression as the illegal and unwanted occupier. Despite these facts, ever-present concerns of absolute destruction move Israeli political leaders to action, or more often, are cynically used by them to whip up public support for military ventures.

Ordinary Israelis who worry about their future bemoan the prospect of conflict with neighbouring Arab states. Those who fear the absolute destruction of their state are moved to sadness and depression because this is a state they love and want to see survive. In contrast, many of Israel's most powerful and significant 'friends' around the world dream of a future war of annihilation in the Middle East, not with sorrow, but with barely-concealed excitement.

The Christian Zionist movement in the United States is the Jewish state's most unlikely supporter. Unlike the Israeli Jews they call their allies, they wish for the biblical Apocalypse to begin as soon as possible. The preachers and leaders of the movement eagerly count down the days like young children waiting for Santa to deliver presents at Christmas. This hyperactive excitement exists despite the almost unimaginable death and destruction that these Christians predict for the region. It will be a biblical destruction during which many of the Jews of Israel, among others, will perish in large numbers on the rapidly disintegrating earth. While at the same time, the Christian Zionists will conveniently enjoy eternal happiness in a more agreeable celestial location.

Israel and the occupied territories are replete with Christian holy sites. Until the outbreak of the second intifada, thousands of Christian pilgrims arrived in the Holy Land from across the globe. Visitors from traditionally Christian countries like Ireland took bus tours to Jerusalem. They walked in the footsteps of the condemned Christ, the Via Dolorosa (Way of Sorrow), praying at the Stations of the Cross, each closer to the site of Christ's eventual crucifixion.

They would wander within the dark corridors of the Church of the Holy Sepulchre, see the various Christian sects who jealously guard their small patches of territory within the building purportedly built upon the site where Christ perished on the cross. The bus tour would also drop into Nazareth, where the young Jesus became a man and began to inspire his followers. The tour would probably enter the occupied West Bank, with an Israeli tour operator of course, and drive to the birthplace of Jesus, the mainly Palestinian Christian town of

Bethlehem. But the rise in bloodshed since 2000 has brought with it a collapse in the number of Christian pilgrims visiting Israel. Understandably, parish tours and most religious congregations have been unwilling to ignore the obvious security risks involved.

With the general tourist sector depressed in Israel, the authorities were happy to see that the American evangelical Christian community kept on visiting the Holy Land despite the intifada. These tourists seemed more battle-hardened and willing to ignore the security threat. If anything, the sharp rise in the intensity of the conflict encouraged more Christian Zionists to come to Israel. A conflict that for some indicated a possible move towards an apocalyptic time.

But if you expect to see these visitors in large tour groups on the usual Christian pilgrimage trail, you will be disappointed. American Christian evangelical itineraries tend to relegate Bethlehem, Nazareth and the site of Jesus's final crucifixion to positions of less importance. Rather, the Christian Zionist tourist is more interested in visiting the classical landmarks of Judaism, the Western Wall, the Jewish sector of the Old City of Jerusalem and modern manifestations of the Israeli state, such as the settlements and the military industrial complexes. It is the final book of the Bible, Revelations, that inspires these people with its lyrical prophesies of global doom. They seem rather less interested in the passages from the gospels where Christ preached peace and cooperation as life's central message.

The evangelical Christian movement makes up a significant section of the 51 per cent of Americans who call themselves Protestant. Its power base within the Republican

Party that it has built in recent decades has been well chronicled by US social commentators and journalists. The two presidential election victories of George W. Bush owe much to this influential sector of society. Hundreds of thousands of evangelical Christians were the theologically-driven foot soldiers of both election campaigns. Through a wide network of community groups, churches, websites, Christian talk-radio shows and TV stations they have had a massive impact on US national politics over the past decade. This influence has come to bear on various areas of policy. In social affairs, the President and his party have reflected the concerns of the evangelical Christians by being strongly anti-abortion, anti-gay marriage and sometimes even questioning evolution. In the realm of foreign policy and the 'War on Terror', the movement has also had a major impact.

Yet it is on Palestine and Israel that some in the evangelical Christian movement have firmly set their sights. The Christian Zionist movement is a sub-set of the wider evangelical community within the United States. The movement's influence on the Bush administration's policy towards the occupation and conflict has been great. The guiding principle of this influence has not been the pursuit of peace and justice between Israelis and Palestinians. Rather the motivation for the movement is to be found deep within the dense text of the Book of Revelations. Its endgame is not the creation of a peaceful two-state solution, but to create the conditions in the Holy Land from which the Apocalypse will begin.

Christian Zionism is growing in organisational strength and influence in the US. Born within the evangelical Christian movement, its adherents argue that the creation of the Israeli state and the return of the Jews to the

Holy Land are events foretold in the Bible. Prophecy also states that, among other things, the Jews will inhabit the entire land of Israel and the Jewish Temple will be rebuilt on the Temple Mount in Jerusalem.

Such events will bring on the end time, the second coming, Christ's followers will be saved, the non-believers will be damned and the Apocalypse will take place. By sticking to this strict futurist timetable of events, the Christian Zionist movement have taken positions on internal Israeli matters, sometimes completely at odds with the opinions and interests of the majority of Israeli Jews. For example, the Christian Zionist movement was against the disengagement from Gaza, because to pull Jewish settlers from the biblical land of Israel would further delay the second coming. One of the leading figures in the evangelical movement, Pat Robertson, publicly speculated that Ariel Sharon's subsequent stroke resulted from God's displeasure with the Gaza plan.

Christian Zionists in the west provide finance and support to some of the most extreme organisations in Israel. A plan to build a new Jewish Temple on the Temple Mount in Jerusalem's Old City is also high on their pre-apocalyptic wish list. Such a construction, supported by only the most right-wing extreme Israeli Jews, would require the destruction of the Dome of the Rock and the Al-Aqsa Mosques currently located on the most contested piece of real estate on the planet. These buildings combine to make up the third holiest site in Islam. Their removal or destruction would provoke apoplectic anger in the Muslim world and spark a regional and possibly global conflict. For this pertinent reason and others, most Israeli Jews would not support such a dramatic measure. But regional and global conflict is all part of the Christian Zionists' jolly timeline, all pointing towards the Apocalypse and Christ's return.

One of my flatmates in Bir Zeit was a young American student who was studying Arabic in his home country. One day after a trip to Jerusalem, he told us about comments he had overheard on a tour of the Tower of David in the Old City. The tower is a restored citadel located close to the Jaffa Gate entrance to the Old City. It is an interesting mix of a building, containing within its walls physical remnants of various religious and political periods of rule in the great city. The tour and exhibition is excellent, although it follows a predictable Zionist narrative with all the inclusions and exclusions to the story of Jerusalem that you would expect.

My flatmate was strolling through the museum when he started to walk alongside an official tour. Most of the people in the tour were American visitors. One of the models on display shows the magnificent Dome of the Rock, whose searing golden beauty dazzles the old city's sky line. The Israeli tour guide spoke of the history of the structure and the importance of it in the Muslim world and as part of Islam's key role in the city's history. At that, one of the American tourists spoke up and added his comments on one of the most cherished and celebrated buildings in the world.

'Why don't we just get rid of it?' he said brutally.

'Sorry sir, what do you mean?' said the Israeli tour guide hesitantly.

'I mean why don't we just get rid of it? By just keeping it there, it gives the Arabs hope, false hope, that they can have Jerusalem. It is better for everyone if it was just got rid of.'

The Israeli guide mumbled something inaudible in response and quickly moved his group on to the next exhibit.

The casual destruction inherent in the American tourist's interjection is typical of much of the cheerleading from Israel's extreme supporters in the US. Tending on the side of violence, these supporters show little regard for what the actual implementation of their desires would mean on the ground for Jews as well as Arabs.

The Christian Zionist movement has sunk roots deep within Israel, particularly in Jerusalem. Opening offices, lobbying politicians and intervening to promote their unique views on how the conflict should be 'resolved'. It is perhaps telling that when the late Palestinian writer and intellectual Edward Said returned to visit his old Jerusalem home that his family had fled in 1948, it was not inhabited by a Jewish family as he had expected, but the offices of a Christian Zionist organisation. That Said's family were Palestinian Christians adds a further ironic twist to his own tragic history.

While Zionism was partially a product of virulent European anti-Semitism, its secular followers, such as David Ben-Gurion, believed the movement to be a part of modern European Enlightenment thinking. Rather than seeing it as a militaristic colonial project, Zionists regarded it as modernist and civilising. In contemporary Israel, the influence of the United States now far outweighs that of Europe in the arena of popular culture as well as politics. Some Israelis bemoan this, arguing that a closer reliance on Europe, rather than a hawkish Washington administration, would be preferable. At the same time, they also criticise the growing influence American pop culture has on the young.

But the Israeli political establishment is firmly wedded to the US, even to such an extent that an alliance with the evangelical Christian movement is encouraged by the Israeli government. This despite the fact that much of the evangelical motivation for support for Israel does not come from any intrinsic long-term concern for Israeli Jews or the State of Israel itself, but rather from a theological desire to begin the Apocalypse, an event in which, as many evangelical Christian theologians agree, Jews will not as fare well, with many perishing and facing eternal damnation.

The alliance between the Israeli state and the US Christian Zionist movement is one of the most bizarre in contemporary world politics. It may have short- and medium-term political benefits for Israel, but its long-term consequences may not be so advantageous.

*

If Israel is not blessed with the best international friends, at least they are powerful. Hundreds of thousands of activists, global justice campaigners and ordinary citizens across the world support the Palestinian cause, but in the corridors of power, particularly of the world's superpower, the Palestinian case is not often championed. The Palestinians are not so fortunate when it comes to the political states that actually do express rhetorical loyalty to their struggle.

One night in Rami's restaurant in Bir Zeit, I got talking to a local Palestinian, Khaled, about university. He said that he could not afford to attend the local Bir Zeit University.

'It costs too much money, I really would like to go to university but it is just not possible,' he said forlornly. 'My cousin who is a refugee went to university in Iraq,' he added.

'Iraq?' I said surprised.

'Yes. Saddam was good to the Palestinians. He treated us well. University was cheap for the Palestinians in Iraq.'

I was a little shocked at this information.

'I know he did not treat his own people well,' Khaled continued, 'but he did care about the Palestinians. At least he was someone who cared about us.'

On one side of the Manara Square in Ramallah you can purchase black and white chalk portrait drawings of some of the leading figures in the Arab world. The prominence that each painting receives in the display is a good guide as to how the Palestinian public regards the local Arab potentates. The late Yasser Arafat's picture is front and centre, while current Palestinian leader Mahmoud Abbas is towards the back, beside the leader of Hezbollah. One picture always at the front is of a young, suave-looking Saddam Hussein. The former Iraqi President is unshaven, while smiling and smoking a cigar. There are good reasons why the late Baghdad despot garnered support among Palestinians, while the rest of the world despised him.

While most Arab states talked of striking out against the 'Zionist entity', Saddam actually did. During the First Gulf War, Palestinians on the West Bank stood on their flat-roofed buildings and cheered at Saddam's SCUD missiles as they soared low overhead towards Tel Aviv. The missiles struck various neighbourhoods in Israel, but they were inaccurate, many were shot down by the Israelis with American support and some of the SCUDs were empty. Some Arab dictators supported the intifada with flowery rhetoric. Saddam sent money to the families of suicide bombers and Palestinians wounded during the uprising.

Most of all, Saddam never ceased his proclamations of fidelity to the Palestinian cause, no matter how difficult the situation. In March 2003 at the height of the US-led invasion, Saddam made his final appearance on Iraqi state TV. In an awful maudlin address as befitting a dictator who was watching his rule crumble, Saddam's final words on Iraqi TV were not addressed to Iraqis, but to the Palestinians.

> God is great, and let the losers lose. Let Iraq
> live. Long live Jihad and long live Palestine!

A little more than three years later, in the video recorded on a mobile phone that the whole world saw, Saddam defiantly roared out again, 'Long live the people! Long live the Palestinians!' The hooded hangman then roughly wrapped the noose around Saddam's neck.

Many Palestinians would have felt pride pulsate through their bones when they heard Saddam make these defiant statements. Yes, they knew he was a murderer, the head of a reprehensible regime that crushed human rights and in the case of the Kurds, their national rights. But when you are in a dismal position like the Palestinians, support from any sector whatsoever is gratefully accepted.

If you listened to the official statements from the Arab governments, you would assume they were going to liberate the occupied territories in the morning. The tightly-controlled media in the dictatorial regimes across the Middle East launch daily attacks on the 'Zionist entity' while praising the Palestinian resistance.

I visited the Syrian capital just after its so-called elections in May 2007. The posters from that election were plastered everywhere on the walls. They all displayed the only standing candidate for the presidency, Bashar al-Assad. Unsurprisingly, al-Assad won the election with a fulsome 97.62 per cent. The Syrian Interior Minister told journalists that the result showed 'the political maturity of Syria and the brilliance of our democracy'. Beside the pictures of the Syrian leader were many Palestinian flags fluttering in the dry air. On the radio, there were clearly many references to Palestine distinguishable even though my Arabic is poor. Assad has tried to manoeuvre himself into a leading role in the Palestinian cause. Arab leaders always talk but do little about Palestine.

Their motivations for highlighting the Palestinian plight are suspect. It cannot principally be a concern for human rights that motivates the Arab leadership. They rule countries that severely curtail the rights of their citizens. In fact a functioning, democratic Palestine could destabilise their rule and act as an inspiration for their own people looking for democratic reform. Simple notions of Pan-Arab solidarity cannot explain it either. Anyone remotely acquainted with the history of bitter rivalry between the Arab states in modern times would be aware that solidarity with their Arab neighbours is not always top of their agenda.

Many commentators believe that the Arab despots use anger at the Israeli occupation to divert discontentment and frustration from within their own countries. Calls for greater economic, social and political reform are deflected by focusing everything onto the Palestinian situation. The Arab leadership helps to deflect potential anger against its own rule, channelling it into anger against the Israeli state. The Palestinians are the pawns in this geo-political game.

Nonetheless, it must also be said that opinion polls have shown that there is widespread sympathy, concern and solidarity among the ordinary citizens of the Arab states for the Palestinians and their liberation struggle. The Arab street is solidly behind the Palestinian cause and unlike their rulers they have no ulterior motive. They want to see the Palestinians gain their freedom, with Jerusalem as their capital.

*

I sat on one of the benches along the Tel Aviv promenade not far away from the Old Jaffa port. Watching the hand-gliders work their aerial magic across the bright blue sky, I sipped at my hot Arabic coffee.

At the next bench to my right two Ethiopian Jews were working, painting the arms and legs of the empty seaview seat. They sauntered through their work speaking to each other slowly and sporadically in Hebrew. In the burning hot spotlight of the afternoon sun, work was always going to take place at a snail's pace.

To my left, a couple of American tourists in their sixties wandered down the promenade. They fitted the cliché well: he wore casual sports gear with a bum bag over his shorts. She was talking loudly to him, complaining good-humouredly about the sticky heat and his failure to keep pace with her slightly more rapid strides.

He bid me a good day in a strong southern American accent, while waving in my direction. I returned the polite greeting. When he faced me, I could see that he was wearing an Israeli Defence Force baseball cap. When they reached the next bench, the woman kept on walking slowly ahead. The friendly gentleman stopped and looked intently at the two Ethiopian workers. They were both on their hands and knees painting opposite legs of the seat. He stood there for a minute or so, overseeing this mundane process. Eventually one of the Ethiopian workers lifted his head to look at this looming figure. His face looked inquisitively at the American gent.

'So where are you guys from?' the American roared in a confident, cheerful voice.

The other painter who had not spotted this man raised his head rapidly in fright, banging his crown against the leg of the bench. He rolled over on his back to face the American, while all the time rubbing his sore head. His face was covered in paint splashes and he squinted into the sun. He mumbled something that was inaudible to me.

'Ethiopia, yes,' said the American loudly.

The two painters now lying on their backs looked up at this sizeable man but remained silent. For 10 or 20 seconds the American stood beaming down at them with a benevolent smile.

'C'mon now. Let those guys get back to work,' his female partner shouted back at him.

'OK,' he waved back at her. He smiled down again at the painters.

'I just want to say, that is some great work you are doing there. That is just some great work,' he said to the bemused and perspiring painters.

It wasn't really 'great work'. It wasn't that it was bad work either, it is just that it was two guys painting the legs of a bench, nothing much to write home stateside about. Maybe this man was by nature enthusiastic about everything. But it was hard not to see his interaction with the painters as reflecting more general reactions among Americans to Israel. American supporters of Israel tend to see greatness all around them when they arrive in the Holy Land. Like old-school communist sympathisers who travelled to Soviet Russia, they walk around emphasising the positives looking at the society through uncritical eyes.

*

The size of American support for Israel is simply staggering. By 2005 Israel had received a total of $154 billion in economic and military assistance from the US. Israel now receives an average of $3 billion in direct foreign assistance each year from the US. This is one sixth of the total US direct foreign assistance budget. This makes up 2 per cent of total Israeli GDP, and in plain language works out as a direct subsidy of more than $500 per Israeli citizen. A nation of just 7 million citizens receives one sixth of the US direct foreign assistance budget annually.

Almost three-quarters of this assistance is in military aid and Israel can choose its arsenal from the top range of

US hardware. Egypt receives the second-biggest instalment of US direct foreign assistance, in which each citizen receives the equivalent of just $20 per person. Countries far more impoverished than Israel receive nothing close in terms of aid.

In return for the aid, Israel does not have to account for its spending, unlike most other countries. In effect, the aid to Israel is unconditional. Israel also receives huge donations from private American citizens estimated at $2 billion a year. The US supports Israel at the United Nations and all other international bodies. The figures above require little additional commentary, except one vital question – why?

The more romantic and idiosyncratic reasons given for this 'special relationship' between Israel and the United States can be discarded fairly quickly. There are those who argue that it is cultural, as both countries were built upon a pioneering spirit of adventure. Both are immigrant societies constructed in part upon a barren frontier with troublesome indigenous populations. The hardy Israeli kibbutz worker in the field making the desert bloom was much like the cowboy taming the western frontier, making it safe for civilisation.

But these cultural ties cannot explain this $3-billion-a-year special relationship. Those who believe American foreign policy is built on such whimsical notions are foolhardy in the extreme. The US has built relationships with South American repressive regimes and Arabian despotic monarchies as well as with functioning democratic states. Cultural bonds do not have to exist for the US to build alliances with other states.

A more serious reason for the relationship proposed by academics is the existence of the very strong Israeli lobby in Washington. This undoubtedly powerful body wields important influence over US foreign policy. It comprises a number of well-organised groups that have built upon many decades of experience in winning the support of US politicians for Israeli actions. Its members are most certainly not all American Jews. A huge number of Israel's biggest supporters in the US are Christians. The important neo-conservative movement is also fundamentally pro-Israel.

Some recent high-profile books from academics have argued that the power of the Israeli lobby has influenced American foreign policy to such an extent that the US government has made decisions that are not in its own interest. Rather, the Israeli lobby has moved the US into a stance of unconditional support for Israel, which actually harms American interests. However this is pushing the analysis too far. Decisions such as the recent invasion of Iraq or support for Israel during the Second Lebanon War were in the end taken by the American President and his administration. It was they, not the Israeli lobby, who made the final decision.

In the final analysis, US support for Israel is about naked self-interest. It is hard-headed realpolitik, pure and simple. Israel is an obedient client state of the US in a region that is hugely important because of its oil reserves. It will do the bidding of the US in the Middle East, no questions asked. It is an ever-present American foothold in the Holy Land, a strategic asset allowing the US to influence the region. The conflict and friction between Israel and its neighbouring Arab states is arguably in the interest of the US.

If the Arab region was democratic and developing in the interest of all its citizens, Washington could have more problems. The Arab street could well vote for leaders who want to use their oil reserves for political leverage or to nationalise the oil industry for the benefit of all society, in some ways like what President Hugo Chavez has undertaken in Venezuela. This would not be in the interests of the US. It is easier to 'influence' a ruling clique in a repressive state than to win the hearts and minds of a majority of its populace in a thriving democracy.

Israel works as a vital outpost for American power, in an area of the world that is crucial for its interests, its interest in oil. Ominously for Israel, there is only one thing you can be certain about in a region dominated by uncertainty – the oil reserves will not last forever.

*

When I was walking towards Williamsburg in Brooklyn I felt like I was back along the sombre streets of the development towns in southern Israel. After my summer in the West Bank in 2005 I flew almost immediately to New York to stay with friends on a short holiday. They were living in a miniscule flat in Brooklyn. What it lacked internally it made up for externally, located as it was in the heart of the ethnically mixed and unendingly interesting Brooklyn community.

One day we went on a long journey by foot through historic Brooklyn, the old Irish areas and the now bustling streets that are home to thousands of Puerto Ricans. Our destination was Williamsburg, an area of New York that has become increasingly hip during the past decade. It is an artistic and musical colony with a long stretch of bars, cafes and live music venues, a bohemian enclave forced into exile from Manhattan because of soaring rent prices on the island.

As we got closer to Williamsburg we walked along the edge of the Jewish district. School buses with Yiddish and Hebrew lettering and kosher stores made up the distinctive urban landscape. A series of fairly decrepit-looking blocks of flats were built in a long row. Religious male Jews walked around the drab area that looked like it needed some financial investment. Shutters had come down on supermarkets and small grocery stores. Buildings lay idle, and a general atmosphere of industrial decay hung in the air. A Navy base located nearby took up much of the space in the area.

For the anti-Semite who believes that Jews control the world's levers of economic power, a quick trip to this part of Brooklyn will put them straight. Not all Jews in New York are living a life of luxury and influence. If anything, the industrial and residential area of Williamsburg reminded me most of the poor development towns I visited in southern Israel. The mundane blocks of flats, the generally tawdry feel to the area was reminiscent of Netivot. The writing on the buses and shops in Brooklyn was in Yiddish, in Netivot it was in Hebrew, but that was the only major difference. Urban decay seemed, on the surface at least, to be the uniting theme of both areas. One was surrounded by one of the most spectacular cities in the world, the other isolated and ringed by a barren desert.

On another night we were talking to two lads in a bar on the Lower East Side. They were members of a local band called the WMDs. They were full of information about the local music scene. One of the guys worked in the property sector, but it was clear that the band and its music were what really motivated him. They gave us a free CD of their music, which was pretty good if you're into that style of rock.

'We are a band from the Lower East Side, so if we are playing upstate or outside New York that is a good thing to be able to say, it sounds pretty cool. But here, we are just another band from the Lower East Side, and it can be difficult. It is hard work,' said the taller of the two lads.

As the friendly conversation developed, I spoke about my recent time in the Holy Land, and it transpired that they were Jewish. My friend, who was in the period of life where buying property had come to the fore, mined the lads for information about house and apartment prices in Manhattan and Brooklyn. I mined them for their attitude to Israel, Jewish identity and the diaspora.

'The Holocaust, that was only a generation ago right? So that is not that long ago, it could happen again. If it happened once why could it not happen again?' asked the taller guy.

'You really think that?' I replied.

'Yes. It is just over 50 years ago, we are not talking ancient history here. Look, Israel provides a safety net. I might not want to go there now, but if things got bad, like really bad, I know there is a place out there for me.'

'But, let's say every Jewish person on the planet went to live in Israel. Would the Jewish people not lose something that you get from living in the diaspora? And would the rest of the world not lose something, considering what the Jewish people have given the world of culture and civilisation?'

While I listed out these questions, I feared that I sounded somewhat sanctimonious.

'Well. That is a really nice thing to say, man, and I would say thanks for saying that. And I am not saying I want to go and live in Israel. It is just nice to know, considering what we have been through – it's just nice to know that it is there.'

I had never actually spoken to a Jewish person in the diaspora who articulated these views so clearly. The idea of Israel as a last point of refuge for the world's Jewish population, in case of some apocalyptic scenario like another Holocaust is obviously a strong one, and difficult for a Gentile to understand. The irony, however, is that with wars in every decade the land of Jerusalem has been a dangerous place for Jews since the foundation of the state of Israel in 1948.

*

The plaza in front of the Damascus Gate is a microcosm of Arab life in Jerusalem. The imposing and impressive structure is the entry point to the Muslim Quarter of the Old City of Jerusalem. There is always an excitable sense of commerce and community in the vicinity of the gate. Unlike the sleepy vicinity around the New Gate or the Zion Gate, this historic opening into the contentious and religiously important Old City is always buzzing with activity. If you sit high on the steps outside the gate you can watch Arab boys hurriedly carrying containers of fruit and vegetables into the Muslim Quarter to be sold in the busy souks along Al-Wad Road. Elderly Palestinian women sit on the ground with their legs folded and yell out the prices of the spices they are selling, while teenagers balance small cups of orange juice on trays as they try to tempt a couple of shekels from the passing public.

Teenage Arab women in hijab walk together, smiling giddily as they enter the Arab quarter for an afternoon of shopping. Alongside the rudimentary stalls of the souks, there are also boutique stores inside the Old City's walls to tempt the fashion conscious woman. Families make their way inside to eat and shop. Middle-aged Muslim men quickly march under the gate on their way to prayers at the Al-Aqsa Mosque. Intermittently, ultra-orthodox Jews in their distinctive black clothing walk at high speed out through the gate, up the steps and towards the Jewish communities of modern West Jerusalem. There is always noise: roars from the market stall holders, cries from the few beggars who sit in front of the gate or the laughter and screams from the young boys who work in the souks with their fathers.

There is also a robust police and military presence. Armed Israeli police stand in groups at the top of the steps, others stand either side of the gate itself. Inside the Muslim Quarter, they patrol the Arab-owned market stores. On significant days, like Friday, the Muslim day of prayer, when thousands of Muslim men attend prayers at the Al-Aqsa Mosque, the armed presence is even tighter.

If you sit for any length of time on the steps outside Damascus Gate you will witness armed police stopping young Arab men and asking for ID. There will be a short conversation and then the ID card will be taken from the Arab by the Israeli guard. He will order the Arab civilian to sit at the top of the steps. At any time there will be three or four Arab men sitting in the usual spot at the top of the steps. They wait there while the Israeli officer goes off to check their ID against some database. The Arab can be left there for long lengths of time sitting under the sweltering sun. Sometimes things can get heated, with angry exchanges between the police and young men. Sometimes, the police just whisk them off in the back of their patrol jeeps.

Of course, situations like these are nothing compared to the oppression of the Palestinians in the occupied territories. However, this ID-checking and armed police presence is not seen anywhere else around the Old City, not at the Jaffa or New Gates, the traditional entry-points into the Jewish or Armenian quarters of the Old City.

East Jerusalem and the Old City were captured by the Israelis in 1967. The Israeli government later proclaimed the whole of Jerusalem as the 'undivided and eternal capital of Israel'. This was despite United Nations resolutions that required Israel to reverse its annexation of the city. The city is not regarded as the capital of Israel by the international community and most countries locate their Israeli embassies in Tel Aviv in recognition of this. Since 1967, the Israeli government has initiated a policy of building Jewish settlements in the east of the city, with the consequential confiscation of Palestinian land around Jerusalem. This has been done to increase the Jewish character of Jerusalem.

The Palestinian minority of around 30 per cent in the city have complained that they do not receive a fair distribution of resources from the local Israeli administration. The Palestinians in East Jerusalem live within a tangled web of complicated identity and residency laws. They must carry annually-renewable blue Israeli ID cards that allow them to reside in East Jerusalem, but not to vote in national elections. Holding on to your ID can be a precarious process and it can be rescinded by the Israeli authorities for various reasons.

The Old City is home to religious sites that are important to Jews, Muslims and Christians. Palestinians believe that although the city must be the capital of their future state, most will accept a political division of the city. Many religious and right-wing Israelis cannot countenance even partial Palestinian sovereignty over the city, while for the Christian Zionists the city is a pivotal part of their apocalyptic future.

The contested, divided, holy city remains a key aspect of the conflict.

Epilogue

It had been an emotionally arduous journey through the Jenin Refugee camp. We had visited the 'martyrs' cemetery' where the graves of the Palestinian fighters and civilians who had died in the camp during the 2002 Israeli invasion were buried.

An old man was sobbing hard while kneeling by a graveside, his shoulder hunched up and his head rocking. From the perimeter of the cemetery two Palestinian kids started firing stones from catapults in the general direction of me and my three international companions. We waved at them to stop. They came over shyly and introduced themselves. They then started to display their impressive expertise, hitting glass bottles with rocks from great distances. We were led through the camp by these two local youngsters. Other children ran up and down the camp's empty alleys, kicking footballs and chasing each other hyperactively. Over 40 per cent of the camp's 12,000 inhabitants are under the age of 15.

The Jenin camp was the scene of an infamous battle that resulted in incredible destruction and suffering. The Battle of Jenin in April 2002 caused the deaths of many Palestinian civilians, militants and Israeli soldiers. The camp itself was destroyed during the brutal Israeli attack, dwellings bulldozed, whole sections razed.

The Jenin boys led us to a long high wall built in the centre of the camp. The wall was decorated by carefully painted murals of flowing rivers, gushing waterfalls and lush green meadows. It was a perfect vision of a pastoral paradise. Beside the rural utopia, there was a painting on the wall of a little boy facing away from us. He stood with his arms held behind his back. He was barefoot, with sparse scraggily hair, a ragged T-shirt and ill-fitting shorts. He was not looking at the rural landscape, but into an empty distance.

One of the boys who had brought us through the camp pointed at the illustration.

'Handala,' he said and smiled, begging us to take his photograph while he and his friend stood beside the mural.

American kids have Mickey Mouse, Palestinian children have Handala.

Handala is the creation of the late Palestinian cartoonist Naji al-Ali. He is drawn by Palestinian children on walls across the occupied territories and in the refugee camps in the Arab states. He is always sketched with his back facing the viewer; his face is never shown.

Handala is a Palestinian refugee forced to leave his home at the age of 10. He has remained that age, unable to grow older in his frozen exodus. He is motionless in time, incapable of ageing until he returns to his homeland, where his stolen life can continue. He looks forlornly into the distance, back towards his childhood home of Palestine. He will not turn around to face us the viewer until he has won back his freedom.

The young Jenin children then brought us around another corner and through a door into a large open garage. Once inside, a middle-aged man with a long and tangled moustache ran over to us and shook our hands. He welcomed us fulsomely in Arabic. The man in charge was welcoming in the Arabic tradition, and he instructed one younger boy to bring us cup after cup of sweet coffee.

The one room building worked as a rudimentary community centre. Young teenagers shot pool at one table, while other younger boys crowded around two computer screens, screaming and yelping as they played video games. We played pool with the teenagers for an hour or so. Neither the man nor the boys had much English, so the conversations were conducted in very rudimentary Arabic with a splattering of English. Despite the problems in translation, they found out where we were from, why we were in the West Bank and what football teams we supported.

The walls in the room were plastered with elaborately designed posters and colourful photographs. The images were not of famous international soccer players or world renowned musical stars, but the determined smiling faces of *shahids*. The eyes of the local martyrs from the Jenin Refugee camp gazed out from the posters and down upon their younger brothers. These were the young boys' heroes, their future.

I walked across and peeked over the shoulders of the screaming, excitable kids enjoying the computer video games on one of the PCs. They were playing a high-paced, first-person shooter game called *Counter Strike*. At the start of each mission in the game, the player gets to choose whether to join either a terrorist or a counter-terrorist team. There was little surprise as to the team the young Palestinian players selected.

*

You can board the *Af-Al-Pi-Chen* ship at the Clandestine Immigration and Navy Museum in Haifa. Meaning *Nevertheless* in Hebrew, the ship illegally carried 434 refugees, many Holocaust survivors, into Palestine in 1947. In the well-preserved hold of the ship you watch a documentary that chronicles the history of the vessel, as well as many other boats that the Zionists used to bring immigrants to Palestine following the Second World War. Of course the presentation focuses on the famous story of the *Exodus,* which has been retold in bestselling novels and a Hollywood movie. That iconic vessel set sail from Europe for Palestine in 1947 laden down by 4,500 passengers, most of them Holocaust survivors. It was prevented from docking in Palestine by the British and, horrifically, was eventually forced to make the journey back to Germany.

This documentary narrative of course reinforces the Zionist story of Israel becoming the safe home for the Jews. Over 200,000 Jews were homeless in post war Europe, living in displaced persons' camps across the continent. The illegal immigration to Palestine of these survivors, organised clandestinely by the Zionist parties, may have been somewhat motivated by humanitarian concern, but it also helped the Zionist aim of flooding Palestine with

Jewish immigrants, to influence the ethnic demographic balance.

But as you focus on the faces of those immigrants looking out from the photographs and you hear their testimony relayed over the sound system, you get a glimpse into the nightmare of their lives. For the Holocaust survivors who crowded onto the decks and into the belly of ships leaving for Palestine, Zionism did seem to provide an answer. They had witnessed unimaginable horror, watched their families, friends and communities wiped out in a few short years. Zionism promised them a home and a safe exit from a murderous continent, escape from a Europe in which they and their forebears had lived for centuries, but in the end had become the setting for the attempted annihilation of the Jews.

The survivors arrived in Palestine, traumatised, broken, orphaned, homeless and distraught. It is a special soul indeed who is improved by suffering. Most of us are not enhanced by misery. To expect the survivors of the Holocaust when they arrived in Palestine to have concern for the plight and circumstance of the indigenous Arab population is to ask for the impossible. When you have emerged from a community in which six million have been gassed and violently murdered, simple survival is your priority. Your own victimhood is so all consuming that to immediately empathise with other victims is unfeasible.

But the Holocaust is now a vital aspect of Zionist and Israeli identity. Modern Israel has to be strong, brutal and harsh with its enemies, because never again will the Jews be coerced into the gas chambers. The Arab and Palestinian enemy has at times been portrayed as Nazis by Israeli politicians and pundits. With every war against them, the historic spectre of the Holocaust is raised and a future annihilation of the Jewish state is predicted.

For modern Israel, the most influential site for warrior-like heroism is the ancient fortress of Masada, which rises high above the Dead Sea. Here the Jews rose up against the Roman Empire. The zealots, as they were called, bravely held Masada in the face of a Roman siege. Over time they eventually realised they were outnumbered and doomed. Rather than surrender to the Romans, all 960 plus of the ancient Hebrew warriors committed mass suicide. IDF soldiers are now brought to Masada for their swearing-in ceremony, where they pledge that 'Masada shall not fall again'.

It is in such acts of ancient suicidal resistance that modern Israeli militarism finds its inspiration. In contrast, the modern Jewish state's military machismo is also at least in part a rejection of the perceived lack of military defiance by Jewish victims during the Third Reich.

This is a tragic reaction to history. There was brave resistance to Nazi rule by both Gentile and Jew. But to die at the blood-drenched hands of a vicious militaristic state is not shameful. A successful struggle against such a sadistic government for a largely unarmed civilian population was unfeasible. There is no dishonour carried by the powerless, and the victims of Hitler. It is the powerful who planned and executed the mass extermination of the Jewish people who are guilty. The Holocaust must be mourned by all of humanity, but it cannot be avenged even by a modern muscular Jewish state.

As with the Holocaust survivors, it is also problematic to lay blame for the Nakba on individuals in the

Mizrahim Jewish communities who came to Israel in the 1950s. The position of that community within the Arab countries became extremely challenging following the creation of the state of Israel and the resulting conflict with the neighbouring Arab states. The Mizrahim were to be wrenched from the Arab community and culture they had lived in and developed for centuries. Many faced decades of difficult assimilation in the Ashkenazi-dominated Israel. But the Palestinians were the victims of the Nakba, so therefore, there were by definition perpetrators who carried it out.

The British state played an appalling role from the penning of the Balfour Declaration in 1917 until their final months in charge of Mandate Palestine in 1948. Still responsible for providing security in the dying days of its rule, it did nothing to prevent the Zionist attacks on Arab villages and the expulsion of the Palestinian population. They had already partially abandoned their accountability by passing on to the UN the task of finding a workable 'solution'. The British Empire left the Holy Land, like so many other places, in a dishonourable way.

The young UN certainly did not have an easy task when the British passed the precarious Palestinian parcel to them. But by proposing a partition plan in 1947 that was so obviously unfair to the Arab community, it helped to push the Holy Land further towards the violence that engulfed it. Feelings of guilt that were rightly felt in Western capitals over the massacres of European Jewry during the war meant that sympathy for Zionism grew rapidly. By supporting a Jewish state in another people's land, the international community helped to partially expunge its own guilt, but in so doing began another horror for another people and another nation.

But it is the Zionist movement and its international sponsors who must bear the brunt of responsibility for creating the conditions for the Palestinian exodus and its resulting disaster. Many of its leading figures were directly involved in carrying out the Nakba itself. The organisers of the movement had been perfectly aware from the earliest days that an Arab people lived in Palestine. In 1897 two rabbis from Vienna visited Palestine and reported that, 'the bride is beautiful, but she is married to another man'.

But the Zionist movement at best decided to wilfully ignore this Arab man's existence, and at worst it consciously planned how it would steal his beautiful wife from his loving embrace. Zionism at its core was a colonial project, and has been championed at different times in the capitals of imperial power, London and Washington.

The Nakba and the 750,000 initial refugees that resulted is a fact of history. For real peace, its historic reality and the millions of Palestinian refugees now living across the Arab world must be recognised by the Israeli state. Israeli leaders must accept the role Zionism played in the destruction and dispersal of another nation and its people.

*

It should be simple, really. The American President says that he is in favour of it, as does the Arab League, the European Union, the United Nations, the Israeli government and the Palestinian Authority. All say that they believe in the two-state vision. Israel will have internationally recognised borders and there will be a new Palestinian state living alongside it as its neighbour.

But if the world's most important powers and the parties directly involved are positively disposed to it, then why all the trouble? Obviously, rhetoric is one thing and action is another. The US President George W. Bush has made much of his declared support for a 'viable Palestinian state'. But he has not condemned further Jewish settlement construction in the West Bank or the building of the Wall in Palestinian territory, and he supports every brutal Israeli attack on occupied towns and cities. History has conclusively taught us that no matter who the next president in the Oval Office may be, their administration will continue the United States's unconditional support for Israel.

The state of Israel claims to want a Palestinian state, but does everything in its considerable power to make such an eventuality impossible. Since the peace process began in the early 1990s, the construction of Jewish settlements has intensified and become increasingly extensive, the occupation is more brutal than ever and the Israeli state refuses to discuss fundamental issues such as the Palestinian refugees. It may be in Israel's strategic interests in the future to allow the creation of some sort of Palestinian 'state', but such a state would be weak, divided and not economically viable.

The PA wants two states. Hamas has offered a long-term ceasefire if Israel retreats to the 1967 borders. The Arab League has promised Israel recognition if it leaves the occupied territories, including the Golan Heights which it captured from Syria in 1967.

For a two-state solution to be viable, Jerusalem would need to be divided as a capital for Israel as well as Palestine. The majority of the Jewish settlements would have to be removed. If any of the massive settlement blocks were to remain in place, the Palestinian state would have to receive adequate compensation in a fair land-swap arrangement. Nonetheless, tens of thousands of settlers would have to be pulled out of their homes by the Israeli state.

The military occupation would have to end, and the IDF retreat behind the Green Line. The Gaza Strip and the West Bank would have to become connected land under Palestinian control. The Palestinians would be allowed to open Gaza International Airport and a seaport. Political prisoners would be released from Israeli jails. The Wall would have to be pulled down from inside the West Bank. The Israeli state would accept its responsibility in finding a solution to the Palestinian refugee issue through a combination of compensation and resettlement. Finally, an Israeli government should apologise to the indigenous population and nation that was dispersed and oppressed in 1948, much like the Australian and Canadian governments have done in recent years with their own indigenous communities.

On the Palestinian side, a referendum on the comprehensive treaty would have to be held not only in the occupied territories, but also in the refugee camps abroad for it to carry full legitimacy. The refugees would have to give up their legal right of return under an agreed compromise settlement. The Palestinians would be required by the Israelis to accept the state of Israel as a Jewish state. The new Palestinian state would have to foreswear armed struggle and clamp down hard on elements within the society that wanted to continue military attacks on Israel.

There are numerous problems with this two-state vision, quite apart from all the 'woulds', 'shoulds' and 'coulds' involved that make its fruition very difficult to visualise. Firstly, both leaderships, if they signed up to such a deal, would have significant difficulties selling it to their own constituencies. A majority of the Palestinian public, even the refugees, would probably accept such a scenario. It would be regarded as a far from perfect deal, but one that offered to free them from their current misery. The PA has already accepted the concept of a Palestinian state consigned to the West Bank and Gaza, and even Hamas has offered a long-term truce if Israel retreats to the Green Line.

However, it is difficult to see any Israeli leader able to sell the above scenario to a majority of Israelis in a referendum, even if he or she wanted to. A majority of Israelis may say in opinion polls that they are in favour of two states, but when the niggling nuts and bolts of such a deal are discussed, Israeli support wanes. The centre of political gravity in Israel has shifted to the right, and the parties that would oppose such a peace deal would be able to whip up substantial opposition into an angry crescendo.

The generation of famous Israeli leaders who stalked the political scene like big beasts, Yitzhak Rabin, Ariel Sharon and Menchaim Begin are either dead or dying. Maybe leaders like that could have carried, if they had so desired, a united Jewish nation towards reconciliation with the Palestinians. There is no current Israeli political leader or party who could so unite the country. Israeli politics are fractured, often petty, corrupt and quarrelsome. There is no personality on the present Israeli political scene who possesses the moral authority needed or courage required to lead the nation towards a just deal with the Palestinians.

Secondly, such a two-state solution would undoubtedly cause major strife within Israel even if it were somehow implemented. But as of now there is no significant pressure on Israeli society to even contemplate such a move. Life in the northern suburbs of Tel Aviv, on the beautiful slopes of Mount Carmel in Haifa or in the apartment blocks in West Jerusalem and elsewhere seems 'normal', even pleasant.

Yes, there are significant problems within Israel because of the occupation, but on a day-to-day level, the occupied West Bank can seem a very long way away when you are sipping coffee on the Tel Aviv beachfront. An economic boom over the past decade, rising tourist numbers and greater political acceptance abroad has improved the mood of a nation. Why make big concessions in any peace deal which would disrupt the tranquillity of everyday life?

Thirdly, there is little real desire in Washington for such a settlement. Most US politicians are hawkish on the conflict and would not support any agreement opposed by a sizeable number of Israeli politicians.

Fourthly, the two-state solution would mean that Israel would remain a Jewish state. This would ensure that the Arab population within Israel would continue to be treated as second-class citizens. That Arab community's campaign, supported by a small but increasing number of Jews, for Israel to change from a Jewish state to a 'state of all its citizens' would be doomed.

Finally, the physical reality of the extensive nature of the Jewish settlements within the West Bank, the Israeli military installations in the occupied territories and the existence of the Wall means that actual separation into two states would be extremely difficult. Cutting the land in two, would require a sharp diplomatic and military knife. Even done with precision, it is probable that much blood would be lost during the operation.

It is often argued that the only thing more unlikely than a peaceful two-state solution is a one-state solution. But the reality on the ground makes a two-state solution increasingly unlikely. It is hard to visualise any Israeli government pulling tens of thousands of settlers out of the West Bank. The settlements are now part of the physical geography of the West Bank. If Israeli and Palestinian peace activists have to wait for an Israeli government with the political will, courage and strength to confront the powerful settler lobby, they could be waiting a long time indeed. Other options are being put forward from some quarters in order to fill this vacuum.

A bi-national singular democratic state for both Jews and Arabs would be the most preferable for a small but increasing number of activists on both sides of the divide. The vision of one secular state for all the people who live in the Holy Land has much to recommend it. In fact, since 1967, there has essentially been one state, but it has been far from secular and democratic. The Israeli government controls the land from the Mediterranean to the River Jordan. The lives of hundreds of thousands of Palestinians in the occupied territories have been ruled for decades by successive Israeli governments which they could not elect. Supporters of the bi-national option do have to concede, however, that the history of such states is not unproblematic.

Many Israeli commentators speak of the occupation as if it has been an aberration in the history of the state. But Israel has occupied the territories for 40 of its 60 years; it is intricately woven into the very fabric of Israeli culture, geography and politics.

Those on the Israeli political left, who argue that the occupation must end and at least some settlements removed, have fundamental questions to pose to themselves. If the occupation and uprooting of Palestinian society in the occupied territories from 1967 was wrong and needs to be addressed, then how come the exact same procedures carried out in 1948 are not regarded as wrong and do not require to be addressed?

A growing number of Palestinians, some in high-profile political positions, have called for the abandonment of the fight for a state in the West Bank and Gaza. They argue that it is clear that the Israelis have no interest in a viable Palestinian state. They have concluded that the Israelis want to manage, rather than resolve the conflict. Thus it would be better for the Palestinian Authority to be dismantled, they say. The next step would be for the Palestinian street to launch a civil rights struggle alongside the Arabs within Israel, for equality in one singular state. Such a struggle is a nightmare for the Israeli elite, as it would clearly expose the oppression and racism in the state.

There are a small number of Israelis in the peace movement who have come to similar conclusions. A viable two-state solution is more distant than ever. The Israeli government has no interest in real peace so therefore some believe one singular state for all Jews and Arabs is the most preferable solution to the conflict.

On both sides of this discussion lies an understanding that the divided land must be shared, between an Arab Palestinian community who have lived there for centuries and a Jewish immigrant society for which the land is now also home. It has to be the potential paradise for the two peoples. These miniscule movements in Israel together with the growing body of similar thought within Palestine hold the best hopes for a long-term sustainable peace in the Holy Land.

*

Whether it is a one- or two-state solution, there is no significant dynamic within Israeli society pushing for a just arrangement with the Palestinians. Such an impetus can only come from abroad.

It will not come from the US, as Washington continues to support Israel's most hawkish policies. It looks unlikely to come from the European Union, either. The EU has grown closer to Israel in recent years. The Euro-Med agreement that Israel signed with the EU gives it unique access to the continent's markets. The EU has also supported a boycott on Palestine since the Hamas 2006 election victory. So the EU places an economic blockade on the occupied, while handing out preferential treatment to the occupier.

A large number of Palestinian civil bodies, academics and trade unions have called for an international boycott and divestment campaign against Israeli institutions. They maintain that it is a way of encouraging Israel to make peace and end the occupation. A boycott is controversial. It is not a perfect option for those in the international community who care deeply for the Palestinian plight but wish no ill will towards ordinary Israelis. But it is a tactic that the global justice and civil rights movements have utilised before, most famously in the case of the Apartheid regime in South Africa. It can have an impact on public and political opinion within Israel.

Recent controversies in Britain surrounding an academic boycott against Israeli institutions have received blanket coverage in Israeli media. Israeli society still cares deeply about how it is perceived in Europe. Cultural and sporting events in which Israel partakes like the Eurovision Song Contest or the European Soccer Championship carry massive importance in the country. Israel still sees itself as the democratic and civilised nation in the region, but an international boycott would provoke questions and self-doubt. Some, of course, will say that such a boycott is motivated by anti-Semitism. But the boycott is not aimed at individual Israelis, but rather at institutions. It will also undoubtedly provoke some debate within Israel about the cost of the occupation, a debate that is not currently taking place.

Israelis are understandably defensive to such suggestions. 'Why us? No country is perfect,' some will say. This is true, and indeed there are many aspects of Ireland's domestic and foreign policy that are disagreeable. Just one example would be that Ireland, supposedly a 'first-world country with a third-world memory' as President Mary McAleese has called us, has severely diluted its traditional policy of neutrality on international military matters. The US armed forces' use of Ireland's Shannon Airport during the invasion and continuing occupation of Iraq is shameful. It links Ireland to an imperial adventure that has cost the lives of thousands and destroyed an Arab nation.

But the Irish state, for all its numerous faults, is not a serial human rights abuser, it is not militarily occupying another people and its independence, although bloody, was not won following the dispossession and dispersal of an indigenous people. Israel is all these things, and its claims to being both democratic and civilised are fatally undermined because of them.

There are many thousands of Israelis of conscience who fight each day against the occupation and try to make their society fairer and just. But they are currently in a minority. Pressure must come from outside to move Israeli society towards finding an accommodation with the Palestinians.

*

Focusing in so much detail on one conflict, like the Israeli-Palestinian one, can help magnify its unique qualities, but may also dim its universal aspects. This book is not a detailed economic and class analysis of the global system that creates discord and inequality, like that which exists in the Middle East. But globalisation and imperialism are the forces that produce the iniquitous and deeply divided world we live in. The oppression of the Palestinian nation is part of a wider system that rewards military might and crushes the powerless.

Looking at recent world events through the eyes of the Arab street for just one moment can be instructive. You watch a US President launch an unprovoked attack on an Arab country spark a series of events that has spread a fire of death and destruction across Iraq. He did so principally because of oil. That is not according to some tree-hugging peacenik or Arab politician, but the conclusion of a scion of the American establishment, former Federal Reserve Bank Chief, Alan Greenspan.

So a war motivated by greed for resources has destroyed an Arab people and a nation, unleashing further havoc across the region. From the point of view of the Arab citizen, surely they would think in a global system with even a modicum of fairness that such a President would not be spending the last weeks of his time in office on a friendly farewell tour sitting down in the Oval Office preparing his long retirement holiday at his ranch. He would not be happily spending the final decades of his life sipping soft drinks under the Texas sun.

No, that President should be employing the best international lawyers money can buy in a desperate attempt to keep himself out of the dock at the International Criminal Court in The Hague. He would be joined by his junior but ever-so-willing partner in the crusade in Iraq, the former British Prime Minister.

But the former British Prime Minister, who supported a war over weapons of mass destruction that did not exist, is not having to face legal questions over his role in the Iraq catastrophe. His name is not ruined, nor his legacy lambasted on the international diplomatic circuit. No, because in a career move that would be funny if it was not so appalling, Tony Blair is now a peace envoy to the Middle East on behalf of the EU, the UN, the US and Russia. The man who helped to bomb Baghdad is telling the Palestinians and others how they can achieve peace.

A majority in the West opposed the war in Iraq. Most would be critical of how George Bush and Tony Blair conducted themselves. But it is on the Arab street that the sheer scale of hypocrisy in the West's dealings with the Middle East is most clearly witnessed and felt. Many

Palestinians and Arabs shrug their shoulders and acknowledge that the world is unfair, but what can be done? But others seethe with understandable bitter resentment at an international system that creates such discrimination and hypocrisy.

The fight for justice and against inequality is a global one. War, modern imperialism, centralised political control and rampant capitalist exploitation of people and the planet has produced a varied worldwide resistance movement. The international elites, who launch invasions and horde the bounty they extract by exploitation, thrive on maintaining division, suspicions and hatred between ordinary people in the East and the West.

Those who oppose the worst excesses of globalisation in the economic and military field must also attempt to articulate a set of principles for, and a vision of, a more equitable, just world that reaches out to the widest possible support base, both in the East and the West.

There has to be room for all cultures, religions and races at the rendezvous of victory, and one of the prerequisites to any successful fight for global justice will be a liberated and free Palestine.

Glossary

Al-Aqsa Mosque – Considered to be the third holiest site in Islam where the Prophet Muhammad visited during his 'night journey'. Located in the old city of Jerusalem.

Aliyah – Meaning 'ascent' in Hebrew, this refers to Jewish immigration to Palestine before 1948, and since then, to the state of Israel. Each separate wave of aliyah has had different ethnic and political characteristics.

Arab League – A regional organisation of 22 Arab states in the Middle East and North Africa. Palestine is a member, despite having not yet achieved statehood.

Arghileh – A water pipe very popular in the Arab world and surrounding areas and with Middle Eastern Jewish immigrants in Israel.

Ashkenazim – Jews whose background is usually from Eastern Europe. The elite in Israeli society tend to come from the Ashkenazim.

Balad – An Arab political party operating in Israel which campaigns to make Israel a 'state of all its citizens' rather than a 'Jewish state'.

Balfour Declaration – A letter written in November 1917 by British Foreign Secretary Arthur James Balfour, stating that the London government favoured the establishment of 'a national home for the Jewish people' in Palestine.

Bedouin – Desert-living nomadic people, or formerly nomadic people, living across the Arab world.

B'Tselem – Israeli human rights group that focuses on Israeli military actions within the occupied territories.

Birthright Tours – Free ten-day trips to Israel available to any young Jewish person in the world, organised by a Zionist group and supported by the Israeli government.

British Mandate – British rule over Palestine from 1920 until 1948.

Burka – Long garment covering the entire head, face and body of a woman with a mesh over the eyes, used in some Islamic cultures but rarely seen in Palestine.

Dome of the Rock – The most famous part of the ancient Jerusalem skyline. The beautiful golden dome over the main mosque is located close to the Al-Aqsa Mosque.

Druze – Religious community living principally in Israel, Lebanon and Syria. Although disputed in theological circles, it is generally regarded as a religion derived from Islam.

Falafel – Fried balls of chickpeas served in pitta bread with sauces, salad and hummus, popular across the Middle East.

Fatah – The major secular Palestinian party, militant organisation and leading faction within the PLO. Until recently, the Fatah was the undisputed party of the majority of Palestinians. Fatah was initially led by Yasser Arafat, and since his death in 2004, by Mahmoud Abbas.

Gaza Disengagement – The removal of over 7,500 Jewish settlers from the Gaza Strip by the Israeli state in August 2005.

Geneva Accord – An unofficial 2003 peace proposal drafted by Palestinian and Israeli academics and politicians.

Greater Israel – A vision of an Israeli state that exists on both sides of the River Jordan. Once very popular among right-wing Zionists and only adhered to by small numbers on the political fringes in contemporary Israel.

Green Line – The border between Israel and the territories it conquered in the 1967 War.

Gush Emunim – 'Bloc of the Faithful', the major Israeli campaigning group that called for the establishment of Jewish settlements in the West Bank and Gaza after they were occupied in 1967.

Gush Shalom – 'Bloc of Peace', small but active Israeli peace organisation calling for the end of the occupation and the establishment of two states, Israel and Palestine.

Haaretz – Israel's most prestigious, but far from its most popular, daily paper. It is Zionist and liberal in editorial outlook.

Hadash – Small, left-wing Israeli party supported by many Arabs and some Jews. Like Balad, it campaigns to make Israel a 'state of all its citizens' rather than a 'Jewish state'.

Haganah – The pre-1948 Jewish paramilitary force, which became the IDF in 1948.

Hamas – The major Islamic political party in Palestine. Its military wing has carried out many attacks on Israel over the past 15 years. Won the January 2006 PLC elections and currently controls the Gaza Strip.

Haredim – The community of strictly observant religious Jews, sometimes also called Ultra-Orthodox.

Herut – The modern Herut is a small right-wing Zionist party in Israel.

Hijab – Headscarf worn by some Islamic women that covers the head, hair and neck.

Holy Koran – The central religious book of Islam.

ICJ - International Court of Justice is the judicial organ of the United Nations. In 2004, the ICJ ruled that the Israeli Wall in the West Bank was illegal.

IDF – Israel Defence Force. The army of the state of Israel, founded in 1948.

Intifada – Means 'shaking off' in Arabic and refers to the two recent uprisings by the Palestinians against the Israeli occupation. The first intifada ran from 1987–1991 and the second began in late 2000.

Irgun – Pre-1948 right-wing Jewish violent paramilitary organisation, subsumed into the IDF after 1948.

ISM – International Solidarity Movement. A global network of activists who support the Palestinian cause.

Jewish Bund – Socialist and strongly anti-Zionist Jewish organisation that had much support in Eastern Europe and Russia in the late nineteenth and early twentieth centuries.

Kadima – Currently largest party in Israel. Founded in 2005 by Ariel Sharon after the split in Likud. Following Sharon's stroke in January 2006, it was led by Ehud Olmert.

Keffiyeh – Popular scarf worn in the Arab world. In Palestine, the colour and design of the scarf can denote what political faction the wearer supports.

Kibbutz – Communal farms established in the Holy Land by Jewish immigrants.

Knesset – The Israeli parliament.

Labour – Historically the largest party in Israel, but its popularity has decreased since 1977.

Law of Return – Passed by the state of Israel in 1950, it allows any Jewish person in the world to migrate to Israel and receive full citizenship.

Lehi – An extreme pre-1948 right-wing Jewish paramilitary organisation.

Likud – The largest right-wing party in Israel.

Machsom Watch – An all-female Israeli human rights group that observes abuses at checkpoints in the occupied territories.

Meretz – A small left-wing Zionist party in Israel.

Mizrahim – Jewish immigrants from Middle Eastern and North African countries.

Moshav – A cooperative farm established by Jewish immigrants to the Holy Land.

Nakba – 'Catastrophe'. A term used by Palestinians to describe the events of 1948 when 750,000 Palestinians fled their homes in what is now Israel.

NRP – National Religious Party. A right-wing Israeli party supported by religious Jews and settlers.

Occupied Territories – An area covering the West Bank, the Gaza Strip and the Golan Heights, all occupied by Israel since the 1967 War.

Operation Defensive Shield – The Israeli invasion of the major Palestinian cities on the West Bank in 2002.

Orange movement – The Israeli political movement that was formed in opposition to the Gaza Disengagement Plan.

Orr Commission – Israeli judicial inquiry established following the killing of unarmed Arabs in northern Israeli towns in late 2000.

Oslo Accords – Signed in 1993, the first peace agreement between the Israeli government and the PLO.

PA – Palestinian Authority. The administrative body established following the signing of the Oslo Accords that gives limited partial Palestinian control over areas of the West Bank and Gaza.

Peace Now – An Israeli lobby group which supports a two-state solution and an end to settlement construction in the West Bank.

PFLP – Popular Front for the Liberation of Palestine. A left-wing Palestinian political and military faction.

PLC – Palestinian Legislative Council. The body that serves as the Palestinian parliament in the West Bank and Gaza.

PLO – Palestine Liberation Organization. The political and paramilitary organisation regarded by most international bodies as the ultimate representative of the Palestinian people. Unlike the PA, it also represents the millions of Palestinians who live in exile in the refugee camps.

Right of Return – What Palestinian refugees regard as their legal and moral right to return to the homes and villages they fled in 1948.

Sabra – An Israeli-born citizen of Israel.

Settlers – Hundreds of thousands of Jewish residents of the settlements built in the West Bank and Gaza Strip since 1967.

Shahid – A Palestinian martyr. Refers to those who have died in military attacks including suicide bombings on Israeli military and civilian targets. Any Palestinian, civilian or militant who has died at the hands of Israeli forces.

Sherut – Local mini-bus service in Israel and Palestine.

Shesh Besh – Arabic name for backgammon, very popular across the Middle East.

Shoah – The Hebrew name for the Holocaust.

Souk – An Arab market.

The Wall – The construction stretching for hundreds of kilometres inside and around the West Bank. The same structure is called an 'Anti-Terrorist' or 'Security Fence' by the Israeli government. For much of its route it is made up of extensive fencing but in populous Palestinian areas it is made of concrete. For this reason, it is referred to as 'the Wall' in this book.

This Week in Palestine – A liberal guide to politics and the arts in Palestine, written and produced in Ramallah.

Torah – The first five books of the Hebrew Bible, known to Christians as the Pentateuch.

Transfer – The political idea, popular among some of the Zionist right in Israel, of removing the Arab population living in Israel and forcing them to live in neighbouring Arab countries.

Western Wall – Located in the Jerusalem old city, it is the most holy place in Judaism. Often called the Wailing Wall, it is said to be the remaining wall of the Second Temple.

Yishuv – The pre-1948 Jewish community in the Holy Land.

Yisrael Beiteinu –A right-wing Israeli political party, supported mainly by the Jewish Russian community. The name means 'Israel is Our Home' in Hebrew.

Zionism – The political movement in favour of the establishment of a Jewish state in the Holy Land.

Zochrot – A small Israeli organisation that attempts to highlight the Nakba and the 500-plus formerly Palestinian villages that have been destroyed since 1948.

Acknowledgments

This book of literary reportage found its inspiration in a wide range of events, interviews, literature, conversations and interactions with people – from Beirut to Belfast, from Dublin to Washington DC – over the past three years.

Spending the 2005 summer studying and living in the West Bank was one of the most rewarding experiences of my life. The staff at Bir Zeit University Palestine and Arabic Studies department – Muna, Ibtisal, Rasha, Sami and Sa'd – made the time all the more pleasurable. I would urge Western students, young and old, to go. It's worth the three hours (or more!) interrogation at Tel Aviv Airport and the problems inherent in living under military occupation.

I'd like to thank the Palestinian friends I made then and since. Because of the extensive nature of the Israeli occupation, Palestinians are understandably worried about revealing too much information. Thus, regrettably, all Palestinian names, apart from those who agreed to official interviews, have been altered in my book.

Thanks to all the international students I spent time with, especially German Toby Thiel, whose knowledge of Israel was particularly helpful, and Englishman Ben Gibbons; my flatmates Philip Carl and Judd Kennedy, and the many others whom I spent time with, especially Sara Husseini, Gergey Pasztor, Simon Davis, Irene O'Dowd, Chris Harker and Stephan Schmidt; Israeli friend Atalia and the Reznik family, who very kindly welcomed me into their Tel Aviv home for a St Patrick's Day meal in 2006. I repaid their hospitality by rudely spending the evening questioning them about every aspect of Israeli state policy.

The many Palestinians and (particularly) the Israelis I have met may have significant reservations about the observations I make about their conflict. However, I hope all realise that it comes from a sincere hope for a 'solution' based on justice and peace. *Salam-Shalom.*

I want to thank everyone who worked in the Belfast offices of *Daily Ireland*, including publisher Máirtín Ó Muilleoir. Sadly the newspaper folded, however I was very proud to work for it; The *Sunday Business Post* and Simon Carswell, who in 2005 was editing the international page; and my former journalistic colleagues at the *Leinster Leader* and elsewhere, in particular Henry Bauress.

Thanks to everyone at New Island who showed faith in this project, especially the former editor Deirdre Nolan.

Friends and family have been a constant and important source of encouragement, ideas, comments and pleasurable distractions.

Acknowledgments

Just to mention Stephen Griffin (1978–2004) in whose memory I dedicated my first book. When I think of the mischievous glint in his eye and the empty space left in time since his life was lost so young and so far away from home, it still makes me, and all those who knew him, profoundly sad.

I was lucky to leave university with more than an MA. My two closest friends Mark Walsh and Simon Dunne have been comradely companions for 12 years or more since our innocent days in NUI Maynooth. Despite vast distance and different life paths, thankfully we remain tighter than ever. Mark also provided feedback on early chapters of the book.

My late twenties have been happily spent in Dublin 8 in the company of friends, often on long, murky, liquid nights that now flow through my memory like the River Liffey that I live beside. Whether playing football or talking about the 4-4-2 system, global politics, or hundreds of other often enjoyably nonsensical topics, thanks to Clifford Burke, Donal Collins, Paul Hartnett, Triona Lynch, Morgan Treacy, Dave Parkes, Donal O'hAodha, Alan Logan and to all those with whom I've shared a pint or two, or bored talking about this project in recent years.

My family, parents David and Marie Lynch, who have provided unconditional support in everything I have done. This book is dedicated to them.

My talented sister, photographer Julie Lynch, read very early drafts, helped with computer problems, map design, cover design and author photographs. I am grateful to her also.

Finally my debt of gratitude to Anne Marie Quinn is embarrassingly vast. Whether in her forensic editing of early drafts, sharing experiences of life in the Northern nationalist minority or in occupied nations like Tibet, her international law expertise, or as the perfect companion on our trip to the beautiful but broken Lebanon, her influence has been colossal. Over the past decade, her loyalty, friendship and belief in my writing has helped me negotiate virulent self-doubt, and she more than anyone has made this book possible.

David Lynch